MODULA-2 PROGRAMMING

Ed Knepley

Robert Platt

A RESTON BOOK
PRENTICE-HALL, INC., Englewood Cliffs, New Jersey 07632

Library of Congress Cataloging in Publication Data
Knepley, Ed.
    Modula-2 programming.

    1. Modula-2 (Computer program language) I. Platt,
Robert, 1951–   . II. Title.
QA76.73.M63K64   1985   001.64′24   84-27660
ISBN 0-8359-4603-7 (case)
ISBN 0-8359-4602-9 (paper)

10 9 8 7 6 5 4 3 2

Printed in the United States of America.

CONTENTS

PART II A CLOSER LOOK

APPENDICES

PREFACE

WHY MODULA-2?

Modula-2 is a relatively new programming language. It was first implemented in 1979 by Niklaus Wirth, who also created Pascal. During the 1970s Pascal gained widespread acceptance among educators and computer users. Pascal was originally designed to teach programming, however, and it had a number of deficiencies as a software development language. Modula-2 corrects these deficiencies but retains most of the logical structure and features of its predecessor. In addition, powerful new features have been incorporated into Modula-2. Modula-2 also combines many of the best features of the languages Ada and C, without their drawbacks. The result is a legitimate competitor to Ada and C.

Because of Modula-2's origins and the fact that it reflects the modern trends in programming, we believe that Modula-2 will sweep the programming community during the 1980s just as Pascal gained popularity during the 1970s. If you are going to invest the time in learning a programming language, we recommend Modula-2. Knowing Modula-2 will be a valuable skill for years to come.

AUDIENCE

This book is written for experienced computer programmers or hobbiests, persons familiar with Pascal, or students in a classroom situation. The complete novice may experience some difficulty with the material without access to an experienced programmer. The book provides a complete coverage of Modula-2 programming, but does not go into the details of general programming fundamentals. For a programmer who is familiar with Pascal, learning Modula-2 is a one- to two-week task. New programmers can learn the language with help. Programmers aspiring to learn Ada could do far worse than to learn Modula-2 first. Many of Ada's concepts have direct parallels in Modula-2.

GOALS

We had two goals in writing this book. The first was to provide an introduction to Modula-2. The second was to describe the problems that surround the development of large programs and to indicate how modern structured languages such as Modula-2 help solve these problems. We felt that it was not sufficient to merely explain the rules for writing valid program statements in Modula-2. It is equally important that you understand why certain features are included in Modula-2 for the development of large programs that are reliable, maintainable, and easy to understand.

This book covers every feature of Modula-2. After finishing it, you will be able to write complete Modula-2 programs with an appreciation of the role of various Modula-2 features in the context of large software projects.

Once you learn enough to write a Modula-2 program (no later than Chapter 5), we encourage you to study Modula-2 at the keyboard of a computer. No one ever learned to ride a bicycle by just reading about it. The same is true for programming. Numerous examples and sample programs are included to foster this approach.

ORGANIZATION OF THE BOOK

This book is intended for either self-study or for use as a text in a one-semester programming course. The book assumes that the reader has very little programming experience and no advanced mathematical background. In fact, we have avoided numerical programming examples in favor of programs that work primarily with text.

The book is divided into three parts. The first two chapters make up Part I and give an overview of Modula-2. Part II is made up of the next six chapters. These chapters cover the fundamentals of Modula-2. (Chapters 2 through 6 present material that makes up an estimated 80% to 90% of the lines of code in the typical program.) Significant programming tasks can be undertaken after

Part II is completed. The final part of the book, Advanced Topics, contains Chapters 9 through 12. Some input and output topics in Chapter 9 might be considered essential, rather than advanced, by many programmers. Throughout, you will want to refer to the reference material in the Appendices.

THE WORD PROCESSOR PROJECT

Modula-2 can best be learned with concrete examples. Many examples are used in this book. They start out extremely simple because we want the reader to concentrate on the language feature being introduced and not be confused over a complex algorithm for finding prime numbers. Furthermore, we try to come back to the same small set of simple examples as each new language feature is introduced. Once again, the emphasis is on "What does this feature do, and how does it work compared to what we have seen so far?" and not "Look at the neat algorithms I know."

As the language fundamentals are completed after the first six chapters, the examples begin to pick up in terms of complexity and realism. In the later chapters, useful software "tools" are presented.

A major strength of Modula-2 is its suitability for large software development projects. This strength is difficult to illustrate in the typical one-page tutorial program. To remedy this problem, a complete word processing program is designed and developed in the final chapter of the book. Some of the software tools developed in earlier chapters are used as library routines. This word processor provides a full-screen text editor and output formatter. This package allows text files to be created, modified, and output. The formatter provides for complete page and margin specification, headers, page numbering, line filling, spacing, and justification—all by means of a fully error-trapped menu system.

END OF CHAPTER PROBLEMS

Each chapter ends with a set of simple questions and problems to test your understanding of the concepts presented in the chapter. Answering these questions should take no more than five minutes and will confirm that you picked up the key points. Checking the sample programs at a computer will take longer than five minutes, but will be time well-spent.

Each chapter also includes a set of supplemental problems. These more challenging problems are part of a single larger problem that spans the entire book. The larger problem is the development of a calculator program. This problem could form the basis for a semester project. Appendix E provides the listing of a calculator program which is an answer to the supplemental problems.

Good luck with Modula-2. You'll find learning the language an interesting and rewarding experience.

Ed Knepley
Robert Platt
Reston, Virginia

ACKNOWLEDGMENT

The authors would like to acknowledge the contribution of reviewer Thomas J. Ahlborn who suggested the program which appears in Appendix D.

PART I

BASICS

CHAPTER 1

INTRODUCTION

NEW CONCEPTS: Structured Programming
ISSUES: Program Transportability, Machine Dependence

1.1 BACKGROUND

Learning to write good programs is, in many ways, similar to learning to write good compositions. Both involve learning rigid rules of grammar together with general rules of style, and both require lots of practice. Good programming style comes with time and is based upon habits picked up from studying the work of others.

Fundamentally, programming involves logically analyzing a problem and then expressing the steps necessary to perform the solution in the clearest possible manner. Although this description applies to problem solving in general, programming requires that the solution steps be expressed in terms that a computer can "understand."

There were no programming languages, as such, for the first computers. Their instructions were entered either one bit at a time or by modifications to the computer. Later, programming languages were developed to help people express problem solving steps in more natural terms. Early languages, *assemblers*, allowed each machine instruction to be expressed with mnemonic symbols such as LDA, STA, and NOP. This made programs easier to write and modify, but the programmer still had to think out each instruction in machine-level terms that were dictated by the design of the particular computer. No simple instructions existed for everyday tasks such as "print this result." Also, since assembly language is unique to a specific computer, programs had to be totally rewritten before they could be run on a different machine.

In order to promote ease of programming and the ability to transport programs between different makes of computers, more elaborate programming languages were designed. These new languages achieved both ease of use and portability by using English-like words such as READ, WRITE, and DO instead of machine-specific assembly language mnemonic symbols. The new languages also avoided reference to machine-specific parameters, memory addresses, and devices. WRITE meant WRITE regardless of the computer being used. These "higher level" languages required special programs called *compilers* to translate the programmer's code into "lower level" machine code. A compiler had to be written for each language on each different type of computer. Because compiler design and programming language design were new fields, early efforts were lacking by today's standards.

Among the most popular early programming languages were FORTRAN (FORmula TRANslation language), for technical applications, and COBOL (COmmon Business Oriented Language), for business applications. Both of these languages are still in wide use today, mainly due to large corporate investment in operational programs (estimated to be in the billions of dollars). However, these languages do not take full advantage of the progress made in computer science. With advances in the fields of programming, language design, and compiler design, better languages have evolved. Among the more modern languages are Pascal, C, Ada, and Modula-2.

These modern languages have several features in common. Among the most important is that they support *structured programming*. A structured programming language reflects the organization of a program in the syntax, or rules of grammar, of the language. Logically related statements and actions are grouped together. In a non-structured language, only the self-discipline of the programmer prevents related portions of the program from being scattered over hundreds or thousands of lines of code. Often, discipline alone is not enough. It is very difficult to understand a program when its structure is removed or hidden. Programs written in a structured language are easier to develop, understand, and maintain than those written in non-structured languages such as FORTRAN or BASIC. Later sections, especially Chapters 8 and 12, will cover the subject of structured programming in more detail.

1.2 ORIGINS OF MODULA-2

In 1970 Niklaus Wirth, a Swiss computer scientist, created Pascal, an early structured programming language. Wirth believed that computer programs should consist of well-defined data structures and well-structured procedural steps, or algorithms. As a result, Pascal places great emphasis on explicitly defining the data structures used in a program. Pascal is relatively easy to implement on microcomputers, and it teaches good programming habits. Thus, beginning in the late 1970s, Pascal became one of the more popular programming languages.

One of Pascal's strengths is that its logical structure makes it relatively easy to learn. In fact, Wirth designed Pascal for use in teaching introductory programming classes. Pascal's features also include the ability to define a wide variety of different data structures, structured programming syntax, dynamic allocation of variables, and flexible subprogramming that includes recursion.

However, Pascal also has certain weaknesses. The input and output operations, which Wirth defined for his student programming language, are not well-suited for general purpose computer applications. The "official" version of Pascal, among other things, does not include string variables, an exponentiation operator, or a means for sharing libraries of subprograms. Further, some of Pascal's syntax is awkward. A programmer is constantly grouping statements with the words BEGIN and END to the extent that complex situations become confusing. Wirth addressed these shortcomings in Modula-2.

Modula-2 is an outgrowth of Pascal and a circa 1975 experimental language of Wirth's called Modula. It was also influenced by Wirth's experience with the language Mesa at Xerox Corporation's Palo Alto Research Center in 1976. Development of Modula-2 began in 1977 and was first implemented on a PDP-11® minicomputer in 1979.

1.2.1 Features of Modula-2

Modula-2's major areas of improvement relative to Pascal include

- Simplification of Pascal's grammatical rules.
- The ability to break large programs into smaller pieces called *modules.*
- The ability to perform low-level programming such as that required for the development of computer operating systems.
- Support for multiprogramming.

Other, less important, features that were incorporated into Modula-2 will be described in subsequent chapters.

In general, Modula-2 is a rich and expressive language. It can represent relationships and programming concepts that are not possible in many other

PDP-11® is a trademark of Digital Equipment Corporation.

programming languages. The following paragraphs give a short introduction to Modula-2's major features. Each item will be covered in detail later.

Modula-2 is intended to be *machine independent* so that the same Modula-2 program can be run on a variety of different types of computers without being rewritten. Usually, machine-independent languages can only be used for high-level, or general application, programming tasks such as accounting and payroll packages. However, Modula-2 is designed to be used in low-level programming as well. For example, Wirth used Modula-2 to write a complete operating system for the Lilith minicomputer.

Most languages cannot be used to write operating systems because operations are required on machine-level information that is unique to a particular computer. Modula-2 allows any action that can be specified in a machine's native language to be described in Modula-2. It does this via modules, which are used to hide the details of a program that must vary between makes of computers. Thus, most programs can be transported easily across computers. The sample programs in this book were run on both an IBM® Personal Computer (IBM PC) and an Apple.®

Most programming languages are capable of performing only one task at a time. Yet, in some applications, such as an airline reservation system, a program must handle multiple activities at the same time. One person will be canceling a reservation while another is getting a boarding pass. The ability to perform several tasks at once is called *concurrent processing*, and Modula-2 is one of the few languages with commands to describe such operations.

Data abstraction and information hiding are modern programming concepts that aid in reducing program complexity and increasing program reliability. For example, this book will cover disk input and output. The details of how data is organized on the disk is left to the programmers of the operating system for a particular computer. The details are hidden in a module and may be different from machine to machine. This has no adverse effect on a user. All the user needs is a high-level procedure to do the disk input/output tasks, e.g., Open(filename), Read(twoblocks, filename).

A final Modula-2 feature is separate compilation. This feature makes the development of reusable programs stored in libraries feasible. Library modules are divided into a definition part, which the user sees, and an implementation part, which only the programmer sees. The definition part is all that is needed in order to compile user programs. The implementation part houses the actual application programs that perform the desired functions. User programs, definition modules, and implementation modules are all compiled separately. (Version control and checking is enforced by the system.) Changes can be made to the implementation portion of library routines without affecting the programs—and therefore the clients—that use them. This feature and the concept of data abstraction and information hiding go hand in hand.

1.2.2 A Simple Modula-2 Program

Listing 1.1 presents a simple Modula-2 program. The program displays a message on the screen and writes the numbers from 1 to 10 in a column. The purpose of discussing a program at this early stage is to show the "lay of the land." You, the reader, need a feel for the overall structure of a Modula-2 program even before the details of the language are introduced. Inexperienced programmers will have to accept most parts of this program on faith until they are discussed in detail in subsequent chapters.

The first two lines of Listing 1.1 contain comments, which are enclosed between the (* and *) symbols. These are programmer's remarks and are ignored by the compiler. The third line—MODULE Sample;—and the last line—END Sample.—mark the beginning and end of the program. The word Sample is the name of the program. Any name which follows certain rules could have been used.

The next line will appear in many of the early examples—FROM InOut IMPORT WriteInt, WriteLn, WriteString;. Without going into detail, this line allows us to use standard input/output routines from a system library. The statement:

WriteString ("This program counts to ten.");

LISTING 1.1

```
(* Listing 1.1 - Sample Modula-2 program *)
(* This program writes the numbers from 1 to 10. *)

MODULE Sample;
    FROM InOut IMPORT WriteInt, WriteLn, WriteString;
    VAR i : INTEGER;
BEGIN
    WriteString("This program counts to ten.");
    FOR i := 1 TO 10 DO
        WriteLn;
        WriteInt(i, 6);
    END;
END Sample.
```

is an example of a system library input/output instruction which displays the message enclosed in quotation marks. Similarly, the statement:

```
WriteInt (i, 6);
```

will cause the number that is assigned to i to appear on the screen. The statement WriteLn; starts a new line.

The line VAR i : INTEGER; is an example of a declaration. It declares that a variable will be used, that its name is i, and that it is an integer. Modula-2 is a strongly typed language, and every object in a program must be declared before it can be used. In a big program, this section can be quite large.

The program section beginning with the declaration (in this specific example, the line VAR . . .) and ending with the final period in End Sample. is called the program *block*. The portion within the block from BEGIN to END Sample. is the program's main body. These are the instructions that are executed when the program is run.

The overall syntax and indentation reflect the program structure. Do not worry about understanding this example in detail yet. We will return to it several times with explanations.

The advantages of structured languages are realized in the development of large programs, and Listing 1.1 barely qualifies as a small program. The word processor, which is developed in Chapter 12, is better suited to demonstrate the advantages of Modula-2.

1.3 MODULA-2 IMPLEMENTATIONS

Although there is a standard definition of the Modula-2 language, there are major elements that are not part of the language. Most prominent is the lack of input/output statements as part of the language. Wirth recommended standard library units for inclusion with Modula-2 implementations. The module InOut that was used in the program of Listing 1.1 is an example of one such library unit. You can expect that most of these recommended modules will be provided with each Modula-2 implementation. However, the final decision is in the hands of the various software houses that implement Modula-2.

1.3.1 The Language and Its Surroundings

The official definition of Modula-2 is contained in Wirth's book *Programming in Modula-2* (Springer-Verlag 1982). The book also defines a standard library of routines that forms an important part of Modula-2. It is important to realize that these standard modules are *not* part of the language proper—merely recommendations.

In a sense, Modula-2 is not only a group of language rules but also an expandable set of language features. For example, although input/output is *not* a part of the language definition, library routines such as WriteString in Listing 1.1 are used to perform this essential function. This book presents both Wirth's official language and also his suggested environment. We will note when we shift between the two, because although the language will be the same, Modula-2 system implementers may differ on how they implement the environment. When we encounter details that are not addressed in Wirth's book, we will use the Volition Systems implementation of Modula-2. This is an excellent implementation and is available on the largest variety of microcomputers.

1.3.2 A Typical Implementation

A typical Modula-2 implementation consists of more than just a compiler. A text editor is needed for entering and modifying programs. A Modula-2 compiler translates the source code from the editor into object code that the computer can understand and execute. Library management utilities are required to file and maintain system and user library programs so that the routines can be called when needed by other Modula-2 programs. A *standard library* of frequently used routines, such as those recommended by Wirth, should be available. A file system to manage the large number of files used by the system is essential.

Given the fact that several different programs will interact with a given Modula-2 routine at different times, an overall *operating system* is needed. The operating system orchestrates the actions of programs such as the text editor, librarian, compiler, drivers for display devices, and disk drives. It also manages the files used by these programs.

The examples in this book were developed using the Volition Systems Modula-2 implementation. Other implementations can be expected to differ slightly in the area of standard library routines.

1.3.3 Availability of Modula-2

At the time that this book goes to press, there are several sources of Modula-2 compilers. Volition Systems offers an implementation for a variety of microcomputers such as Apple, IBM PC (and compatibles), and Sage. The Volition Systems implementation runs under the University of California at San Diego (UCSD) p-System and PC-DOS.® The Modula-2 Research Institute implementation runs on IBM PC-compatible microcomputers. Logitech's Modula-2/86 runs on microcomputers with MS-DOS® or CP/M-86® operating systems. Wirth's home base, the Eidgenossische Technische Hochschule (ETH) in Zurich, Switzerland, has a Modula-2 compiler for the Digital Equipment Corporation's PDP-11® family of microcomputers. Finally, the University of Hamburg, Germany has a compiler for the Digital Equipment Corporation VAX-11 family of minicomputers.

These products are just the start of a growing number of implementations. Other groups have announced Modula-2 compilers that will be available in the near future. To get the most out of this book, get access to a Modula-2 compiler and try out the sample programs and problems. In selecting a compiler, make sure that it is faithful to the official definition of Modula-2.

1.4 PROGRAMMING TECHNIQUE

Modula-2 encourages good programming habits and techniques. This is a topic that we will return to throughout this book. The value of learning Modula-2 is diminished if you do not take advantage of these features. The following are some important questions to keep in mind while progressing through the book:

1. Have you analyzed the problem and broken the program into small and easy-to-understand pieces that reflect the logical structure of your solution? One of Modula-2's greatest strengths is its feature for breaking down large, complex problems into small, independent, and readily understood pieces. Learning Modula-2 is synonymous with learning how to use these features.

2. Is the program readable? Modula-2 format is free form and allows program lines to be indented and spaced to reflect the program's structure. Also, liberal use of comments and the selection of descriptive identifier names are very helpful. You may have to modify the

PC-DOS® is a trademark of IBM Corp.

MS-DOS® is a trademark of MicroSoft.

CP/M-86® is a registered trademark of Digital Research, Inc.

program long after you have forgotten its details. Never assume that you will be the only person to read your programs.

3. Is the program portable; that is, can it be easily transported between different types of computers? If parts of your program must be machine specific, have they been isolated into a single module? In this manner, converting the program to run on other machines will not entail hunting through the entire program for machine-specific details.

In addition to the programmer's view, consider the program's design from the user's perspective. Most programs are made to be used by people, and the man-machine interface requires close attention. All of the elegant code, algorithms, and data structures in the world will not help if the user cannot figure out how to make the program work. Ask yourself these questions:

1. Are the input formats convenient, logical, uncluttered, and consistent (friendly)?
2. Does the program protect itself, the user's data, and the user from the effects of bad input data (error trapping)?
3. Is the program sufficiently flexible so that it can be adapted to perform related tasks (modular and reusable)?

The answer to these three latter questions are not independent of the previous three issues. The man-machine interface may be a factor that dictates the use of machine-specific (i.e., non-portable) code. The challenge is to utilize the modular features of Modula-2 to construct reusable system library procedures for these recurring user interface functions—for example, screen input/output handlers and menu development utilities. Do it right once, and you will see the advantage.

SUMMARY

This chapter discussed the origins of Modula-2 and the general characteristics of the language. The remainder of the book will describe Modula-2 in detail. By the end of the book, every feature and detail of the language will have been explained and demonstrated.

PROBLEMS

Each chapter ends with two sets of problems. The first set is easy and tests your understanding of the basic concepts presented in the chapter. The problems of the second set (labeled *supplemental*) are more challenging. These latter problems are all parts of a larger problem that spans the book from Chapters 1 through 11.

In the supplemental problem set, a program to emulate a calculator is developed. Each chapter either adds to the capabilities of the previous chapter's calculator or reformulates earlier solutions using new Modula-2 features from the most recent chapter. Appendix E provides the listing of a calculator program that addresses most of the questions posed in the supplemental problems.

SUPPLEMENTAL PROBLEMS

Problem 1

There are two different types of calculators. They differ in the order that operands and mathematical operators are entered. One entry type is referred to as Algebraic notation and the other is Polish notation. In an algebraic calculator, if we want to subtract two numbers and display the result, the following four steps are performed:

```
Press 5
Press −
Press 2
Press =
        3   (result is displayed).
```

To perform the same operation using a Polish notation model, we would perform the following steps:

```
Press 5   (and press enter key)
Press 2   (and press enter key)
Press −
        3   (result is displayed).
```

The calculator to be developed uses Polish notation. If you are not familiar with this type of calculator, learn to use one. Problems in subsequent chapters will assume that you have this knowledge.

Problem 2

What functions should our calculator perform besides the obvious (i.e., +, −, * and /)? What functions are available on pocket calculator models? How do these functions differ from an algebraic notation model and why?

Problem 3

Why would anyone use Polish notation? What implementation advantages does it provide (if any)?

CHAPTER 2

THE ELEMENTS OF MODULA-2

NEW CONCEPTS: Syntax Diagrams, Statements, Constants, Variables, Data Types, Control Structures, Modules
ISSUES: Standard Input/Output, Syntactic vs. Semantic Rules

INTRODUCTION

Many programming topics represent classic "chicken and egg" situations. Topic number one makes little or no sense without knowledge of topic number two, which, in turn, makes little or no sense without knowledge of topic number one. For example, it is difficult to present a meaningful description of the language features for reading and writing data without having first introduced variables because the data we are reading and writing are assigned to variables. However, it is likewise difficult to provide demonstrations of variables without first discussing input/output because reading and writing is typically the means by which the variable's values are obtained and displayed. Which should be introduced first? No matter what order is chosen for the introduction of a language feature, inevitably some subject that follows is a prerequisite for the current topic. This is something that must be recognized and accepted. Throughout the book, there are references to topics in subsequent and previous chapters when necessary.

In an attempt to minimize the problem just described, this chapter gives a general description of the major elements of Modula-2. This discussion is not detailed; the details come in later chapters. Each key part of the language is previewed so that the detailed discussion of these items in subsequent chapters can be viewed in the context of the total language.

2.1 SYNTAX DIAGRAMS

A major part of this book is about the rules of grammar for the Modula-2 programming language. The grammatical rules for a programming language can be best summarized pictorially. The pictorial representations for these rules of grammar are called syntax diagrams. (See Figure 2.1.) A syntax diagram describes the rules for writing a syntactically (grammatically) correct program. A syntax diagram consists of two basic components—nodes and directionalized paths. There are two types of syntax diagram nodes: One is rectangular in shape, and the second is either circular or a box with rounded corners. The rectangle contains a name, which references yet another syntax diagram that must be substituted in the current diagram at that point. The circular or rounded nodes contain a word or character that must be substituted literally at that point. The directionalized path describes legal routes through the syntax diagram and may contain branches. At a fork in the path, any branch may be taken so long as it follows the directional arrows. A simple example will illustrate the use of syntax diagrams.

Figure 2.1 is a syntax diagram for writing a whole number of Modula-2. To use the diagram for determining the syntax of valid Modula-2 whole numbers, we must begin at the left side of Figure 2.1a, which is labeled Whole Number. This is the standard starting point for every syntax diagram. A syntax diagram is used by following a path until it branches or until a node is encountered. In the case of Whole Number, the starting path leads to the rectan-

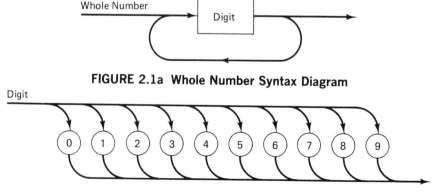

FIGURE 2.1a Whole Number Syntax Diagram

FIGURE 2.1b Digit Syntax Diagram

gular node labeled Digit. Since this node is rectangular, and not circular or rounded, another syntax diagram must be substituted at this point in the construction of a whole number. The next syntax diagram is called Digit, and is shown in Figure 2.1b.

Starting at the left of the digit syntax diagram, we encounter a branch in the path before encountering the first node. At this juncture, we can take either fork in the path. A number of additional branches may be encountered prior to the first node, depending on which node we intend to reach. For example, there are three path branches en route to the node which is labeled 2. Assuming we follow the direct path to node 2, since this is a circular node, the character 2 must be placed in our whole number construction at this point. All paths leaving the circular digit nodes lead to the same place, i.e., to the end of the digit syntax diagram. This is a syntax diagram requirement. Every syntax diagram must eventually provide a path to the end of the diagram.

Reaching the end of the digit syntax diagram is equivalent to exiting from the right side of the rectangular whole number node labeled Digit. The value of the whole number, thus far, is 2. The saga of the whole number syntax is picked up at this point. Leaving the Digit node in Figure 2.1a, we encounter a branch in the path. One fork in the path takes us to the end of the whole number syntax diagram. The second fork takes us back to the beginning, and thus back to the Digit node. Assuming that 2 was not the entire whole number to be constructed, the loop in the path would be taken. On the second pass through Digit, assume that the node labeled 4 is reached. Then the character 4 is written at the end of the current whole number construction, giving us 24.

Continuing in this manner—that is, going from path to node or branch, substituting node contents or choosing a path direction until the end of the syntax diagram is reached—provides us with a syntactically correct whole number. All syntax diagrams are used in the same fashion. Notice that the syntax diagram says nothing about the maximum number of digits in a valid whole number. This information is supplied separately.

The loop around the box containing the word Digit says that a whole number must have at least one digit, but can also be a string of more than one digit. Any of the following examples are syntactically correct in terms of the rules of Figure 2.1:

2   24   248   1234567890

Strings of characters that contain any character other than a digit do not match the syntax prescribed by Figure 2.1 and are invalid. For example,

2X   4.5   248W   A5   1,000

are all invalid whole numbers.

The notation used in drawing syntax diagrams is easy to understand. Items that must appear literally in your program—for example, digits, keywords such as END, and punctuation marks—are enclosed in circles or boxes with rounded corners. Boxes with square corners mean that an item defined by another syntax diagram must appear at that point in the program. The program can select one of several alternatives when a branch in a path is encountered.

To see if your program follows Modula-2's syntactic rules, all you have to do is follow the syntax diagram paths and compare each word, symbol, or punctuation mark of your program with the corresponding elements in the diagram. If you can follow a series of syntax diagram paths that link all of the elements of your program, then you can be sure that the Modula-2 compiler will not object to the program on grammatical grounds. Of course, your program still may not perform the function that you intended since the syntax only guarantees that the grammar is correct. This brings up an important distinction. Every language has both *syntactic* and *semantic* rules. The diagrams in this book summarize the syntax of Modula-2. You must still master the semantic rules, which are covered in the rest of the book, in order to give your programs meaning.

We will use syntax diagrams throughout the book to define legal Modula-2 grammar. Appendix A contains the complete set of syntax diagrams for Modula-2. An alphabetized index is presented with the diagrams for ease of reference. The terminology and the order of appearance of the diagrams coincide with the syntax appendix in Wirth's book. This should facilitate cross-references with the language "standard." Throughout the book we will make reference to these syntax diagrams—for example, see Figure A.7 for the digit syntax diagram. The reader is encouraged to use these diagrams. They form the definitive rules of grammar for the language.

2.2 THE BUILDING BLOCKS OF MODULA-2

Modula-2 has a number of items that appear so frequently in programs that using them becomes second nature. They are similar to words and punctuation in English. In this chapter we will review the syntax diagrams of these items. Later chapters will cover the issues involved in using these program elements to create more complex structures.

2.2.1 Identifiers

Modula-2 permits a programmer to assign names to various objects. Such names are called *identifiers*. Figure A.1 is the syntax diagram for creating a legal identifier. An identifier is composed of one or more characters, either letters or digits, with the requirement that the name must begin with a letter. For example, the following are five legal identifiers:

   a   A   OneOverDelta   x12   AVeryLongIdentifier

and the following are four illegal identifiers:

   2a   a 1   One-way   Version.1.

Modula-2 is a "case-sensitive" language that distinguishes between upper- and lower-case letters. For this reason, a and A are different identifiers that represent two separate objects. (Some implementations of Modula-2 provide an option to ignore the difference between upper- and lower-case letters. This option is for those computer systems that do not use both upper- and lower-case letters.)

A Modula-2 identifier has no restriction on its length. Furthermore, every character in the name is recognized by the compiler. (Compare this to Pascal, in which the name length is unlimited but the compiler uses only the first eight characters.) Thus,

   AVeryLongIdentifier1   and   AVeryLongIdentifier2

are two valid and distinct Modula-2 identifier names. In Pascal, they are the same identifier—AVERYLON.

The selection of an identifier that will help make a program readable and understandable is an important programming technique. Since Modula-2 does not impose any limitations on the length of an identifier name, meaningful names can always be used. For example, the identifier qlj does nothing to explain the object it represents. However, identifying the average value as AverageValue adds to the readability of the program and reduces the chances of referring to the wrong identifier. Multiple-word identifiers should be written using capital letters at the start of each word—AverageValue and not average-value—in order to improve readability. The underscore character, which is valid in some Pascal implementations (average_value), is illegal in Modula-2.

Certain Modula-2 identifiers have predefined meanings. When you use these *standard identifiers*, they automatically take on the meaning established by the system. In some circumstances, you can redefine any of these identifiers to assume another meaning of your choice. This redefinition, which is not a common occurrence, is allowed only in procedures (procedures are described in Chapter 8), and not in the main portion of the program. Once redefined within a procedure, the standard meaning is unavailable in that section of a program. Here is a list of the standard identifiers. These standard identifiers must be learned. Their meaning will be explained in later sections of this book.

ABS	HIGH
BITSET	INC
BOOLEAN	INCL
CAP	INTEGER
CARDINAL	NEW
CHAR	NIL
CHR	ODD
DEC	ORD
DISPOSE	PROC
EXCL	REAL
FALSE	TRUE
FLOAT	TRUNC
HALT	VAL

In addition, certain key words act as punctuation in Modula-2 programs and because of their special role may not be used as identifier names. These are called *reserved words* and are listed below. These words, like the standard identifiers, must also be learned. Their usage is explained in subsequent sections of this book. Unlike standard identifiers, reserved words cannot be redefined in a program.

AND	ELSIF	LOOP	REPEAT
ARRAY	END	MOD	RETURN
BEGIN	EXIT	MODULE	SET
BY	EXPORT	NOT	THEN
CASE	FOR	OF	TO
CONST	FROM	OR	TYPE
DEFINITION	IF	POINTER	UNTIL
DIV	IMPLEMENTATION	PROCEDURE	VAR
DO	IMPORT	QUALIFIED	WHILE
ELSE	IN	RECORD	WITH

2.2.2 Program Structure and Comments

If identifiers make up most of the words of Modula-2, what makes up the space between the words, and how are the words combined into program lines? In general, one or more spaces or carriage returns (new lines) must appear between words in a Modula-2 program. (A carriage return contains an implicit space.) Program lines can start in any column. Line numbers, such as those used in BASIC and FORTRAN, are not used in Modula-2. Punctuation marks and spaces are not allowed in the middle of identifiers. The following example illustrates that the free form of Modula-2 permits a program to be indented in order to indicate its structure.

```
MODULE FormatDemo;
   IMPORT InOut;
   VAR
      i : INTEGER;
   BEGIN
      FOR i := 1 TO 10 DO
         InOut.WriteInt(i, 6);
         InOut.WriteLn;
      END;
   END FormatDemo.
```

Although there are no firm rules regarding the structure and form of a Modula-2 program, an indentation style, such as that in the previous example, is recommended in order to improve readability. At the other extreme, the following version of the same program—which uses the minimum allowable spacing and no indentation—is legal but almost incomprehensible.

```
MODULE Demo;IMPORT InOut;VAR i:INTEGER;BEGIN FOR i:=1 TO 10 DO
InOut.WriteInt(i,6);InOut.WriteLn;END;END Demo.
```

In this example, certain elements of Modula-2 punctuation, such as the semicolon, constitute valid substitutes for spaces. (These elements of punctuation will be covered later.) Aside from spaces, carriage returns, and comments, the only symbols that may appear between words in a Modula-2 program are the punctuation marks that appear in the round boxes in the syntax diagrams. For example, if the syntax diagram includes a circle with a comma at a given point, then a comma must appear at that point in the program. Failure to include that comma will result in an error message from the compiler. Similarly, an error message will also result if a comma appears at a point in the program where the syntax diagrams do not indicate that one is expected.

Modula-2 permits a comment to appear *anywhere a space is allowed*. Comments make Modula-2 programs more readable and understandable by including remarks pertaining to various aspects of the program's operation. A program with meaningful identifiers and good comments should almost be self-documenting. Comments are skipped by the compiler, and thus have no impact on the performance of the program. This is not the case in some languages, such as interpreted versions of BASIC, where comments can have adverse effects on the speed of execution. A comment is written as

(*This is a comment; any character string is legal.*)

where the symbol pairs (* and *) are the comment delimiters. The Pascal delimiters { and } are not valid in Modula-2. The previous sample program is repeated here with comments.

```
(*This demonstrates one comment possibility*)
(*Comments can go here*) MODULE (*here*) Demo (*or here*);
(*Notice that several comments can go on one line*)

  IMPORT InOut; (*Comments can also span
                     several lines*)
  VAR
    i : INTEGER;

BEGIN          (*Main program body*)
  FOR (*loop index*) i := 1 (*start*) TO 10 (*finish*) DO
    InOut.WriteInt(i (*Write value of i*), 6 (*In 6 space field*));
    InOut.WriteLn; (*New line; Comment inside parameter list above*)
  END (* of FOR i. . . *);
END Demo. (* End of an "over commented" program*)
(*The End.*)
```

Comments can contain any information that the programmer believes will be helpful in understanding the program. In addition, some vendor's implementations of Modula-2 use comments to activate and control compiler options. For example, the Volition system will set compiler options (such as ignoring upper- and lower-case differences) based upon comments that begin with a dollar sign ($).

Another use for comments is to temporarily remove a section of a program without physically deleting that portion from the source text file. Modula-2 makes this easy by allowing comments to be *nested* and to extend across any number of lines. For example, Listing 2.1 will display only the words Hello. Goodbye. Lines 2 through 5 of the program's main body are treated as comments, including two statements that would normally be executed.

LISTING 2.1

```
(* Listing 2.1 -- Example of nested comments *)

MODULE Comments;
  FROM InOut IMPORT WriteString;
BEGIN
  WriteString("Hello. ");
  (* ----Start of outer comment
  WriteString("This will not be displayed");
  (* This nested comment is contained in the outer comment *)
  WriteString("Modula-2 will treat this as a comment");
  End of outer comment---- *)
  WriteString("Goodbye.");
END Comments.
```

2.2.3 Numbers and Numeric Constants

As you can see from the sample program in the previous section of this chapter, Modula-2 not only refers to items by identifiers such as i but also by numbers like 1 and 10 and by *numeric constants*. The syntax rules for numbers and numeric constants are shown in the syntax diagrams of Figures A.2 through A.8.

Modula-2 is able to refer to numbers in four separate ways. In mathematics, a number can be written using different number *bases.* Modula-2 permits whole numbers to be written using three different bases—octal (base 8), decimal (base 10), and hexadecimal (base 16). For example, the ordinary decimal (base 10) number 23 can also be written as 17 in hexadecimal (base 16) or as 27 in octal (base 8). In addition to these three representations for whole numbers, numbers containing a decimal point—called REAL numbers—are used in Modula-2. Section 3.1 covers this fourth type of numeric constant.

Examination of Figure A.3 shows that a decimal constant follows the same syntax rules that were described in Section 2.1 for a whole number. Octal constants follow the same basic syntax rules as do decimals except that, whereas the allowable decimal digits are

0 1 2 3 4 5 6 7 8 9,

the octal digits do not include 8 and 9. The octal digits are

0 1 2 3 4 5 6 7.

One additional difference between decimal and octal constants, as shown in Figure A.3, is that the octal constant ends with the letter B (or C, as we will see when we discuss characters).

Hexadecimal constants are constructed in a manner similar to that for decimal and octal constants. The hexadecimal digits are

0 1 2 3 4 5 6 7 8 9 A B C D E F.

Figure A.3 indicates that hexadecimal constants end in the letter H. Note that a hex number cannot begin with the letters A through F. For example, F0H is illegal and must be written 0F0H. In summary, Modula-2 constants for the decimal number 23 could be expressed as 23, 17H, or 27B.

2.2.4 Data Types

The numbers in our examples thus far have been whole numbers, or integers. However, we realize that there are also real numbers and non-numeric items as well. This brings up the point that items handled in Modula-2 programs not only have data values but also *data types*. INTEGER, CARDINAL, REAL, BOOLEAN, and CHAR (character) are data types. (They are also standard identifiers.) It is as important for the computer to know the *type* of the data as it is to know its *value*.

Each data element used in a program requires space in the computer's memory. In addition to memory space, every element has predefined operations that may be performed. Finally, every data element has a set of legal values that it can assume. The amount of memory required, the valid operations specified for an element, and the values it may assume depend on the element's type. For example, storing the string of characters "This program counts to ten" will take up much more space than storing the number 1. Further, certain operations, such as addition, make sense for integers like 1 but cannot be performed on strings of characters. Lastly, an INTEGER data type cannot have a value such as c, since c is a character and not an integer. In order for the computer to allocate the proper amount of space for the various items of a program and to know what operations and values are valid for each item, the data type must be explicitly specified for every program element.

Modula-2 has a number of predefined data types. It also permits you to define your own data types within a program. A constraint comes with this flexibility, however. Modula-2 does not allow operations on mixed data types. For example, Modula-2 will not add the number 1 to the character string 'hello.' This sort of operation would result in a compile time error.

The requirement that the data structures upon which each program acts be well-defined is reflected in Modula-2's syntax. As stated in the Chapter 1 discussion of Listing 1.1, Modula-2 expects the data type of each object to be defined before that item is used in the program. The only limited exception to this rule is for constants. The specification of a constant such as

PageLength = 66   or   Message = 'Hi there'

provides an implicit definition of the type as part of the value declaration. A simple number is assumed to be an INTEGER, or a type of integer called a CARDINAL. Strings of characters enclosed in quotation marks are assumed to be STRINGS. As each data type is covered in Chapters 3 and 6, the rules for writing constants of each type will also be explained.

A compilation error results if the syntax rules regarding type declarations and operations between incompatible types (1 + 'hello') are violated. This is standard operating procedure for all syntax errors—"No correct syntax, no compiled program."

2.2.5 Expressions and Operators

We have looked at the words of Modula-2. What about the rules for combining these words into simple phrases? The phrases of Modula-2 are called *expressions* and can consist of one object or a combination of objects. Each expression has a value. The value can be given by a single item (like the numeric constant 4), or can result from the evaluation of a combination of objects.

When several items appear together in an expression, *operators* determine how the items are to be combined. All operators must be explicitly stated. Multiplication cannot be implied. That is, 3(2+5) must be rewritten as 3*(2+5) if the intent is to multiply the sum (2+5) by 3. Here are a few examples of correct Modula-2 arithmetic expressions:

```
3 + 2
(2 * 6) − 7
10 DIV 2
5
```

All of the above expressions have 5 as their value.

Table 2.1 summarizes Modula-2's arithmetic operators. Other operators and the type of data that they act upon are covered in Chapter 3.

TABLE 2.1

```
                     Modula-2 Arithmetic Operators

    OPERATOR     NAME              EXAMPLE    COMMENT
       +         Addition          3 + 2      Applies to any number
       −         Subtraction       3 − 2       "      "  "      "
       *         Multiplication    3 * 2       "      "  "      "
       /         Division          3 / 2      For REAL numbers only
      DIV        Division          3 DIV 2    INTEGER & CARDINAL only
      MOD        Remainder         3 MOD 2     "      "      "      "
```

Modula-2 has two different types of expressions:

• *constant expressions,* whose values are known at the start of the program and cannot change, and

• *regular expressions,* whose values can change while a program is running.

The four examples of correct Modula-2 arithmetic expressions are all constant expressions because their values will always be 5 and will never change during the execution of a program.

Figures A.12 and A.41 give the syntax diagrams for constant expressions and regular expressions. Operators can occur in any order as long as the operator appears between the two items (operands) it is to act upon. (In other words, adding 3 and 2 is written 3+2, not + 3 2 or 3 2 +.) The only exception to this rule is that a plus or minus sign may appear in front of an item to indicate whether its positive or its negative value is to be used. For example, − 3*(4+2) is legal (with a result of − 18), but 3*−(4+2) is illegal. Two operators can not appear side by side.

The arithmetic operators are divided into two categories called Add-Operators (Figure A.15) and MulOperators (Figure A.17). The difference between the two classes of operators comes into play in determining the order in which the operations are to be performed. Three rules govern the order of operations when evaluating expressions:

1. Any expression inside parentheses is evaluated before operations outside the parentheses. Therefore, 3*(2+1) is 9, not 7.

2. MulOperators are performed before AddOperators. Therefore, 1+2*3 is 7, not 9.

3. If there is a tie after applying the first two rules, proceed from left to right. Thus, 18/3*2 is 12, not 3.

If you have difficulty in applying the last two rules, follow the first rule and use parentheses to clear up any uncertainties. You can never go wrong by using extra parentheses.

Although the above examples all use *integer* constants and produce numeric values, expressions can be used to combine other types of data, as described in Chapter 3. The important point to remember is that an expression gives precise rules for combining data objects by specifying the use of defined operators in a particular sequence. Depending on what data types, values, and operators are used, the result of the expression will be a data object of a particular type and value.

2.3 THE MAJOR COMPONENTS OF MODULA-2

We now move from the words and phrases of Modula-2 to the sentences and paragraphs of the language. The remainder of this chapter will summarize the major components of Modula-2's syntax.

One of Wirth's fundamental assumptions in designing both Pascal and Modula-2 was that well-written programs result from a successful combination of precisely defined data structures and structured algorithms. (An algorithm is the procedural steps used to solve a problem.) Wirth summarized this idea with the equation:

Algorithms + Data Structures = Programs

The following subsections introduce the elements of Modula-2 that are used to describe the algorithms and data structures of a program. Bear in mind that each element presented plays an important role in spelling out these two key program ingredients.

2.3.1 Statements

A *statement* corresponds to one sentence in the algorithm, or in the description of the actions that the computer is to perform. In our sample program in Listing 1.1, the step that sends a message to the screen,

```
WriteString("This program counts to ten");
```

is an example of a statement. The purpose of a statement is to have the computer perform some action. The syntax diagram for a statement is given in Figure A.46. This figure shows that there are a number of different types of statements in Modula-2, including the If statement, While statement, and Loop statement, among others. Each will be described in subsequent chapters.

Note that a statement may consist of nothing, and it can also contain other statements. A fundamental concept in programming is the notion of sequential actions. A computer algorithm is a sequence of actions to be performed by the computer. Since actions correspond to statements, this leads to the idea of the statement *sequence*. A statement sequence is made up of one or more statements (which may be the null statement) separated by semicolons. The semicolon is referred to as the statement *separator*. As an extreme case,

```
;;;;;;;;;
```

is a valid statement sequence indicating a series of null statements separated by the semicolon statement separator.

Expressions, introduced earlier in this chapter, play a major role as statement building blocks.

2.3.2 Constants

We have already seen some Modula-2 constants. Constants are objects whose values do not change while a program is being executed. From our earlier example, the statement

```
WriteInt(i, 6);
```

uses the constant 6.

Names can be assigned to constants as long as you follow the rules for creating identifiers given in Section 2.2.1. The assignment of names to constants is a recommended programming practice. It greatly simplifies changes to a program, as will be shown in Chapter 3.

In addition to having a value that does not change during the execution of a program, constants have a second property, a data type. For example, the numbers 1, 2, and 5 are all constants of data type INTEGER, but the constant 2.5 is a REAL number.

Most constants are simple values such as 5734. However, Modula-2 also defines a special type of expression called a *constant expression,* whose value can be determined from other constants before a program is run. The expression 2*5 is a constant expression because both 2 and 5 are constants, and its value, 10, can be calculated by the system before the program starts running. Figure A.12, described earlier in this chapter, gives the syntax diagram for a constant expression.

2.3.3 Variables

If all the values used in a program had to be known and specified before the program started, computers would not be very useful. Instead, the power of the computer comes from its ability to describe actions to be performed on general groups of items whose values can be specified and changed *after* the program starts to run. Consider the problem of computing a company's payroll. If every employee's name, wage, and hours worked had to be specified explicitly in a statement, the utility of the program and of the computer would be greatly diminished. We would be forced to write

```
JonesPay := 40.0 * 5.85;
SmithPay := 40.0 * 6.77;
      :
      :
      :
PlattPay := 10.5 * 18.11;
```

with a line for every employee in the company. Even worse, the hours and wage data would have to be changed every pay period, which would, in essence, require that the program be continually rewritten and modified.

What we really want is to have the computer do the work of looking up the number of hours that each employee worked and mutiplying that number by the employee's hourly wage. The result can then be used to print a paycheck for the employee. In Modula-2, the statement

```
EmployeePay := HoursWorked * WageRate;
```

can be used to perform this operation. This single statement replaces the multiple statements in the example above. Furthermore, the program will not require changes each pay period. Of course, the number of hours worked, wage rate, and pay can be different for each employee in the firm and are stored in a data file. The computer can then perform the necessary operations for each employee's record.

At some time while the program is running, a place in the computer's memory holds the value for the number of hours worked by the first employee. (This value is read by the computer from a payroll data file.) When the processing of that employee is complete, a similar value for the second employee is read and stored in this same location, and so on. Likewise, memory locations are reserved for the changing values of WageRate and EmployeePay. Because the values stored in EmployeePay, HoursWorked, and WageRate can change during the program's execution, such items are called *variables*.

Variables are names for places in the computer's memory where values can be stored and recalled. Each variable must be assigned a name (using the rules for identifiers in Section 2.2.1) and must have a data type. The allocation of memory space for each variable is made by the compiler based on the variable's data type. For example, in Listing 1.1, the variable i changed values as the program counted to 10, and i was defined to hold an INTEGER data type. Therefore, it would be allocated two bytes of computer memory space in a typical implementation. More will be said in subsequent chapters regarding variables and their use in Modula-2.

2.3.4 Control Structures

In some ways, writing a program is like writing a cookbook recipe. The steps in solving a problem are written in the order that they are to be performed. At times you may need to repeat groups of operations. For example, "For each apple, remove its core and place on a cookie sheet." This repetition of groups of instructions can be specified in Modula-2 without explicitly writing the statement every time that it is needed. (Indeed, you may not know ahead of time how many apples are in the bushel.)

Statements that cause instructions to be repeated or skipped or to otherwise depart from the listed sequential order are called *control structures.* They are covered in detail in Chapter 4.

2.3.5 Procedures

A Modula-2 program can be divided into smaller pieces. One advantage of breaking down a problem into parts is that it enables you to write and test a complex program one step at a time. Also, if a particular set of steps has to be performed in several different locations within a program, you can give those steps a name, or identifier, and then merely write the identifier wherever those steps are to be performed, thus eliminating the need to repeat each step associated with the identifier. A named group of steps is called a *procedure.* (In some of the other programming languages, procedures are called functions, subroutines, or subprograms.)

The sample program in Listing 1.1 used several procedures for writing information to the computer's screen. These procedures—WriteInt, WriteLn, and WriteString—were defined by the system implementers and then stored in a system library. The use of procedures not only saves typing time, but it means that if programmers debug a procedure once, they do not have to worry about errors if the procedure is reused elsewhere. Procedures and procedure libraries are described in Chapter 8.

2.3.6 Modules

Modules are the centerpiece of Modula-2. A module is a group of procedures and data-structure definitions combined to form a basic Modula-2 program unit. As will be described in Chapter 8, there are several different types of modules. For example, every program is a module. Complex programs typically consist of more than one module and also use procedures from one or more library modules.

When several programmers are working on a project, it is useful to hide the *details* of each programmer's work from the others so that one programmer does not accidentally interfere with the others' components. Modules permit the programmer to specify which details can be altered by other parts of the program, and which "hidden" elements can not be changed from outside the module. A fairly routine example would involve identifier names. Conflicts in the names of identifiers (more than one identifier with the same name) usually leads to adverse results of one form or another. Modules make it possible for two programmers to use the same identifier name without fear of adverse consequences.

In addition, suppose that a procedure in a module has to be changed because a mistake was discovered, or because a more efficient way was found to achieve the same result. The use of modules allows these changes to be made without affecting other programs that rely on these procedures. Modules or programs that use the changed module would not normally need to be altered or recompiled.

In the sample program from Listing 1.1, the entire listing represents a single *program module.* A program module can stand alone as a main program. This is in contrast to other modules that merely reside in the library until used by program modules, for example, InOut in Listing 1.1.

2.3.7 Separate Compilation

Separate compilation is a powerful feature of Modula-2. Separate compilation supports the development of large programs, particularly when multiple-person program teams are involved. Separate compilation makes the development of software libraries practical. Common functions and procedures can be programmed once and placed in a library for use by any program.

The features provided by separate compilation protect the user from unannounced changes to library routines by maintaining strict version control checking at the system level of the language. This safety feature is lacking in Pascal implementations that extend the language to include library units. Implicit advantages provided by Modula-2's separate compilation feature are program reliability, maintainability, and decreased development time. Separate compilation is covered with modules in Chapter 8.

2.3.8 Input/Output—The Component That "Wasn't There"

Most programming texts begin by showing how to write a message to the computer terminal. It is a simple task that makes a reader feel progress is being made. The problem with reading (input) and writing (output) in Modula-2 is that the language does not contain any statements for this purpose!

The reason for this, which is not unique to Modula-2 (consider Ada and C), is that input and output are very system dependent. However, Modula-2 language implementations are supposed to come with library modules that contain input/output procedures as defined by Wirth. Although these library input/output procedures are not part of the language, the net effect on the programmer of having no built-in input/output capability is almost nil. Whether an output procedure called WriteLn (which means, write an end of line to the current output device) is provided in a library unit or as part of the language (as in Pascal) makes little difference to the end user—just as long as it is available. The Modula-2 approach offers certain advantages to the programmer in terms of program efficiency.

The basic input/output procedures can be expected to be the same on all Modula-2 implementations. These standard routines are described in Chapters 5 and 9 and in Appendix C. Unfortunately, different software vendors have introduced subtle differences in their library procedures for the more advanced input/output capabilities (see Chapter 9), and industry attempts at standardization are still in progress.

SUMMARY

This chapter has provided a brief overview of Modula-2. You now have the basic vocabulary and background necessary to understand the details of the Modula-2 language as it is presented throughout the remainder of this book.

At this point, it is important that you understand how to read a syntax diagram. These diagrams will be used throughout the book to define Modula-2 language rules. It is also important that you grasp the concepts of identifiers, constants, variables, expressions, data types, and statements, all of which are fundamental to the material that follows. The information presented on program structure, control structures, procedures, modules, separate compilation, and input/output will be covered in detail in later chapters.

QUESTIONS AND PROBLEMS

1. Pick out the three illegal identifiers:

   HiThere   I'mOK   a   aA   B52   Array
   ThisIsAReallyReallyLongIdentifier   1B52   ARRAY

2. Write the whole numbers 5 and 10 in the three different Modula-2 formats for whole numbers.

3. What is the difference between a constant expression and a regular expression? Examine the syntax diagrams carefully.

4. What are the values of the following expressions? (*Hint:* The sum of the answers is 25.)

   3*(2+1)   3*2+1   1+3*2   −(1+3)*2
   4+4−3+2   4+4−(3+2)

5. What is the difference between a constant and a variable?

(Did you remember that hex constants must begin with a digit when you wrote 10 in problem 2? It is 0AH and not AH.)

SUPPLEMENTAL PROBLEMS

Pseudo-code is a mixture of English and programming language that is used to describe computer algorithms. Pseudo-code is often used in the early stages of the development of a program. The following is a pseudo-code example for a procedure that determines how many digits are in a number that the user enters into the calculator.

```
Initialize the Length of the number to zero;
WHILE (there is another digit to be counted)
    Increment the Length counter;
END of the counting loop;
```

There are no formal rules for the syntax of pseudo-code. As you learn more of Modula-2, you should attempt to conform as closely as possible to the syntax of Modula-2. The above example uses minimal Modula-2 syntax—a WHILE . . . END loop (see Chapter 4) and a structured (indented) layout.

The idea is to describe the algorithm (solution steps) as accurately as possible. Later, each step is expanded to one or more lines of actual program code. PROCEDURE Length of the calculator program in Appendix E is the actual Modula-2 implementation of the above pseudo-code example. Note the similarity between the pseudo-code and the comments in the actual code.

Problem 1

Write the description of a simple Polish notation calculator using pseudo-code. Assume that the calculator can perform the standard operations of addition, subtraction, multiplication, and division. Your code should address *what* is to be done and the *logical flow*—do not worry about the details of "how" yet.

The pseudo-code should consider program initialization, the actual data processing steps (user input, error checking, computation, and display), and program termination.

You should consider the following questions in your solution: How many numbers should the calculator be capable of storing for pending operations?

What must we do with the result of an operation (it should be available for subsequent operations)? What kinds of errors are possible and what action should be taken?

Problem 2

Stacks play a key role in the implementation of a Polish notation calculator. Sometimes a *stack* is referred to as a Last In First Out (LIFO) device. (This is common in other disciplines such as queueing theory.) A physical example of a LIFO device is the spring loaded dish holder/dispenser used in a cafeteria. The top dish on the stack (last in) is the next dish to be taken (first out). A computer stack is analogous to the dish stack—data elements are kept in an area of storage referred to as a *stack* and the last data element added to the stack is the first element removed.

Data entered in our Polish notation calculator will be kept in a stack. If you have never heard of the term *stack* in reference to computers, do some research on this topic. Some issues to investigate are:

- The size of the stack (i.e., how many elements can it hold and what happens when it's full or empty).
- How should the stack be implemented—common choices are arrays (Chapter 6) and pointers (Chapter 7).
- How to add and delete items?

Relate these issues to your pseudo-code.

PART II

A CLOSER LOOK

CHAPTER 3 ====

DATA ELEMENTS

NEW CONCEPTS: Types, Standard Types, Declaring Identifiers, Scope of Identifiers
ISSUES: Use of Constants

INTRODUCTION

In Chapter 2, we saw that variables and constants not only have values but also have a property called a data type. This chapter will introduce the more commonly used Modula-2 data types. These types are predefined as part of the Modula-2 language. It is also possible to define your own data types to meet special needs. Discussion of programmer-defined types as well as several more complex predefined types is taken up in Chapter 6.

The purpose of associating a data type with a variable or constant is to provide information to the computer regarding storage requirements and allowable values and operations for each data element. This information is used by the computer both at compilation time and at run time. At compilation time, the computer checks expression operands for type compatibility. For example

```
x := 1 + 'Hi there';
```

is not allowed because addition is not an allowable operator for the string 'Hi there'. This kind of error would be identified by the compiler.

Besides ensuring that type compatibility rules are satisfied, the compiler also makes storage allocations for the program elements based on their type. At run time, the system *may* check the value of data assigned to variables to ensure that the type rules are being followed. As an example, the assignment of a value larger than the largest whole number available on a particular computer would represent a range error that could not be detected until the program is executed. In this case, although the value is valid in the sense that it is an integer and the associated variable is an integer type, the value of the integer is outside of the range of valid integer data values for this system. There is no guarantee that errors of this type will be identified by the system as they occur. The programmer should guard against them.

Every variable in a Modula-2 program must be explicitly assigned a valid data type. In this chapter, besides introducing the most frequently used types, we will describe how these types are assigned to variables. Lastly, this chapter will introduce "scope" rules for identifiers. As a general rule, all identifiers cannot be accessed (used) in all parts of a Modula-2 program. The scope of an identifier controls which portions of the program can and cannot access the identifier. This topic will be covered in depth in Chapter 8.

3.1 STANDARD DATA TYPES: PROPERTIES AND OPERATORS

Knowing how to select the appropriate data types is essential for a correctly functioning program. Factors which enter into this selection process include knowledge of the operations to be performed on the data and the range of values that the data can assume. In most instances, for the types to be covered in this chapter, this selection will be obvious. For example, in the payroll example of Chapter 2,

```
EmployeePay := HoursWorked * WageRate;
```

it is clear that a decimal and not a whole number is the appropriate data type for all three elements of this statement. The choice of a data type for more unusual or complex types is sometimes more difficult and will be covered in Chapter 6. For each of the data types introduced in this chapter, we will present its purpose, the range of values that it can represent, examples of constants used to represent such values, and a list of operators that can be used with the type.

3.1.1 INTEGER

Integers are whole numbers. (See Figure A.3.) Integer arithmetic is generally faster than arithmetic on other numeric data types, and integers take up less memory than other types. When the problem involves numeric data, and whole numbers are adequate to represent the problem data, integers or cardinals (see the next section) are the type to use for overall efficiency and simplicity. Of course, if the nature of the problem is such that decimal digits are required—for example, monetary data with dollars and cents—then INTEGER is not the correct data type and cannot be used.

Every Modula-2 implementation has a minimum and a maximum value that can be represented by integer variables. These smallest and largest values vary from one make of computer to another. In the Volition Systems implementation, the constant named MaxInt, which is defined in the SystemTypes Module (see Chapter 11), specifies the value of the maximum. On the Apple® II computer, this MaxInt value is 32767. Similarly, the constant MinInt specifies the smallest value, which is −32768. These same values for MaxInt and MinInt are found in the Volition Systems implementation for the IBM PC. This is interesting since the Apple II is an 8-bit system and the IBM is a 16-bit system. The same values appear in the 8-bit Apple due to Volition's manner of implementation. This implementation, by means of software, gives the appearance of running on one standard 16-bit computer—regardless of the actual machine being used. This feature is a great advantage in terms of moving programs from one computer to another.

If a value outside the range defined by values such as MaxInt and MinInt is stored in an integer variable, an overflow results and the value is lost. Programs should protect against overflows since the results are unpredictable. You cannot depend on the operating system to help detect these errors. It may or may not detect them, depending on the specific implementation being used. If we wrote the result of MaxInt + 1 using the Volition system, we would get the value −32768 (which happens to be MinInt). Similarly, the result of MaxInt + 2 is −32767, MaxInt + 3 yields −32766, etc. If you are familiar with the internal representation of integers, you can see what the system is doing. (If this is something new to you, finding out the answer is a good exercise for the reader.)

Note that negative, zero, and positive numbers can all be stored in integer variables. Sample integer constants are −6, 42, and 10000. Note that commas may not be included in the number, even if it is over 1000.

Table 3.1 shows the arithmetic operators for integers. There are two categories of operators—arithmetic and relational.

Considering the arithmetic operators first, the addition (+), subtraction (−), and multiplication (*) operators perform the normal functions associated with these operators. The DIV operator will divide two integers, and the result

---

*Apple® II is a registered trademark of Apple Computer, Inc.

TABLE 3.1

```
          Integer Variable Operators

  OPERATOR    NAME        EXAMPLE    RESULT
     +        Add          3 + 2       5
     -        Subtract     3 - 2       1
     *        Multiply     3 * 2       6
    DIV       Divide      3 DIV 2      1
                          4 DIV 2      2
    MOD       Remainder   3 MOD 2      1
                          4 MOD 2      0
```

is equal to the whole number portion of the quotient. Any fraction or remainder will be lost. Thus, 7 DIV 5 is 1, not 1.4. On the other hand, the MOD operator gives us the remainder from a division operation. Thus 7 MOD 5 is 2 (and 8 MOD 5 is 3, 9 MOD 5 is 4, etc.).

The relational operators are used to determine whether

a equals b (a = b)

a does not equal b (a # b, or a <> b)

a is less than b (a < b)

a is greater than b (a > b)

a is less than or equal to b (a <= b)

a is greater than or equal to b (a >= b)

where a and b are integers.

3.1.2 CARDINAL

Integers are limited to numbers less than 32768 (MaxInt) on a typical 16-bit computer. Although a range of values from 0 to 65535 can be described using 16 data bits, the integer loses half of this range in order to represent negative numbers. That is, if the sixteenth bit (most significant bit) is a one, the system interprets the result as a negative number when dealing with integers. Therefore, only half of the value range (2 raised to the power of 15, minus 1), or 32767 values, can be used for positive numbers. However, if we know that negative numbers are not required for a particular problem, it would be convenient to be able to use the entire range of values from 0 to 65535. Enter the

CARDINAL data type! (Also enter a clue to the answer to the question from the last section on why MaxInt plus one equals MinInt.)

Cardinals can only represent zero or positive values. The constant Max-Card is 65535 on a system whose value for MaxInt is 32767. It is the largest value that can be stored in a CARDINAL variable. The smallest value is 0. The same operations listed in Table 3.1 for integers can also be performed on two cardinal variables or constants, or a combination of the two.

Just as the use of an integer value outside of the range defined by MinInt and MaxInt can cause strange and unpredictable results, similar problems can occur with cardinals. For example, what happens if a negative value or a value greater than MaxCard is assigned to a cardinal variable? Not all Modula-2 implementations automatically check for such errors. In the Volition system, if a value of −1 is assigned to a cardinal variable it will be interpreted as 65535; a value of 65536 is interpreted as 0; 65537 is 1; etc. This logic is similar to that seen with integers.

Do not count on results such as those just described even within a single implementation such as Volition's, much less across all implementations. For example, if 65536 is entered from the keyboard in response to a program input statement that reads a cardinal value, the Volition system will interpret the number as 6553. Note that if 65536 had been computed, it would appear to be a zero, but the same number, input from the keyboard, is interpreted to be equal to the first four digits entered. Upon some reflection, there is a consistent logic to all of this. However, the message is clear: Build safeguards into your program to protect yourself against out-of-range values for integer and cardinal data. You cannot depend on the system to do it for you.

Examples of cardinal constants are 0, 6, 34567, and 65123. Note that values in the range of 0 to 32767 can be assigned to both integer and cardinal variables. Values less than 0 are uniquely integer, and values greater than 32767 (or whatever MaxInt is) can only be cardinal. This relationship between the range of values for integers and cardinals can be shown as

```
INTEGER→      MinInt..0..MaxInt
CARDINAL→          0..MaxInt..MaxCard
                   ^ ^ ^ ^ ^ ^ ^

                   Overlap
                   Region
```

Even though cardinals and integers are both whole numbers, they are distinct data types and may not be freely mixed together in expressions. This is true even if the integer and cardinal values are in the common region for the two types. For example, if IntVar is an integer variable, and CardVar is a cardinal then

```
IntVar + CardVar
```

is an illegal expression regardless of the values of the two variables. We will have more to say about this in a later, more general discussion on type and assignment compatibility.

Normally, the choice between declaring a variable to be of type INTEGER or CARDINAL would depend on the value range of the data; i.e., are there negative numbers (in which case it must be INTEGER), and what is largest value that is expected? In some instances, however, the decision may stem from various library routines that require the use of one type and not the other. In the case where either type is acceptable, bear in mind that some arithmetic operations may be faster when using cardinal variables.

3.1.3 REAL

The REAL data type is used to store values with fractional parts or values that are too large to be represented by type INTEGER or CARDINAL. This is not to imply that whole numbers in the range of valid integer and cardinal constants cannot be represented by real constants—they can. However, arithmetic on real numbers is extremely slow in comparison to integer arithmetic, and is avoided except when absolutely required.

Real number representations are made up of two parts. Consider the following examples of Modula-2 real numbers.

```
1.  1.0  1.2  123.4567  12345.67  1.234567E4  1.234567E+4
1.E+6  1.0E6  1.1E12  1.E−6  1234567.E−6
```

The syntax diagram for REAL data types is shown in Figure A.4. (Pascal programmers will notice differences here.) Note in the examples and in the syntax diagram that the two distinct parts of the real number are a fractional part and an optional scale factor. The fractional part is everything that precedes the letter E; the scale factor is everything from the letter E through to the end. The scale factor, e.g., E+4, is read as "10 raised to the power of 4" (10 raised to the power of n is a 1 followed by n zeroes). The fractional part of the real number is multiplied by the scale factor. Therefore, the example 1.E+6 is read as 1 times 10 raised to the power of 6 (or one million, i.e., 1×1000000).

Unfortunately, there is a maximum number of digits that can appear in the fractional part of a real number. This reflects the precision of the representation, and may vary from one implementation to another. Precision is equivalent to accuracy of representation. Once the number of digits in two different numbers exceeds this maximum, the system may not be capable of distinguishing between them. For example, if the precision is seven digits, the two real numbers 1.23456789E3 and 1.23456711E3 will both be interpreted to be 1.234567E3. Similarly, there is a maximum value that can appear in the scale factor. This number represents the range of potential real numbers. Range affects the largest and smallest numbers that the system can handle. For example, if this number is 38, then the largest value the system can represent is on the order of one followed by 38 zeroes (a very big number). Conversely, the smallest non-zero value is represented approximately by a decimal point followed by 38 zeroes and, finally, a one. Actually, the largest and smallest values using the Volition implementation are 3.40282E38 and 1.17549E−38. (As we said before, assume that it is 10 raised to the plus or minus power of 38.)

A typical Modula-2 microcomputer implementation only provides space for seven digits in the fractional part of the real number. The range of values that can be stored in a REAL variable varies between computers. The scale factor is typically a value in the range of −38 to +38. Because REAL values are stored in a fixed amount of memory, real arithmetic is inherently imprecise. As a result, it is necessary to be particularly careful when testing two REAL values for equality. In order to be on the safe side, a test for equality should instead test for equality plus or minus delta, where delta is some very small value that reflects the imprecision of the operation.

Table 3.2 summarizes the operators that act upon REAL values. The only notable difference between real operators and the operators for integer and cardinal types is the division operator. Note that the slash symbol, /, indicates REAL division. This is in contrast to DIV, which indicates integer division. REAL division produces a REAL quotient, including a fraction. For example, 2./5. is 4.0E−1, but 2 DIV 5 has the value 0.

TABLE 3.2

Real Variable Operators			
OPERATOR	NAME	EXAMPLE	RESULT
+	Add	3. + 2.	5
−	Subtract	3. − 2.	1.
*	Multiply	3. * 2.	6.
/	Divide	3. / 2.	1.5
		4. / 2.	2.

3.1.4 Characters (CHAR)

A character is a single symbol selected from the computer's character set. Most computers use the ASCII character set, which associates numeric codes with all of the symbols that appear on a keyboard, plus approximately 30 additional characters that do not appear on the keyboard. (See Appendix B.) For example, the ASCII code number entered into the computer's memory when you type the capital letter A is 65, B is 66, and so on. There are 128 unique symbols that are defined by this industry standard with codes spanning the range from 0 to 127. Some 33 of these characters are non-printable characters such as line feed, carriage return, backspace, bell, and other control characters. Many computer manufacturers have designated other special meanings (such as graphics symbols) to another 128 internal code numbers. Thus, each character variable can hold a value from 0 to 255. It should be recognized that no standard exists for the manufacturer's extensions.

Modula-2 provides two different ways to represent a character constant. The most obvious way is to place a symbol in either single or double quote marks: "A" or 'A'. However, because some symbols cannot be typed directly on a keyboard, Modula-2 also permits a character constant to be specified by its internal code number. ASCII code numbers are often presented in reference books as octal numbers. Modula-2 also uses the octal value of the ASCII code, followed by a capital C. This explains the two forms for octal digits shown in Figure A.3. For example, 15C is the constant for a carriage return character, and 7C will cause the computer's bell to ring if this character is written to the computer's standard output device (i.e., the terminal). The octal representation for characters is not limited only to characters that cannot be typed or printed. The letter "A" or 'A' could be written as 101C (the ASCII code for "A" is 65 decimal, which is 101 octal).

In Modula-2, the character data type is designated by the symbol CHAR (and not CHARACTER). As with the other data types we have introduced thus far, CHAR is a standard identifier that is built into the language. Table 3.3 lists the operations that can be performed on character variables.

TABLE 3.3

Character Variable Functions			
FUNCTION	EXAMPLE	RESULT	COMMENT
CHR	CHR(65)	"A"	Returns character whose ordinal value is 65.
ORD	ORD("A")	65	Returns ordinal value of "A".

3.1.5 STRING

This section is out of place because STRING is not actually a standard Modula-2 data type. It is, however, a frequently used data type that serves an important function and that exists in a number of languages. Modula-2 does define string constants such as 'Hi there'. Wirth recommends that standard library module procedures (ReadString and WriteString—see Chapter 5) be provided with every system implementation to handle string input and output. However, when it comes to a standard data type of STRING, there is none. String constants are supposed to be assigned to variables that are "an array of characters." In Chapter 6, when the topic of arrays is introduced, the techniques for constructing string data types will become apparent. These techniques will be useful if a library unit is not available or if you want to replace existing library modules.

String types and procedures to operate on string data can be expected to be found in library modules that are provided with system implementations. For example, the Volition implementation has a library module named Strings. Operations such as string comparison and concatenation are provided.

Frequently messages made up of a sequence of characters are used in programs. Such a sequence is called a string. In the sample program from Chapter 1, "This program counts to ten" was a string constant. The difference between a character and a string is that a character may only hold a single symbol, while a string can hold a sequence of characters. Strings have an additional property besides value and type—each string has a length. The length of a string variable can change during the execution of a program, just as its value can. (Note that a single character string is of type CHAR.) In order to mark the current end of a string, a special end-of-string character, 0C (ASCII nul), is automatically placed after the last character of a string provided that the string length is less than its maximum, which must be specified by the programmer.

Modula-2 has two ways of writing string constants. If the string does not contain an apostrophe symbol ('), the constant can be written by enclosing the sequence of symbols with two apostrophes:

'This is a string constant'.

Otherwise, if the string does not contain a quote symbol, the constant can be surrounded by two quotes:

"Hi there."

If the string contains a single quote, double quotes *must* be used as the string delimiters:

"Can't use single quotes here".

Similarly, if the constant contains a double quote, then single quotes must be used to delimit the string. *Note:* There is *no way* to mix apostrophes and quotes within the same string constant. In this case, the string will have to be broken into smaller parts that satisfy this constraint. Figure A.9 gives the syntax diagram for strings.

A few points are worth noting or repeating. String constants must contain more than one symbol, or they will be treated as character constants. Also, STRING constants may not extend past the end of the line of source code; i.e., a string constant cannot be longer than one line. Finally, unlike other data types, STRING is not a standard identifier and must be declared before it can be referred to in a program. Declarations of strings will be covered in Chapter 6.

3.1.6 BOOLEAN

Most computers need to record values that represent whether something is true or false. For example, an employee record system might keep track of whether each employee is covered by group health insurance. Variables that are either true or false are called Boolean variables in honor of the English mathematician George Boole who invented the field of symbolic logic. Table 3.4 summarizes operations that can be performed on Boolean values. In Modula-2, there are two BOOLEAN constants: TRUE and FALSE. Note that these values have an order assigned and, therefore, can be compared using relational operators just as numeric types can be compared. In this ordering, FALSE comes before (is less than) TRUE. FALSE, TRUE, and BOOLEAN are all standard identifiers that are automatically defined by the system.

TABLE 3.4

BOOLEAN Variable Operators			
OPERATOR	NAME	EXAMPLE	RESULT
AND	Logical AND	A AND B	TRUE, if A and B are both TRUE; FALSE otherwise
&	(Alternate form for AND, see above)		
OR	Logical OR	A OR B	TRUE, if A or B or both are TRUE; FALSE otherwise
NOT	Logical NOT	NOT(A)	TRUE, if A is false; FALSE otherwise

Boolean values arise most frequently from comparing values in Boolean expressions. Relational operators act upon two values of a given data type and produce a result of data type BOOLEAN. For example, if a and b are of type INTEGER, the expression:

a > b

results in a BOOLEAN value that is TRUE if a is larger than b, or FALSE if b equals or exceeds a. Table 3.5 summarizes these relational operators and gives examples of Boolean expressions.

TABLE 3.5

```
                        Relational Operators

OPERATOR    NAME            EXAMPLE    RESULT
    =       Equal           A = B      TRUE, if A equals B
    #       Not equal       A # B      TRUE, if A doesn't equal B
                            A <> B     (alternate symbol)
    <       Less            A < B      TRUE, if A is less than B
    >       Greater         A > B      TRUE, if A is greater than B
    <=      Less or equ     A <= B     TRUE, if A is less than or equal to B
    >=      Greater or equal A >= B    TRUE, if A is greater than or equal to B
    IN      Included in     A IN B     See chapter 6.


    These relations apply to INTEGER, CARDINAL, REAL, CHAR, BOOLEAN, as well
    as enumerations and subrange types (covered in Chapter 6).  The operators
    = and # (<>) apply to sets and pointers (Chapters 6 and 7 respectively), in
    addition to the previously noted types.  The operators <= and >= have a
    special meaning when applied to sets (Chapter 6).
```

Boolean values can be stored in variables and can be acted upon by operators. Because BOOLEAN expressions can be combined by using the operators from Table 3.4, complex logical relationships can be expressed. For example, if "GovtmtEmployee" and "SocialSecurity" are BOOLEAN variables, then the statement:

SocialSecurity := (NOT GovtmtEmployee) AND (Salary < 32400);

would place a BOOLEAN value in SocialSecurity. Here, the BOOLEAN variable SocialSecurity represents whether social security payments should be withheld. It will be TRUE only if the employee is not a government worker and the salary is less than $32,400. If GovtmtEmployee is TRUE or if the salary equals or exceeds $32,400, the value FALSE will be stored. Note that parentheses are important in complex expressions. The expression

    a < b AND c < d

is invalid and must be written as

    (a < b) AND (c < d).

This requirement stems from the precedence rules for relational and BOOLEAN operators. Among the BOOLEAN and conditional operators, NOT has the highest precedence, followed by AND, then OR, and lastly by the relational operators. This hierarchy would cause our illegal example to be interpreted as

    a < (b AND c) < d

which is not what was intended.

3.2 DECLARING CONSTANTS

As we mentioned, a constant can be given an identifier name. The advantage of giving a name to a constant, and then referring to that name rather than to the constant's value, is that programs become easier to read, understand, and modify. For example, if the sample program in Listing 1.1 were to be changed to count to 20 instead of 10, the programmer would have to read through the entire program looking for the number 10 and then would have to decide whether each occurrence of the constant 10 should be changed to 20. Although this is trivial for Listing 1.1, in a program of any size, this would be a time consuming and error-prone process. Using a named constant makes the process much easier, as shown in Listing 3.1.

The constant in Listing 3.1, named MaxCount, is defined to be 10. The name MaxCount is used in place of the constant 10. Later, if a different number is desired, only the line of the program that defines MaxCount needs to be changed.

Figure A.11 shows the syntax diagram for declaring a constant in Modula-2. Each identifier that is used to refer to a constant value must appear

LISTING 3.1

```
(* Listing 3.1 -- Sample program with Constant *)
(* Lines changed or added since listing 1.1 are noted by comment *)

MODULE Sample;
    FROM InOut IMPORT WriteInt, WriteLn, WriteString;
    CONST MaxCount = 10;                              (* New *)
    VAR i : INTEGER;
BEGIN
    WriteString("This program counts to ");          (* Modified *)
    WriteInt(MaxCount, 1);                            (* New *)
    FOR i := 1 TO MaxCount DO                         (* Modified *)
        WriteLn;
        WriteInt(i, 6);
    END;
END Sample.
```

in a constant declaration. More than one constant may follow the keyword CONST.

In Listing 3.1, the order in which the CONST and VAR declarations appear does not matter. (This is a change from Pascal.) Either clause could come first. However, both clauses must come before BEGIN, which marks the end of the declarations and the start of the algorithm. The more general requirement is that declarations must appear prior to the section of the program where the identifier is first used. In Listing 3.1, there is only one program section, and, therefore, there is only one choice for the location of the declarations, i.e., before the symbol BEGIN.

Notice that an equal sign separates the constant's identifier from its value. The value can be either a constant or a constant expression. Because a constant expression can be used, one constant can be defined in terms of other, previously defined constants. For example,

```
CONST
    Size = 20;
    OneLessThanSize = Size − 1;
```

If OneLessThanSize had been defined as 19 rather than Size − 1, and if the program was later modified to change the value of Size, the value of OneLessThanSize would not automatically change. By defining one constant in terms of another, the programmer can be sure that the proper relationships will always be maintained.

3.3 DECLARING SIMPLE VARIABLES

In the first section of this chapter, we saw that variables have both names and data types. Each variable used in a Modula-2 program must be explicitly declared so that its data type can be defined. The VAR block is used to declare variables. The sample programs in Listings 1.1 and 3.1 used the VAR declaration

```
VAR i : INTEGER;
```

Figure A.38 shows the syntax diagram of a VAR declaration.

In a variable declaration, the name of one (or more) variable(s) appears before a colon, and the data type follows the colon. If more than one variable has the same data type, a single statement can be used, but the variable names must be separated by commas. Thus, the following variable declaration:

```
VAR i,j,k : CARDINAL;
```

has the same effect as,

```
VAR i : CARDINAL;
    j : CARDINAL;
    k : CARDINAL;
```

Another equivalent version of the two preceeding variable declarations is,

```
VAR i : CARDINAL;
VAR j : CARDINAL;
VAR k : CARDINAL;
```

the choice of which to use is up to the programmer.

Although lists of identifiers can be used in a VAR clause—VAR i,j,k : INTEGER—the same shortcut may not be used for constants.

A variable (or constant) cannot be used in a Modula-2 program without first being declared. This error is caught during compilation. Furthermore, since the declaration either explicitly (in the case of variables) or implicitly (in the case of constants) defines a type to be associated with the data, only values of the specified type may be used. Type incompatibilities are detected both during program compilation and execution.

This section considered only the declaration of simple variable types. In Chapter 6, more will be said about declaration of variables. Even though the variable types in later chapters may be more complex, the basic rules for declarations are still the same as those presented in this section.

3.4 SCOPE OF IDENTIFIERS

When naming children, parents carefully assign different names to each child. After all, what good is a name if everyone has the same one? The same logic applies to the selection of identifiers for constants and variables. Thus, the variable declaration,

```
VAR i : INTEGER;
     i : CARDINAL;
```

shows a poor choice for the names of the two variables because they are both the same. This is illegal in Modula-2 and would result in an error message (something like "variable declared twice") when the program was compiled. One problem that would result if multiple variables were permitted to have the same identifier name would be that the compiler could not determine which was which in the program. For example, in the case of the two variables above, if the statement

```
i := 2;
```

appeared in the program (i.e., assign the value 2 to the variable whose name is i), which i are we talking about? The compiler has no way of knowing. Therefore, as a general rule, it is illegal to have more than one identifier with the same name.

Note the equivocation at the end of the previous paragraph—"as a general rule. . . ." It is possible to have more than one identifier with the same name in a Modula-2 program. However, the use of these names must be such that no doubt can arise as to which program element is meant when an identifier name is used. Taking the family name analogy one step further, children in the same neighborhood frequently have the same first name. Generally, this does not cause confusion because the combination of a first name with a family last name uniquely identifies each child.

A Modula-2 program is normally broken into a set of smaller parts (or subprograms) using *procedures* and *modules* as described in Chapter 2. The procedures and modules are analogous to the "neighborhood families." The same identifier name can appear in an overall Modula-2 program as long as each occurrence is unique within a separate procedure or module (i.e., unique within its own family). (This will be explained in detail in Chapter 8 when procedures and modules are covered.) Therefore, if the variable i : INTEGER is declared in one procedure and the identifier i is used again in another procedure or module, there is no confusion. The meaning of each identifier is clear. Its meaning and definition are limited to the procedure where it was declared.

The part of the program in which an identifier is defined—for example, the procedure in which the variable i : INTEGER is declared—is known as the *scope* of the identifier. The meaning of the identifier, i.e., i is a variable of type INTEGER, is known only within the procedure in which it is declared. References to i outside of the scope of i, such as in another procedure that has no declaration involving an i of its own, will result in a compiler error message which complains of an "undeclared" variable. Scope is an *important* concept and must be understood in order to write correct programs. Scope rules will be covered in detail with extensive examples in Chapter 8 when procedures and modules are introduced.

There is one additional variation on the rule regarding unique identifier names and the scope of the identifier. This will be covered in Chapter 7 under the topic of records, but it is mentioned here to complete the picture. A record is a collection of data elements, such as a personnel record, which Modula-2 treats as a logical entity. Each element in the collection is named. If one element of a personnel record has the name Age and another variable in the scope of the record (but not part of the record) has the same name, there will be no confusion (to the compiler, at least) and the situation is allowed. The reason for this is that the real name of the personnel record data element is not Age, but something like Employee.Age, where Employee is the name of the overall record. Therefore, the compiler is not trying to differentiate between Age and Age but between Age and Employee.Age, and it has no problem.

The scope of an identifier depends on where it is declared. The identifier is known only within the procedure or module where it is declared and is unknown outside the bounds of these "subprograms." Because identifiers must have the proper scope in order for a program to have its intended meaning, the position in a program of the declaration of an identifier is important. Until Chapter 8, all of our examples will consist of a single program module with no procedures, and the program declarations will appear immediately after the name of the module. As a result, the scope of each identifier will be the entire program. Although this will keep our examples simple, do not assume that all variables will always be known throughout a program.

SUMMARY

This chapter has introduced the most commonly used data types (and their associated operators) defined in the Modula-2 language. These types are adequate for most routine programming tasks. This commonly used set is more extensive than the total set of many other languages. Data types which are more complex than the simple ones introduced in this chapter, plus user-defined types, will be presented in Chapter 6. In addition to defining data types, rules were given for declaring constants and variables. Lastly, the scope rules for program identifiers were explained.

The contents of this chapter constitute the fundamentals of Modula-2. Subsequent chapters will explain how to build programs from these basic building blocks.

QUESTIONS AND PROBLEMS

1. How are the name, type, value, and scope of variables and constants determined?
2. What is the difference between a constant and a variable?
3. Which of the following declarations are *not* legal?

```
VAR i, j, k : REAL;
VAR i j k : REAL;
VAR i = REAL;
VAR i : REAL;
CONST I, m, n = 10;
CONST m : 10;
CONST m = 10;
```

(Did you find 4? The first, middle, and last are OK.)

5. What is the data type of each of the following constants?

"a"	15C	'Enter input:'		24567	34567
3	3.0	TRUE	−3	−24567	1.E−4
"a "	BACH	33B	−4.2778E16		"FALSE"

SUPPLEMENTAL PROBLEMS

Problem 1

In this chapter we've seen that the sizes of integer and cardinal numbers are implementation dependent. Investigate techniques for use in the calculator program that will allow us to work with numbers as large as we please without any implementation constraints.

Problem 2

Identify calculator parameters that should be implemented as constants for ease of program change and maintenance as discussed in this chapter. What are reasonable choices for their type and value?

Problem 3

The user's input is to be interpreted as either a positive number to be "pushed" on the stack or a command. The minimum commands are (the notation s1 and s2 mean the 1st (top) and 2nd numbers on the top of the stack):

COMMAND	MEANING
+	Add s1 to s2
−	Subtract s1 from s2
*	Multiply s1 by s2
/	Divide s1 into s2
C	Clear (empty) the stack
P	Pop (remove) top item from stack
Q	Quit (stop the program)
S	Sign change of s1
X	Exchange s1 and s2 on stack

After each of the four mathematical operations, the original items at s1 and s2 are no longer on the stack and the result of the operation is at s1. Note that only positive numbers can be entered. Entry of a minus sign should cause the calculator to immediately subtract s1 from s2. The S command is used to change the sign of the top number on the stack.

Draw a picture of a stack (assume it can hold more than two numbers) with data in it. Redraw the stack following each of the above commands. How do these commands compare to the list from your answer to Problem 2 in Chapter 1?

CHAPTER 4

ASSIGNMENT AND CONTROL

NEW CONCEPTS: Assignment, Control by Looping and Branching
ISSUES: Assignment Compatibility

INTRODUCTION

This chapter introduces some of the most important features of Modula-2, which are features basic to every programming language. Probably the most fundamental requirement of every programming language is a method for assigning values to variables. In Modula-2, this is done by means of *assignment statements*. Another fairly fundamental part of any programming language is a method for exerting control over how the program is executed—specifically, which parts of the program are executed and when. Modula-2 instructions (statements) are normally executed in the same sequence that they appear within the program. Often, however, it is necessary to alter the order in which the statements are executed. Modula-2 provides a rich assortment of methods—more than most languages—for changing the order in which program statements are executed. These *control* structures can be grouped into two categories—loops and branches.

After completing this chapter, the reader will have the majority of the nuts and bolts of Modula-2. The contents of Chapters 2 through 4 constitute the bulk of the features used in most programs. The remaining pieces are vital, to be sure, but the contents of these first few chapters will comprise most of the lines of code that make up normal programs. The only truly vital part which is missing is input and output. This is covered in Chapter 5, following which complete—albeit very simple—programs can be written. The additional language features of the last half of this book allow large, complex, and reliable programs to be developed efficiently.

4.1 THE ASSIGNMENT STATEMENT

Each action to be performed by the computer is expressed as a Modula-2 *statement*. The simplest and most fundamental action in programming is to assign a value to a variable. The syntax diagram for the *assignment* statement is shown in Figure A.47.

For the time being, consider the definition of the *designator* in the syntax diagram to be the same as that of an identifier, which we saw in Chapter 3 and in Figure A.1. In Chapters 6 and 7, when arrays, records, and pointers are covered, we will see other forms that the designator can take.

The form of the assignment statement is

```
VariableName := SomeExpression;
```

where VariableName is the identifier of a previously declared variable, and SomeExpression is a valid expression. The symbol :=, a colon followed by an equal sign, is the Modula-2 assignment symbol. It means to assign the value of the expression on its right to the variable on its left. There must always be a variable and an expression in these two positions.

You may be surprised by the use of := rather than =. The latter symbol is used in Modula-2 (as in Pascal) as a relational operator to *test* for equality (see Chapter 3). The statement

```
Age := Age + 1;
```

means to add one to the current contents of the memory location assigned to the variable Age, and then store the result back in the Age location. Or, in other words, to increase the value of Age by one. On the other hand,

```
Age = Age + 1;
```

is an *illegal* statement. The symbol = means to test the two expressions on either side of the equal sign and to return a TRUE if they are equal and to return a FALSE otherwise. This operation makes no sense in the context of the above example since there is nothing to assign the true or false value to once the expression is evaluated. We will see the correct use of the = symbol later in the chapter when we consider conditional statements. For now, note that it is impossible for Age = Age + 1 to be true either mathematically or in the context of a Modula-2 conditional statement.

It is important to recognize that an assignment statement is different from a mathematical equation. The assignment statement is *not* a mathematical equation. It simply indicates that the current value of the variable on the left should be replaced with the value of the expression on the right.

Note that a variable and not a constant must appear to the left of the assignment symbol. Any valid expression, including a constant or another variable, may appear on the right. For example, assuming that variables i, j, and k are INTEGERs, b is BOOLEAN, c is CHAR, and variable s is a STRING, we have the following examples of assignment statements:

```
i :=5; (* Assign the value 5 to the variable i *)
j := i − 3; (* decrease i by 3 and assign result to j *)
k := i*j − 1; (* Assign to k, the product of i & j less 1 *)
k := −1 + i * j; (* Same effect as the previous statement *)
b := TRUE; (* Assign the value TRUE to b *)
b := NOT TRUE; (* Assign FALSE to b *)
c := "?"; (* Assign the character ? to the variable c *)
s := "this is a message"; (* Strings can be assigned, too *)
```

As you examine these simple assignment statement examples, the following question is a test of your understanding of expression evaluation and assignment statements: What value is stored in the variable k after the first three statements are executed in the order listed above? If your answer is not 9, you have missed some critical points along the way.

4.1.1 Assignment Compatibility

Not all assignment statements make sense or are legal. It depends on whether the operands of the statement are *assignment compatible*. For example, if i is an INTEGER, the assignment statement:

```
i := "A string constant";
```

is nonsensical and illegal. The variable i can only be assigned integers, not strings of characters.

The basic rule that governs the legality of all assignment statements is that of *assignment compatibility*. The operands on each side of the assignment operator, :=, must be assignment compatible. One way for operands to be assignment compatible is to be *type compatible*.

Two types, Type1 and Type2, are type compatible if they are the same basic type, i.e.,

BOOLEAN, CARDINAL, CHAR, INTEGER, REAL

or if they are declared as

Type1 = Type2; (See Chapter 6, Section 6.2.)

or if Type1 is a subrange of Type2, or both Type1 and Type2 are subranges of the same type. (Subranges are covered in Chapter 6.) Assignment compatibility also includes the case in which the operands are both integer or cardinal or subranges of integer and cardinal. Although integer and cardinal are not type compatible by any of the type compatibility rules just cited, they are assignment compatible. Several examples will clarify this.

```
IntVar1 := IntVar2; (* Obvious compatibility *)
IntVar1 := IntVar2 + 3; (* Once again, obvious *)
IntVar1 := CardVar1; (* LEGAL; special case of ASSIGNMENT compatibility;
                        not type compatible *)
IntVar1 := IntVar2 + CardVar1; (* ILLEGAL; mixed types on right; can't add
                                  integer & cardinal *)
RealVar := 3.1415 * RealDiameter; (* ok *)
BoolVar := TRUE OR FALSE; (* ok *)
BoolVar := (IntVar1 = IntVar2); (* ok; expression on right is TRUE or FALSE
                                   depending on relationship between the two
                                   integers *)
```

Note the difference between type compatibility and assignment compatibility as demonstrated in the third and fourth examples. The third example is legal from the standpoint of assignment compatibility, based on the special rule regarding integer and cardinal types. The fourth example, however, is illegal and cannot be compiled. The reason has nothing to do with assignment compatibility. There is a type compatibility error in the expression IntVar2 + CardVar1. Mixed-type expressions are *never* allowed in Modula-2, as was discussed in Chapter 3.

In order to apply the assignment compatibility rule, a programmer must know how to determine the data type of an expression. The simplest expression is just a constant. As described in Section 3.1, each constant's form dictates its data type. The following program illustrates some of the compatibility rules and also demonstrates the implicit typing of constants.

```
MODULE test;
VAR
    IntVar1, IntVar 2 : INTEGER;
    CardVar1, CardVar2 : CARDINAL;
```

```
CONST
    IntConst = -500;
    CardConst = 40000;
    CardIntConst = 100; (* Is this cardinal or integer? *)
BEGIN
  IntVar1 := IntConst; (* Both integer; legal *)
  IntVar1 := CardIntConst; (* Makes no difference; legal *)
  CardVar1 := CardConst; (* Both cardinal; legal *)
  CardVar1 := CardIntConst; (* Makes no difference; legal *)
  IntVar1 := IntVar2 + CardIntConst;
  CardVar1 := CardVar2 + CardIntConst;
      (* It would seem that one or the other of the above two must be illegal; if
         CardIntConst is cardinal then we have mixed arithmetic in the 1st of the
         two; otherwise the second is mixed. What's the answer? *)
  IntVar1 := IntVar2 + CardVar1; (* ILLEGAL, every day of week *)
END test.
```

From the earlier examples, it is clear that the first four assignment statements are legal. There should be no question regarding the first and third. The second and fourth statements are legal due to the special rule regarding assignment compatibility between integer and cardinal values. It makes no difference whether the constant CardIntConst is interpreted by the system to be a cardinal or integer.

This brings up an interesting question—just how does the system interpret this constant? If it is a cardinal, the fifth statement should be illegal since IntVar2 + CardIntConst would be a mixed-type expression. As we saw in the earlier example, mixed expressions are not allowed. If CardIntConst is an integer constant, however, then the sixth statement must contain an illegal mixed-type expression.

What actually happens is that the system interprets the constant as being *either* cardinal *or* integer, whichever your expression needs. Recall that in Chapter 3 we pointed out an overlap in integer and cardinal values in the range of zero to MaxInt. Therefore, in this very special case, both of these statements are legal. The final statement is included to demonstrate that there are *no* exceptions when it comes to mixing types among operands that are variables (as opposed to variables and constants). This is always wrong.

The following table provides some more examples:

Constant	Data Type
-3	INTEGER
45678	CARDINAL
3	INTEGER or CARDINAL

3.1415	REAL
"A"	CHAR
"A "	STRING (*Note:* Blanks count.)
'A cat'	STRING
"HELLO"	STRING
TRUE	BOOLEAN

The type of an expression corresponds to the type and values of its operands. Mixed types in an expression are illegal. Some examples are:

Expression	Data Type of Result
3 + 4	INTEGER or CARDINAL
3. + 4.	REAL
3 − 4	INTEGER
3 * 20000	CARDINAL
3 / 4	ILLEGAL (invalid INTEGER operator /)
3 * 2.0	ILLEGAL (mixed types)
50000 + (−3)	? (50000 − 3 is cardinal)
a = b	BOOLEAN
i > 5	BOOLEAN
CHR(65)	CHAR (value is "A"; see Chapter 8)

Additional examples will be discussed in Chapter 6 after we introduce subranges. Recall from the discussion of compatible types that subranges are involved in type compatibility rules.

Table 4.1 summarizes which data types are sufficiently related to permit a value of one type to be assigned to a variable of another type.

TABLE 4.1

ASSIGNMENT COMPATIBILITY

DESTINATION TYPE	ALLOWABLE SOURCE VALUE TYPE
INTEGER	INTEGER or CARDINAL
CARDINAL	INTEGER or CARDINAL
REAL	REAL
BOOLEAN	BOOLEAN
STRING	STRING of same or shorter length (Note that this includes CHAR)
CHAR	CHAR

4.1.2 Transfer Functions

A programmer may have a value of one type that must be assigned to a variable of an incompatible type. Fortunately, Modula-2 provides a series of built-in procedures for handling such conversions. If you are unclear about what a procedure is, for the time being think of it as an operation that accepts a single expression (surrounded by parentheses) as input and returns a value of the proper type. Procedures are covered in Chapter 8.

For example, the procedure to convert a CARDINAL value to a REAL value is called FLOAT. So, if C is declared a cardinal variable and R is a real variable, then the statements,

```
C := 3;
R := FLOAT(C + 2);
```

would assign the real value 5.0 to the variable R. FLOAT converts 5, the result of the expression C + 2, to the real number 5.0.

It is also possible to convert other data types. A simple example is the conversion from integer to cardinal and vice versa. This is done as follows:

```
CardVar := CARDINAL(IntVar);
IntVar := INTEGER(CardVar);
```

As shown in these two sample statements, we can use the type names INTEGER and CARDINAL for type conversion. To convert any integer, or integer expression, to a cardinal data type, simply use the CARDINAL procedure. Table 4.2 shows the most common transfer functions.

The capability of using the type name to perform type conversion is available for all data types, including the more complex types and user-defined types to be discussed in later sections. The only constraint is that both types

TABLE 4.2

```
                  TRANSFER FUNCTIONS

NAME              FUNCTION
FLOAT(card)       Converts CARDINAL to REAL
TRUNC(real)       Converts REAL to CARDINAL, drops fraction
CHR(card)         Converts CARDINAL to CHAR
INTEGER(card)     Converts CARDINAL to INTEGER
CARDINAL(int)     Converts INTEGER to CARDINAL
```

involved must occupy the same amount of storage space in the computer's memory. This restriction is due to how this conversion, or type transfer, process is accomplished. In particular, no computation is involved in performing the transfer. All that happens if we use

```
CardVar := CARDINAL(IntVar);
```

is that the computer copies the data in IntVar directly to CardVar as if IntVar were actually a CARDINAL data type. This restriction does not apply to the explicit transfer functions such as FLOAT and TRUNC. The following sample program demonstrates some of Modula-2's general type transfer capabilities. More will be covered in Chapter 6.

```
MODULE test;
FROM InOut IMPORT
     Write,
     WriteInt,
     WriteLn;
VAR
     IntVar : INTEGER;
     CardVar : CARDINAL;
     CharVar : CHAR;
BEGIN
  CardVar := 33;
  IntVar := 2 * CardVar; (* 66 *)
  WriteInt(IntVar, 6); WriteLn; (* 66 written *)
  CharVar := CHAR(IntVar); (*66 is assigned *)
  Write(CharVar); WriteLn; (* Letter B is written *)
  CharVar := CHR(IntVar); (* Table 4.2 procedure *)
  Write(CharVar); WriteLn; (* Letter B is written *)
END test.
```

Notice the fourth statement. The computer's representation for the integer 66 (the value of IntVar) is simply copied over to the storage location for CharVar. The data in IntVar and CharVar are identical (0000000001000010) following this copy operation, i.e., 66 base 2. The WriteInt statement produces 66, and the Write produces the letter B because of the way the computer interprets the same set of data found in two different memory locations. In one case, the type is defined as an integer; in the second, the type is a character. In the sixth statement, CHR() accepts an integer variable as its argument since, for a transfer function, the variable used as the argument need only be assignment compatible with its argument type. Note that the fourth and sixth statements represent two ways to accomplish the same function. The sixth statement uses a built-in (explicit) standard procedure (CHR); the fourth uses the more general type transfer capability. The fourth is more risky. You have only yourself to rely on to stay out of trouble.

4.2 CONTROL STRUCTURES

Modula-2 program statements are normally executed in the same order that they appear in the program. In almost every program, however, there is a need to deviate from this order. A change in the order of execution may be necessary for one of two reasons:

- Some group of statements needs to be executed repetitively.
- One of several different groups of statements must be executed depending on some condition that is tested in the program.

In the sample program in Listings 1.1 and 3.1, most statements are executed in the order in which they appear. Execution begins at the word BEGIN and follows in sequence to the final END statement for the MODULE. However, the program takes a detour in order to print out the numbers between 1 and 10. The break in the normal sequence begins with FOR and continues until the first END. The two write statements included in this group are executed *repetitively*. Statements that cause a departure from the normal sequential flow of execution are called *control structures*.

Modula-2 has a wide variety of control structures to support the requirements of *structured programming*. In structured programming, each segment of the program that is to be executed under certain conditions is grouped together. Structured programs are easier to write, easier to debug, and easier for others to read and understand. As you will see in this chapter, Modula-2's control structures lend themselves to structured programming.

4.2.1 Statement Sequences

A control structure groups statements together to define a group that may be executed out of the usual sequence. This raises the question of how to mark the start and end of such a group. Some languages, like C, use brackets such as { } to mark the start and end of a group of statements. Other languages, like Pascal, use the keywords BEGIN and END. There are almost as many approaches as there are languages.

Modula-2 uses control structure keywords for the combined functions of indicating the type of control structure and marking the start and end of the statement sequence it controls. As you will see from the syntax diagrams in this chapter, most control structures consist of two groups of keywords that come at the start and end of a set of statements. The group of statements that fall within the control structure is called a *statement sequence*. As shown in Figure A.49, a statement sequence is merely one or more statements separated by semicolons, or statement separators. In the sample program from Listing 1.1, the statements WriteInt(i, 6); WriteLn; constitute the statement sequence, which is repeated ten times during the execution of the surrounding control structure.

The rules for the use of the statement separator—the semicolon—should be noted carefully. Every statement pair must be separated by a semicolon. Recall from Chapter 3 that Modula-2 allows a null statement. The null statement is a statement that is empty. The reason for this is that it makes it possible for extra semicolons to appear in a program without causing problems. If the compiler encounters an extraneous separator, it assumes that a null statement is involved and does nothing. On the other hand, if a required separator is missing, a compile time error will result.

4.2.2 Looping Statements

Modula-2 provides four different control structures for *looping*, or the repetitive execution of a statement sequence. These are:

WHILE statement

REPEAT statement

LOOP statement

FOR statement

Each of these control structures allows a statement sequence to be executed repeatedly until some stopping condition is met. The ability to define and check for a condition that stops the repetition is as important as the repetition itself. The control over the stopping condition is what differentiates these four control structures. It is important to note, as each is studied, how the termination condition is implemented.

A key element in the use of control structures is the role of BOOLEAN expressions (Figure A.41) in checking for a stopping condition. For example,

a < b
(a + b) = c

As discussed in the previous chapter, a Boolean expression returns the value TRUE or FALSE, depending on the validity of the relationship in the expression. In the first example, a < b, if a is 5 and b is 10 (or any number greater than 5), then the value of the expression is true. Note that the term *Boolean expression* applies to the type of the resulting value (i.e., Boolean), and has nothing to do with the types of the operands in the expression. The rules for evaluating Modula-2 Boolean expressions differ from some other languages, notably Pascal. If Boolean operators (AND and OR) appear in the expression, the terms of the expression are evaluated from left to right *until* the result is determined. (This is known as short-circuiting the evaluation.) If the expression is

a AND b

the evaluation stops immediately if a is false since the value of the expression is completely determined at that point—i.e., unless both terms are true the value is false. Therefore, we can stop since the result is false regardless of the value of b. This was shown in Table 3.4.

We now introduce the four looping control structures in turn.

WHILE

Listing 4.1 illustrates Modula-2's WHILE statement.

LISTING 4.1

```
(* Modification of listing 1.1 to use WHILE loop *)

MODULE WhileDemo;
    FROM InOut IMPORT WriteInt, WriteLn, WriteString;
    CONST MaxCount = 10;
    VAR i : INTEGER;
BEGIN (*WhileDemo*)
    WriteString('This program counts to ');
    WriteInt(MaxCount, 1);
    i := 1;
    WHILE i <= MaxCount DO
        WriteLn;    WriteInt(i, 6);
        i := i + 1;
    END (*while*);
END WhileDemo.
```

A WHILE statement will repeat a statement sequence as long as the Boolean expression following WHILE is TRUE. The start and end of the statement sequence to be repeated within the WHILE loop are marked by the keywords DO and END. The program in Listing 4.1 accomplishes the identical result as the program in Listing 3.1. While the value of i is less than or equal to MaxCount, or

```
WHILE i <= MaxCount DO
```

the statement sequence

```
WriteLn; WriteInt(i, 6); i := i + i;
```

is executed. Since i is equal to 1 at the start of the loop (by virtue of the initialization statement, i := 1) and since MaxCount = 10, the program will execute this sequence MaxCount (10) times. The stopping condition is checked at the start of the loop, and, therefore, it is possible to bypass the loop's statement sequence entirely if i is greater than MaxCount when the WHILE loop is first encountered. It is important for i to have been assigned a value prior to encountering the loop, or the results are totally unpredictable. Modula-2 does not automatically set the value of program variables to a default value at the start of the program. The syntax of the WHILE statement is summarized in Figure A.53.

The WHILE statement has the following noteworthy points:

1. The BOOLEAN expression is tested before the loop is executed. If the Boolean expression is false at the start of the WHILE statement, the loop will not be executed. This is one feature which distinguishes the WHILE loop from the other loops. It is used when it may be necessary to bypass the loop entirely. Contrast this with the REPEAT loop. A common programming error with WHILE and REPEAT loops is to miscalculate the stopping condition in a way that the loop either performs one iteration too many or too few.

2. The BOOLEAN expression is reevaluated after each repetition of the controlled statement sequence. The statement sequence in the loop will continue to execute until the Boolean expression becomes false. This brings up an important point. Something in the statement sequence must alter the value of the termination condition, or the loop will *never* terminate. In Listing 4.1, it is the statement

```
i := i + 1;
```

Nothing in the system will guard against this potential problem. Infinite loops are legal.

3. A Modula-2 program or procedure must have an END for every WHILE. Any legal statement sequence can go in between. It can consist of the null statement, i.e.,

WHILE TRUE DO END;

which will keep your machine occupied for a long time doing nothing.

4. After the loop terminates, the next statement to be executed is the first statement which follows the WHILE ... DO ... END statement.

REPEAT . . . UNTIL

For situations in which a programmer must ensure that a loop will be executed *at least once*, Modula-2 has the REPEAT ... UNTIL control structure. Listing 4.2 gives another version of the count-to-ten program. This version uses a REPEAT ... UNTIL control structure in its loop. As in the WHILE example of Listing 4.1, the value 1 is assigned to the integer variable i before the loop begins. The keyword REPEAT marks the start of the loop. The statement sequence that starts a new line on the screen, prints the value of i, and adds 1 to the value of i is identical to that of Listing 4.1. The end of the loop is marked by the keyword UNTIL followed by a BOOLEAN expression. At the completion of each execution of the loop, the Boolean expression i > MaxCount is tested. If the expression is true, then the statement after the loop is executed. Otherwise, the loop is repeated.

LISTING 4.2

```
(* Listing 4.2 -- Sample program with REPEAT ... UNTIL *)

MODULE Sample;
    FROM InOut IMPORT WriteInt, WriteLn, WriteString;
    CONST MaxCount = 10;
    VAR i : INTEGER;
BEGIN
    WriteString("This program counts to ");
    WriteInt(MaxCount, 1);
    i := 1;
    REPEAT
        WriteLn;    WriteInt(i, 6);
        i := i + 1;
    UNTIL i > MaxCount;
END Sample.
```

Figure A.54 is a syntax diagram for REPEAT . . . UNTIL. Note these points:

1. The BOOLEAN expression is tested for the first time *after* the loop is executed. Contrast this with the WHILE statement. This is the distinguishing characteristic of the REPEAT loop. You are guaranteed that the controlled statement sequence will be executed *at least once.*

2. The statement sequence in the loop will continue to execute until the BOOLEAN expression becomes true. The same point that was made for the WHILE statement must be made here. Unless something in the controlled statement sequence is done to alter the value of the terminating condition, as expressed by the Boolean expression following UNTIL, the loop will execute forever.

3. A Modula-2 program or procedure must have an UNTIL for every REPEAT. Any valid statement sequence can be included between REPEAT and UNTIL. Since a valid sequence includes the null statement, the following is a degenerate case which executes once and does nothing,

REPEAT UNTIL TRUE;

4. After the loop terminates, the next statement to be executed is the first statement which follows the REPEAT . . . UNTIL statement.

LOOP . . . EXIT . . . END

Thus far we have considered two loop control structures. One was distinguished by the fact that it checked at the start of the loop for a stopping condition. The second checked for termination when it reached the end of the loop. A third control structure—the LOOP . . . EXIT . . . END—tests at the start, interior, and/or end of the loop. The loop terminates when an EXIT statement is encountered (of which there may be several). The syntax diagram is given in Figure A.56.

The LOOP . . . EXIT . . . END control structure provides greater flexibility than WHILE or REPEAT in two respects. First, because an unlimited number of EXIT statements may appear within the loop, any number of different termination conditions can be used. The same termination condition can appear at more than one point in the loop. Second, because the test for the termination condition is not a part of the EXIT statement, additional actions can be taken after the test for the termination condition is satisfied but before actually leaving the loop. The following simple rules govern the use of the LOOP . . . EXIT . . . END control structure:

1. The loop will continue to be executed until an EXIT statement is encountered. Other control structures should be used to test for the exit condition. (The discussion of the example in Listing 4.3 will be deferred until the IF statement is introduced later in this chapter. The IF statement is the most natural mechanism for making the termination check within a LOOP statement.)

LISTING 4.3

```
(* Listing 4.3 -- Sample program with LOOP ... END *)

MODULE Sample;
    FROM InOut IMPORT WriteInt, WriteLn, WriteString;
    CONST MaxCount = 10;
    VAR i : INTEGER;
BEGIN
    WriteString("This program counts to ");
    WriteInt(MaxCount, 1);
    i := 0;
    LOOP
        i := i + 1;
        IF i > MaxCount THEN EXIT END;
        WriteLn;    WriteInt(i, 6);
    END (*loop*);
END Sample.
```

2. The keyword LOOP marks the start of the statement sequence to be repeated, and the keyword END marks the end of the sequence. Note that the absence of an EXIT results in a loop that runs forever. This is not all bad. As will be mentioned in Chapter 11, under the heading of low-level functions, Modula-2 has a use for infinite loops when implementing concurrent programs by means of the Process feature.
3. After the loop terminates, the next statement to be executed is the first statement which follows the LOOP . . . EXIT . . . END statement.

FOR . . . DO . . . END

The final looping control structure is FOR . . . DO . . . END. This was the control structure used in our first count-to-ten program. This structure requires a *control variable* to keep track of the progress in the loop. The FOR loop syntax is shown by the following excerpt:

```
FOR i := a TO b BY c DO
  (*Statement sequence to be repeated*)
END;
```

Here i is the control variable. An assignment symbol := separates it from its starting value a, which can be any expression. The keyword TO separates the initial value from the expression b, which gives the final value of the control variable. The BY c portion of the statement is optional. This tells how the control variable is to be incremented (or decremented) after each repetition. The default is the same as writing BY 1. Finally, the keyword DO signals the start of the statement sequence that will be repeated, and the keyword END marks the end of the repeated sequence.

When the loop is entered, the control variable assumes its initial value, a. The value of the variable is compared to the final condition, b. If it is less than or equal to this value for a positive increment c (or greater than or equal for a negative increment), the statement sequence is executed. Otherwise, control passes to the first statement following the FOR statement. After each repetition of the statement sequence, the value of the control variable is changed. After the control variable's value is changed, it is compared once again to the final value. These steps are repeated until the value of the control variable is greater than the specified final value (or is less than the final value for a negative c). Note that it is possible to bypass the FOR loop entirely if the terminating condition specified by the initial and final values are satisfied from the very start.

The control variable does not have to be a numeric type. The starting and final value expressions must be assignment compatible (see Chapter 3) with the control variable. The term c in BY c must be an integer or cardinal constant expression, regardless of the control variable type. If the control variable is a character, then BY 1 means to start with the initial character specified by a, and after each repetition to increase the value of the character by 1. For example, if the initial character is m, then after the first repetition, it will be changed to n. For the same case, but with a c of −2, after m comes k (the second letter before m) and then i, then g, and so on.

The following program excerpt

```
VAR
  c: CHAR;
  :
```

```
FOR c := 'a' TO 'z' DO
  Write(c)
END;
```

will display the lower-case alphabet.

Although the initial and final values can be any expression of the same data type as the control variable, none of the variables used in those expressions should be changed during the execution of the loop. Similarly, the statement sequence that makes up the body of the loop should not change the value of the control variable. Make it a practice never to allow the control variable to appear to the left of an assignment statement within the statement sequence of the FOR loop. To do so is to invite disaster. However, you can use the value of the control variable within the loop, as was the case in Listing 1.1. As a matter of fact, this is one of the most powerful features of the FOR statement. This feature is particularly useful in manipulating elements of arrays, as we shall see in Chapter 6.

Any constant expression can follow the keyword BY. Each time through the loop, the value of the expression is added to the control variable. If the BY option is not included, the number 1 is automatically added each time.

The control variable must be declared so that it is known in the part of the program that contains the FOR loop. Control variables may not be of type REAL. Regardless of the data type of the control variable, if BY appears, the BY expression must be of type INTEGER or CARDINAL.

The FOR loop syntax diagram is shown in Figure A.55. To summarize the FOR . . . DO . . . END rules:

1. The termination condition is tested *before* the loop is executed. If the initial value is outside the range specified by the final value, the loop will not be executed at all. The feature of the FOR loop that distinguishes it from the other three loop control structures is that an explicit start and stop criteria must be stated. This equates to saying something like "Do the following exactly 20 times," whereas the WHILE and REPEAT loops say something like "Do the following until it's done, whenever that may be." FOR statements find their greatest use with arrays (Chapter 6) where specific numbers of repetitions are common. They are virtually useless for reading or writing data in situations where the number of data elements to be input or output is unknown—the WHILE is better in this case.

2. The statement sequence in the loop will continue to execute until the control variable exceeds the expression following the keyword TO. (If

the constant expression following the keyword BY is negative, the loop will end when the control variable is less than the final value.)

3. A Modula-2 program or procedure must have a DO and END for every FOR.

4. After the loop terminates, the next statement to be executed is the first statement which follows the FOR ... DO ... END statement. *Note:* The value of the control variable is *undefined* after the FOR loop terminates. *Do not count on its value being equal to the final loop condition, or any other specific value.*

4.2.2 Nesting Loops

A statement sequence can be enclosed by more than one control structure. There is no limit to the extent that loops can be nested. There is also no constraint on the different types of control structure loops that may be nested. We can have a FOR inside of a WHILE which is inside of a REPEAT, all of which are contained in a LOOP. For example, if a program were to ask for the temperature once per hour for every day in a month, it might look like Listing 4.4.

LISTING 4.4

```
(* Listing 4.4 Example of nested FOR ... DO ... END *)

MODULE NestedLoops;
  FROM InOut IMPORT WriteInt, WriteLn, WriteString;
  VAR Hour, Day : INTEGER;
     (* Additional declarations would appear here *)
BEGIN
  FOR Day := 1 TO 31 DO  (* Assumes 31 day month *)
    FOR Hour := 0 TO 23 DO
      WriteString("What is the temperature for day #");
      WriteInt(Day, 1);
      WriteString(", Hour = ");
      WriteInt(Hour, 1);
      (* At this point of the program, data would be read & processed *)
      WriteLn;
    END; (* This ends the Hour FOR loop *)
  END; (* This ends the Day FOR loop *)
END NestedLoops.
```

Note that the Modula-2 compiler assumes that each END corresponds to the nearest unended control structure that uses an END to terminate a loop. A loop may be completely enclosed by other loops, but the scope of two loops cannot cross. Listing 4.5 shows an incorrect Modula-2 program in which a REPEAT . . . UNTIL loop improperly includes only a part of a FOR . . . DO . . . END loop.

LISTING 4.5

```
(* Listing 4.5 Incorrect nesting of loop control structures *)
(* Same as listing 4.4 except replace the outer for loop with
   a repeat loop, AND do it wrong.  Note that the structure
   and indentation show the problem clearly *)

MODULE IllegalNestedLoops;
  FROM InOut IMPORT WriteInt, WriteLn, WriteString;
  VAR Hour, Day : INTEGER;
      (* Additional declarations would appear here *)
BEGIN
  Day := 0;
  REPEAT  (* Replace listing 4.4 outer for loop with repeat loop *)
    Day := Day + 1;
    FOR Hour := 0 TO 23 DO
      WriteString("What is the temperature for day #");
      WriteInt(Day, 1);
      WriteString(", Hour = ");
      WriteInt(Hour, 1);
      (* At this point of the program, data would be read & processed *)
      WriteLn;
  UNTIL Day = 31;  (* End of repeat loop.  Oops!  Where's the for? *)
    END; (* This ends the Hour FOR loop *)
  (* Reversing the two previous statements would solve the problem *)
END IllegalNestedLoops.
```

4.2.3 Branching Statements

The four control structures presented in the last section all cause a statement sequence to be repeated. These structures provide *loop control* over the flow of execution within a program. A second type of control structure selects between alternative sets of actions based upon conditions specified by the programmer. These structures are referred to as *branching* control structures because they provide branches in an otherwise straight sequential execution path for program statements. Without branching control structures, all Modula-2 programs would merely execute statements in the order in which they appear, except to possibly loop back over various segments. Branching control structures are essential for writing most programs.

Modula-2 provides two different branching control structures, the IF statement and the CASE statement. The IF statement allows one of several alternative courses of action to be taken based on program results to that point. The CASE statement provides similar capabilities, but is especially useful when a large number of alternative results and/or alternative actions must be considered. Both statements accommodate a form of decision making within the program. They evaluate some current program condition or result and decide, based on the result of the evaluation, what action to perform next. This capability forms the basis for most of what the computer novice associates with the "intelligence" or "reasoning power" of a computer. As we shall see in Chapter 7, under records, the CASE statement is also valuable in dealing with Modula-2 variant record elements.

The IF Statement

The syntax diagram for the IF statement is shown in Figure A.50. The basic form of an IF statement is:

```
IF Relationship1 THEN Statement1
ELSIF Relationship2 THEN Statement2    (*Optional*)
ELSIF Relationship3 THEN Statement3    (*Optional*)
:
:       (* More optional ELSIFs *)
:
ELSE StatementN    (*Optional*)
END
```

The diagram and the generic example show the syntax. The statement begins with the keyword IF. IF is followed by a BOOLEAN expression which evaluates to TRUE or FALSE. Next comes the keyword THEN, which is followed by any valid statement—including another IF, or any other control structure, since these are all forms of statements. The IF statement is completed by the keyword END. This represents the minimum IF statement.

The IF statement can also include optional parts. One is an unlimited number of ELSIF segments, which follow the same basic syntax as that just described for the IF statement, except the ELSIF does not have a separate END symbol. The second, and last, optional part of the IF statement is the ELSE. The ELSE, if it is present, is the last part of the statement before the END symbol is reached. The syntax of ELSE differs from that of IF and ELSIF in that no Boolean expression is present.

What we have just described is the syntax of IF. What about the semantics? What does it all mean and how does the IF statement work?

When the IF statement is executed, the first relation (Relationship1 in the sample) is tested. If the relationship is true, then the associated statement (Statement1 in the sample) is executed and the IF statement terminates. If the relationship is false, and none of the optional parts are present, the IF statement terminates without any action being taken. When the IF statement terminates, control passes to the first statement which follows it.

If an ELSIF is present, and the IF relationship is false, then the ELSIF relationship is evaluated. If it is true, then its associated statement is executed and the IF statement terminates. If the first ELSIF relationship is false, then events proceed just as described for the IF portion of the statement. That is, control either passes on to the next part, if one is present, or the ELSIF statement terminates without any action being performed.

If an ELSE is present and if all preceding Boolean expressions were false, the statement which follows the ELSE is automatically executed. This is why there is no Boolean expression following the ELSE. Hence, if an ELSE is included in the IF statement, we are guaranteed that at least one statement will be executed—either one associated with the IF or ELSIF statements, or failing in both of those, the ELSE statement will be executed. Without an ELSE statement, there would be no statement executed if none of the Boolean expressions were true.

Note carefully that once a true expression is found and the associated statement is executed, the IF statement terminates. None of the subsequent parts are considered. Powerful pseudo-intelligent decisions can be formulated through complex IF . . . ELSIF . . . ELSIF . . . constructions.

When the LOOP . . . EXIT . . . END control structure was presented, we deferred discussion of Listing 4.3 until the IF statement was reached. Returning to this example now, we see that the program's main body is

```
i := 0;
LOOP
   i := i + 1;
   IF i > MaxCount THEN EXIT END;
   WriteLn;  Writelnt(i, 6);
END (*loop*);
```

Once again, it is our old friend count-to-ten. In this example, the IF statement is nested within the LOOP. Recall that the LOOP is executed until an EXIT is encountered, at which time the loop terminates. In the example, each time the IF statement is executed, the expression i > MaxCount is evaluated.

While i is less than or equal to MaxCount (=10), the statement that is nested within the IF statement, i.e., EXIT, is bypassed. When i is finally greater than MaxCount, i.e., after the loop is repeated 10 times, EXIT is executed thus causing termination of the LOOP control structure. This example depicts a more or less classic use of the IF statement.

Note that in this case the statement could also have been written using the optional ELSE as follows:

```
i := 0;
LOOP
   i := i + 1;
   IF i > MaxCount THEN
      EXIT
   ELSE
      WriteLn;   WriteInt(i, 6);
   END (*if*);
END (*loop*);
```

Two of the semicolons in this example are superfluous (but cause no harm). Can you tell which they are? *Hint:* It is neither the first two nor the last one (only three left). *Answer:* The ones following WriteInt and END (*if*).

Keeping things elementary, the above example can be expanded to illustrate the ELSIF portion of the IF statement. First of all, it is necessary to understand the purpose of the WriteLn procedure, which is covered in Chapter 5. WriteLn causes output to begin on a new line. Therefore, in the above example, WriteLn is responsible for the numbers 1 through 10 appearing in a column instead of all on one line. This being the case, we do not need WriteLn until after the first number has been written. This leads to:

```
i := 0;                            i := 0;
LOOP                               LOOP
   i := i + 1;                        i := i + 1;
   IF i > MaxCount THEN               IF (i>1) & (i <=MaxCount) THEN
      EXIT                               WriteLn; WriteInt(i, 6)
   ELSIF i = 1 THEN                   ELSIF i = 1 THEN
      WriteInt(i, 6)                     WriteInt(i, 6)
   ELSE                               ELSE
      WriteLn; WriteInt(i,6)             EXIT
   END (*if*)                         END (*if*)
END (*loop*);                      END (*loop*);
```

In these two examples, a new line (WriteLn) is started only if the number to be written is not 1. The two functionally equivalent versions are presented merely to illustrate that there are many right ways to accomplish the same task. Some are better than others, but syntactically and semantically, several alternatives can always be found. Note that in both examples the ELSE is required for proper program operation.

Nested IF Statements. Like any other control structure, IF statements can also be nested. Listing 4.6 is a trivial example of nesting one IF . . . THEN . . . ELSE . . . END control structure within a second one.

LISTING 4.6

```
(* Listing 4.6 - Example of nested IF...THEN...ELSE...END *)

MODULE Decisions;
    FROM InOut IMPORT WriteLn, WriteString;
    VAR WorkHrs, Raining : BOOLEAN;
BEGIN
    WorkHrs := FALSE;
    Raining := TRUE;
    IF WorkHrs THEN
        IF Raining THEN
            WriteString("Drive to work.");
        ELSE
            WriteString("Walk to work.");
        END (*if raining*);
    ELSE
        IF Raining THEN
            WriteString("Read a book.");
        ELSE
            WriteString("Go jogging.");
        END (*if raining*);
    END; (* IF WorkHrs *)
    WriteLn;
END Decisions.
```

In Listing 4.6, the message displayed on the screen will vary depending upon the values assigned to the Boolean variables WorkHrs and Raining. In its present form, the program will display "Read a book." Note that each of the three IF statements also happen to have an associated ELSE branch. The indentation of the program lines suggests the logical structure of the program. The "Drive to work" and "Walk to work" alternatives constitute the TRUE branch for the IF WorkHrs statement. The "Read a book" and "Go jogging" alternatives constitute the FALSE branch. By revising the two assignment statements at the top of the program to assign all four possible combinations of values to WorkHrs and Raining, each of the four messages can appear. (For this reason, this control structure is called a four-way branch.) Regardless of what values are assigned, the WriteLn instruction will always be executed because it is placed after the END corresponding to the first IF.

By using a number of ELSIFs within an IF statement, multiple branches that handle a large number of mutually exclusive alternatives can be created. One example of such multiple branch structures is a menu routine. In a typical menu routine, a number of alternative actions are displayed on the screen, and the user selects one by pressing an appropriate letter on the keyboard. Depending on which letter was selected, a different routine is executed. The skeleton of a menu routine would be:

```
LOOP
   { Clear the screen }
   WriteString("I)nsert, D)elete, X)change or Q)uit: ");
   Terminal.Read(Response); (* get menu option *)
   IF Response = "I" THEN
      { Insert routine }
   ELSIF Response = "D" THEN
      { Delete routine }
   ELSIF Response = "X" THEN
      { Xchange routine }
   ELSIF Response = "Q" THEN
      { Quit routine }
      EXIT;
   ELSE WriteString("Illegal choice"); { Pause }
   END; (* IF *)
END; (* LOOP *)
```

Each bracketed comment would be replaced with a Modula-2 statement sequence that specifies the actions to be performed in order to accomplish each option's task. After the quit routine is executed, the EXIT statement causes control to pass to the statement following the END statement for the LOOP. Note that the "Illegal choice" message will only be displayed if the user failed to respond with one of the four capital letters: I, D, X, or Q. As we shall see in the next section, the CASE control structure offers a more convenient way of expressing multiple branches. Menus similar to the one above are used extensively in the word processing program described in Chapter 12.

The CASE Statement

In the last example, repeatedly writing ELSIF Response = could get tedious if the list of alternative actions was long. Since this is a frequent occurrence, the CASE statement provides an easier way of representing such situations.

The syntax rules for the CASE statement are shown in Figure A.51. First and most obvious, the case statement begins and ends with the keywords CASE and END. Second, the word CASE must be followed by an expression. Unlike the IF statement, in which the expression must be of the BOOLEAN type, the expression following the word CASE can be any of the types presented in Chapter 3, except type REAL. In addition, the expression can be an enumerated type or a subrange type, as will be described in Chapter 6. The expression is followed by the keyword OF. Third, the phrase CASE expression OF is followed by one or more cases. These cases represent the alternative courses of action to be chosen, as well as the conditions under which each action is to be selected.

Note that multiple elements of the Case Label List (see Figure A.32) may lead to the same action, or statement sequence. In this case, the labels are either separated by commas or, if they are contiguous elements, by the special symbol .. placed between the first and last elements of the contiguous list. For example, if we wanted to check characters for the occurrence of a vowel, the following would work:

```
CASE Character OF
   "A", "E", "I", "O", "U",
   "a", "e", "i", "o", "u" : WriteString("Vowel");
   ELSE     WriteString("Not a vowel");
END;
```

To be more explicit regarding the nature of the non-vowels, we could have written:

```
CASE Character OF
   OC..100C,   133C..140C,
   173C..177C     : WriteString('Non-alphabetic')|
   102C..104C, 106C..110C,
   112C..116C, 120C..124C,
   126C..132C     : WriteString('Upper case non-vowel')|
   'A', 'E', 'I', 'O', 'U': WriteString('Upper case vowel')|
   142C..144C, 146C..150C,
   152C..156C, 160C..164C,
   166C..172C     : WriteString('Lower case non-vowel')|
```

```
    'a', 'e', 'i', 'o', 'u': WriteString('Lower case vowel');
    ELSE     WriteString('Non-ASCII Character');
END;
```

Notice how this last example mixes all possible forms of the Case Label List. This is a more flexible syntax than Pascal's case label. If the xxxC notation has you puzzled, review the explanation of the CHAR (character) data type in Chapter 3, and refer to the ASCII character table in Appendix B. It is easy to see that this example is far easier to write (and read) using the CASE statement than using the corresponding IF statement representation.

Each item of the Case Label List, to be matched against the expression following CASE, must be a constant expression. Also, each item on the list must be of the same data type as the expression following the word CASE. In the example, both the expression, i.e., Character, and each element of the Case Label List are all of type CHAR. If an element of the Case Label List equals the expression following CASE, the associated statement sequence is executed. Once a match is found, no other cases are tested, and the CASE statement terminates.

A final syntax comment: Each alternative statement sequence (except the last) must end with a vertical bar symbol, |. No vertical bar may appear prior to the ELSE statement, if it is present. (See Figure A.51.) Just as the semicolon is called the statement separator, we could refer to the | as the statement sequence separator for the CASE control structure. (It serves the same purpose in the RECORD data type declaration discussed in Chapter 7. The CASE statement is useful for manipulating RECORD data elements.)

LISTING 4.7

```
(* Listing 4.7 - Menu routine with CASE statement. *)

LOOP
   (Clear the screen)
   WriteString("I)nsert, D)elete, X)change or Q)uit: ");
   Terminal.Read(Response); (* get menu option *)
   CASE Response OF
      "I": (Insert routine) ¦       (* Note use of ¦ *)
      "D": (Delete routine) ¦
      "X": (Xchange routine) ¦
      "Q": (Quit routine);
            EXIT ;                   (* No ¦ before ELSE *)
      ELSE WriteString("Illegal choice");   (Pause);
   END; (* case *)
END; (* loop *)
```

Listing 4.7 shows the menu example of the IF statement section revised to use a CASE statement. Although this example contains an ELSE branch to specify what action is to be performed if Response does not match any of the listed values, Modula-2 does not require that an ELSE branch be included. Note that if the expression following the keyword CASE fails to match any of the listed values, and no ELSE branch is specified, execution of the program will halt with an error. The message here is clear—if the cases which follow the word CASE are not totally inclusive, and if the program does not take steps to screen out unlisted cases, you had better make certain that the ELSE is present.

SUMMARY

This chapter introduced key Modula-2 features. It is virtually impossible to write a meaningful program without a firm grasp of this material. The assignment statement is a fundamental action in all programming languages and must be understood. Looping and branching control structures are essential. Without these features, little or nothing useful can be accomplished.

Assignment compatibility and type compatibility are two important concepts that must be understood. These topics will be covered again in Chapter 6 following the description of subranges and type declarations.

QUESTIONS AND PROBLEMS

1. If r is a REAL variable, i is an INTEGER, and c is a CARDINAL, rewrite the following statements to eliminate illegal mixing of data types:
   a. r := i / c;
   b. i := i + c;
   c. r := c;
   d. r := c + 1;
   e. i := r;

2. True or false?
   a. A FOR loop is always executed at least once.
   b. A WHILE loop is always executed at least once.
   c. A REPEAT loop is always executed at least once.
   d. A LOOP..EXIT is always executed at least once.

3. What is the value of the integer i when the WriteInt(i, 6) statement is reached in each of the following:

a. FOR i := 1 TO 10 DO
      i := i + 1;
   END (*for*);
   WriteInt(i, 6);

b. i := 11;
   WHILE i <= 10 DO
      i := i + 1;
   END (*while*);
   WriteInt(i, 6);

c. i := 11;
   REPEAT
      i := i + 1;
   UNTIL i > 10;
   WriteInt(i, 6);

d. i := 11;
   LOOP
      IF i > 10 THEN
         i := i + 2;   EXIT;
      END (*if*);
   END (*loop*);
   WriteInt(i, 6);

e. i := 11;
      IF (i DIV 3) = 0 THEN
         i := 10;
      ELSIF (i DIV 3) = 1 THEN
         i := 12;
      ELSE
         i := 14;
      END (*if*);
      WriteInt(i, 6);

f. i := 11;
   CASE i OF
      0..10 : i := 10|
      20..30: i := 13|
      31..99: i := 50;
      ELSE   i := 15;
   END (*case*);
   WriteInt(i, 6);

Is there a pattern to your answers? There should be. The FOR result is undefined.

SUPPLEMENTAL PROBLEMS

In each of the following problems, if your programming experience and the material covered thus far have not prepared you to write the entire program in Modula-2 then write as much as necessary in pseudo-code (English), but use Modula-2 declarations, variables, assignments, and control structures to the maximum extent possible. No later than Chapter 6, after covering arrays, come back and complete the problems using Modula-2.

Problem 1

Use either the IF...ELSE structure or the CASE structure to control processing of the user inputs to the calculator. Calculator commands are as defined in Problem 2 of Chapter 3. Don't worry just yet how each process will be done; assume that procedures to execute each command exist. Is either structure better suited to this problem? How are you going to handle differences between numbers to be pushed on the stack and commands to be executed? Can numbers and commands be handled in the same control structure?

Problem 2

Use one of the loop control structures of this chapter to write the main control loop for the calculator. This loop should control reading the user input, processing the input using the result of Problem 1, and display results. Are all of the available loops equally applicable to this problem? If not, why?

Problem 3

Write three small programs for use in implementing the stack. One, called Pop, will remove the top element from the stack and make it available for use; all other stack elements move up one place in the stack. The second, called Push, puts a new element on the top of the stack and all old stack elements are moved (pushed) down one place. The third, Clear, initializes (empties) the stack. Consider likely error conditions (e.g., popping an empty stack, pushing a full stack) and take appropriate steps. Use control structures from this chapter.

CHAPTER 5

INPUT/OUTPUT BASICS

NEW CONCEPTS: Data Input and Output, Library Modules, Input/Output Re-direction
ISSUES: Machine Independent Programming, Program Portability

INTRODUCTION

One of the most fundamental requirements of a programming language is the ability to provide data to a program (input) and to get results from a program (output). Modula-2 input and output features are the subject of this chapter, which will provide a brief, overall description of the Modula-2 input/output philosophy—a philosophy considerably different from that of most other languages. This will be followed by a detailed description of the input/output capabilities that are available in standard implementations of Modula-2. These basic functions include entering data from a standard input unit, normally a keyboard, and sending data to the standard output unit, normally a terminal. More advanced topics related to data input and output, topics such as disk files, the redirection of files, and sequential/random file access, are covered in Chapter 9.

5.1 MODULA-2 INPUT/OUTPUT PHILOSOPHY

One of the objectives of Modula-2 is to satisfy the need for an efficient high-level systems programming language that is essentially machine independent. One aspect of computer programming that is in direct conflict with this objective is computer input/output. The basic system programming input and output processes are heavily machine dependent and input/output-device dependent.

So how is the objective to be met in the face of this dilemma? Simple—Modula-2 was designed with *no input/output* statements as part of the language!

Now we would all agree that this seems to be a radical solution to the problem. How is input/output accomplished in a language that has no input or output statements? The solution lies in the use of library routines that can be accessed by any program.

Library routines for handling input and output are expected to be provided with each implementation of Modula-2. These routines are written and tailored for each specific machine and operating system on which the implementation will run. In this way, input/output functions are available to Modula-2 programs even though they are not part of the language proper. The following sections of this chapter will demonstrate that the net result is the same as if the statements were, in fact, part of the language. No problem arises as long as each Modula-2 implementation provides the recommended standard library modules.

The library routines for handling input and output are made possible by the feature of Modula-2 which gave the language its name—the *module.* In this chapter, you are asked to accept the existence of something called a module. The details of modules—what, why, and how—will be covered in Chapter 8. In the meantime, we need to use the input/output capabilities that are provided by some of these so-called standard library modules.

5.1.1 Library Modules

A number of functions, such as input/output, occur over and over again in programs. Continually reprogramming these operations each time that they are required is inefficient and a potential source of error. A better solution would be to program them one time and to put these "canned" functions in a library routine that can be accessed by any program. This is exactly one of the things that modules allow us to do. This particular form of module (there are several, as we shall see later) is called a library module.

In this chapter we will consider two of the recommended standard input/output library modules that are provided as part of a Modula-2 implementation. The specific examples that we use are from the Volition Systems implementation of Modula-2.

We will show how library routines are accessed for use in a program. The standard input/output functions will be identified and described, and their use will be illustrated with examples.

5.1.2 Input/Output Standard Library Modules

When we consider computer input/output as a whole, the number and variety of input/output devices is extremely large. The number of different data types is also very large. In this chapter, we will limit ourselves to the standard system input and output devices—typically a terminal keyboard and screen. We will likewise limit the data types to those that are used to communicate between the computer and the user. This data is made up of the letters and numbers we enter into programs and read on our terminals.

The recommended library modules for a standard Modula-2 implementation include two modules that are capable of handling all of the input/output requirements related to the standard input and output sources. The first of these is the module named InOut, and the second is RealInOut. They are described in the following section.

5.2 BASIC INPUT/OUTPUT LIBRARY FUNCTIONS

5.2.1 The Module InOut

Standard module InOut provides the necessary input/output functions for reading and writing the basic data types with the standard system input and output devices. We will assume that the standard devices are the terminal keyboard and screen. The data types that are allowed were described in Chapter 3. They are CARDINAL, INTEGER, CHAR, and STRING (STRING is an ARRAY OF CHAR, as will be described in the next chapter).

These procedures make no assumptions regarding the details of the data stream being processed except that the stream elements appear in a sequence and that all elements are of the same type. A typical example would be a stream of text characters being typed on a keyboard or being sent to a screen for display.

The input/output functions of this module can be divided into three categories—

- input procedures,

- output procedures, and
- procedures to redefine the identity of the system input and output devices.

Input Procedures

There are four standard input procedures provided by InOut. They are—

- Read(CharacterInput),
- ReadString(StringInput),
- ReadInt(IntegerInput), and
- ReadCard(CardinalInput).

Before covering these procedures in detail, we must point out that the input/output procedures can read and write only a *single* variable at a time. Specifically, the terms CharacterInput, StringInput, IntegerInput, and CardinalInput represent single character, string, integer, and cardinal variables, respectively. This will be a change for Pascal programmers who are used to overloading input/output procedures with forms such as

```
Read(v1, v2, v3, etc . . .),
```

where v1, v2, and v3 are multiple variables of potentially different types that are included in a single input statement.

Since the Modula-2 statements handle only one variable at a time, if you want to read values for four variables in a Modula-2 program, you will have to write four Read statements. This may seem inefficient, and it does take some getting used to. The resulting code is no less efficient than the corresponding Pascal technique. In the Modula-2 approach, some of the previous burden on the compiler has been shifted to the programmer. The overall Modula-2 philosophy regarding input/output is the same in Ada also.

Read (CharacterInput)

The procedure Read gets a single character from the standard input, assigns this input character to the character variable CharacterInput, and echoes the character on the standard output. When the end of the input character stream is detected, a "flag," called Done, is set to FALSE. The BOOLEAN variable

Done is part of the InOut module. This variable allows the status of the most recent input operation to be tested.

When the end of the input has been reached, the null character (ASCII 0) is returned in CharacterInput by Read. The end of stream is implementation dependent. For example, entering Control-C with the Volition Systems implementation results in the end of stream.

Listing 5.1 is a sample program which illustrates the use of Read. Notice the statement IMPORT InOut in the second line of the program. This is the mechanism by which we access the procedures of the InOut library module for use in our program. Within the program body, we see the statement InOut.Read(Chr). The prefix InOut. is called a qualifying identifier because it identifies the library module that is the source of the procedure Read. This will be explained in detail in Chapter 8.

LISTING 5.1

```
MODULE ReadDemo;

IMPORT InOut;

VAR
  Chr : CHAR;

BEGIN (*ReadDemo*)
  InOut.Read(Chr);
  WHILE InOut.Done DO    (* TRUE if not end of text stream *)
    (* At this point, program presumedly processes Chr *)
    InOut.Read(Chr);
  END (*while*);
  (* Now that Done := FALSE, the contents of Chr := 0C *)
END ReadDemo.
```

ReadString(StringInput)

ReadString provides the capability to read a sequence of characters, in constrast to the single character returned by Read. This sequence is a STRING (see Chapter 3) or an ARRAY OF CHAR (see Chapter 6). There are several features of ReadString to note:

- Leading blanks are ignored.
- The operation is terminated by a blank or any control character. (This basically equates to all non-printable characters.)

- The character that terminates input is returned in the InOut module variable named termCH.
- Backspacing is allowed when input is from a terminal.

Listing 5.2 shows the use of ReadString. It is a trivial example that results in the input sequence being read into the variable Str. After this simple example, the same thing is accomplished using the Read procedure that we just described. Or is it the same thing? Let's compare what happens in the program with the four ReadString features listed above. (If you are not familiar with ARRAYS, you may want to skip the remainder of this section on ReadString and return to it following Chapter 6.)

Leading blanks appear to be ignored using the REPEAT loop (and they are). A blank or a control character (any character whose ASCII value is less

LISTING 5.2

```
MODULE ReadStringDemo;

IMPORT InOut;

CONST
  MaxString = 80;

VAR
  Chr : CHAR;
  Str : ARRAY [0..MaxString] OF CHAR;
  i : CARDINAL;


BEGIN (*ReadStringDemo*)
  InOut.ReadString(Str);         (*doing it by the book*)

  (* Is the following the functional equivalent of ReadString?? *)
  REPEAT                          (*suppress leading blanks*)
    InOut.Read(Chr);
  UNTIL Chr # ' ';

  i := 0;
  WHILE (ORD(Chr) > ORD(' ')) & (i <= MaxString) DO
    Str[i] := Chr;                (*can't get here with a backspace*)
    INC(i);
    InOut.Read(Chr);
  END (*while*);

  InOut.termCH := Chr;                    (*set termCH*)
  IF i < MaxString THEN
    Str[i] := 0C;                 (*null goes at end of string*)
  END;
END ReadStringDemo.
```

than or equal to the ASCII value of space—see the ASCII table in Appendix B) terminates the input. So far, so good. Two down and two to go.

Following termination of the WHILE loop, the variable Str contains the input sequence, with leading blanks suppressed up through the terminating character. It seems to work. One last thing—backspacing. Here is where the program fails. Backspacing will terminate the WHILE loop, thus terminating the input. Can you see how to solve the problem? We will come back to it after looking at some of InOut's output procedures.

If you followed the alternate method in Listing 5.2 for accomplishing the ReadString function, you have a good grasp of both Read and ReadString.

ReadInt(IntegerInput) and ReadCard(CardinalInput)

ReadInt is used to read data into INTEGER variables. ReadCard performs the same function for CARDINAL variables. The following basic rules for their use parallels most of the rules for the use of ReadString:

- Leading blanks are ignored.
- The operation is terminated by a blank or any control character.
- Backspacing is allowed when input is from a terminal.
- A potential difference from ReadString is that the terminating character may possibly not be returned in the variable termCH. In the Volition Systems implementation, however, it is returned in termCH.
- A second difference is that if an integer (ReadInt) or cardinal (Read-Card) is read successfully, the InOut variable Done is set to TRUE. In this respect, ReadInt and ReadCard are similar to Read. When all of the input characters are not digits (0..9), or some similar error occurs, Done will be set to FALSE.

  For example, if you entered

  123a4

  in response to the statement InOut.ReadInt(IntVar), Done would be FALSE. The value of the variable, IntVar, would be equal to 123 (but do not count on this).

The proper form for these two procedures is

```
InOut.ReadInt(IntVar); InOut.ReadCard(CardVar);
```

where IntVar and CardVar have been properly declared as INTEGER and CARDINAL variables respectively. These two procedures read a text stream from the standard input unit, convert the stream to the appropriate numeric type, and assign the numeric value to the variable. This conversion is typically accomplished within another module (called Conversions in the Volition Systems implementation), which is invisible to the programmer using the InOut procedures.

Basically, what is done to convert the text stream is identical to what you would have to do yourself if only Read and ReadString were available. You would have to write a small routine to convert the text data which was read by ReadString into its equivalent numeric form. The program segment in Listing 5.3 demonstrates a method for performing this conversion. The variable Str contains a sequence of characters read by ReadString, and Number and i have been declared to be cardinal variables.

LISTING 5.3

```
Number := 0;
i := 0;
WHILE Str[i] # 0C DO   (*Strings are terminated with a null character*)
   Number := 10 * Number + ORD(Str[i]) - ORD('0');
   INC(i);             (*standard procedure; same as i := i + 1*)
END (*while*);
```

This program segment does not take into account the maximum value that a cardinal can assume, which is implementation dependent. It also does not take into account the fact that if Number is an integer, a negative value could occur. How would you modify this program to perform properly on your computer?

This completes the basic input procedures that should be available on all Modula-2 system implementations. These procedures are at the highest level of the input/output hierarchy and can thus be expected to be completely portable across all system implementations of Modula-2.

We see from the examples of Listings 5.2 and 5.3 that only the Read procedure is necessary. Given the Read procedure, we can perform the functions of ReadString, ReadInt, and ReadCard by means of our own programming, without any additional help from library procedures. Furthermore, we can create our own input/output library modules (after we finish Chapter 8) to replace or augment the existing modules, if there is a need.

Output Procedures

The following are the seven standard output procedures provided by InOut:

- Write(CharacterOutput)
- WriteLn;
- WriteString(StringOutput)
- WriteInt(IntegerOutput, FieldWidth)
- WriteCard(CardinalOutput, FieldWidth)
- WriteOct(CardinalOutput, FieldWidth)
- WriteHex(CardinalOutput, FieldWidth)

As was mentioned earlier, the Write procedures, like their Read counterparts, can only write a *single* parameter at a time.

Write(CharacterOutput)

The Write procedure writes a single character to the standard output.

WriteLn;

The module InOut defines a character constant, EOL, which is implementation dependent. EOL marks the end of a line of text. That is, it is a line terminator. The procedure WriteLn terminates a line. It is defined to be the equivalent of Write(EOL).

If the character variable Char1 contained 1 and Char2 contained 2, then the following two program segments illustrate the use (and effect) of WriteLn in conjunction with Write.

	Version 1	Version 2
Program Segment	Write(Char1); Write(Char2);	Write(Char1); WriteLn; Write(Char2);
Output Result	12	1 2

Version 2 could have also been written as

```
Write(Char1);
Write(EOL);
Write(Char2);
```

WriteString(StringOutput)

This procedure writes the string StringOutput to the standard output device. Except for the number of characters involved, its operation is identical to the procedure Write. If you want a new line to start following whatever you have written using WriteString, use WriteLn, as in the above example.

WriteInt(IntegerOutput, FieldWidth)

WriteInt writes the INTEGER value of the variable IntegerOutput to the standard output. The parameter FieldWidth must be a CARDINAL type and is used for output formatting. It defines the width of the space for writing the value of IntegerOutput. If the space required for the number is less than the value of FieldWidth, then blanks are added to the left of the number. If the value of FieldWidth is too small, then the exact amount of space required is used.

Note that WriteInt, WriteLn, and WriteString were all used in the count-to-ten program of the previous chapters. Examine Listings 4.1 to 4.3, and make sure that you understand the function of each output line. Note that the values 1 and 6 are used for the WriteInt field width parameter in these listings. Why does WriteInt(MaxCount, 1) use a width of 1, especially when MaxCount's value is two digits long? To see the answer, ask yourself where MaxCount would appear relative to the string that precedes it if you wrote WriteInt(MaxCount, 40). Most people do not like 39 spaces between words.

WriteCard(CardinalOutput, FieldWidth)

WriteCard writes the CARDINAL value of the variable CardinalOutput to the standard output. The parameter FieldWidth is used in the same manner as was described for WriteInt.

WriteOct(CardinalOutput, FieldWidth)

WriteOct writes the CARDINAL value of the variable CardinalOutput to the standard output in octal format. (Six digits are used in the Volition Systems implementation.) The parameter FieldWidth is used in the same manner as was described for WriteInt.

WriteHex(CardinalOutput, FieldWidth)

WriteHex writes the CARDINAL value of the variable CardinalOutput to the standard output in hexadecimal format. (Four digits are used in the Volition Systems implementation.) The parameter FieldWidth is used in the same manner as was described for WriteInt.

The program in Listing 5.4 illustrates the use of the last three output procedures. When this program is run, the resulting output is

    1024 002000   0400

which, in a seven-space field, represents 1024 in decimal, octal, and hexadecimal.

LISTING 5.4

```
MODULE WriteNumberDemo;

IMPORT InOut;

VAR
  Card : CARDINAL;

BEGIN (*WriteNumberDemo*)
  Card := 1024;
  InOut.WriteCard(Card, 7);
  InOut.WriteOct(Card, 7);
  InOut.WriteHex(Card, 7);
END WriteNumberDemo.
```

We introduced the ReadString procedure by presenting a method to accomplish the ReadString function just using Read. This program for ReadString, in Listing 5.2, worked properly except that backspacing was not included. We deferred the solution of that problem until the output procedures had been explained. The reason was that we needed the Write procedure to cure the backspace problem.

The revised version of the WHILE loop portion of Listing 5.2 is shown in Listing 5.5. The rest of the program is unchanged, with one exception. You will notice reference to a term BackSpace (ASCII backspace) in Listing 5.5. This is the implementation-dependent character constant that represents the value assigned to a backspace character (ASCII 27 decimal for most systems). This value must be declared or obtained from a library unit. Volition Systems includes a library unit called ASCII which would allow all references to BackSpace in Listing 5.5 to be replaced by ASCII.bs.

LISTING 5.5

```
WHILE ((ORD(Chr) > ORD(' ')) OR (Chr = BackSpace)) &
      (i <= MaxString) DO
  IF Chr # BackSpace THEN    (* ^^^ new term ^^^ *)
    Str[i] := Chr;
    INC(i);
  ELSIF i # 0 THEN (*backspace; do something if past the 1st char*)
    DEC(i);                  (*back up character counter*)
    InOut.Write(' ');        (*blank out previous char*)
    InOut.Write(BackSpace);(*move cursor back; Write(' ') moved it*)
  END (*if*);
  InOut.Read(Chr);
END (*while*);
```

The solution to the backspacing problem does not absolutely require the two Write statements in Listing 5.5. If these two statements are deleted, the only difference in operation is that an old character that is backspaced over will not disappear until a new character is typed over it. This latter approach is, in fact, how the Volition Systems implementation works. The recommendations made by Wirth for the standard library module InOut do not specify which of these two alternatives is to be implemented. We personally prefer to have the letters disappear.

Procedures to Redefine System Input and Output Sources

The module InOut has a third category of procedures in addition to the input and output functions that have been described thus far. This final category provides the capability to redefine the source of the input text stream and the destination of the output text stream.

The default values are normally the system's terminal, i.e., the keyboard and screen. With these additional InOut procedures, we may select other devices for our input and output units. As an example, we might choose to get our input from a disk file and send our output to the printer. This capability is referred to as input/output redirection.

We will have more to say about redirection in Chapter 9 when we cover more advanced input/output topics and also in Chapter 12 when we present a word processing program that uses redirection extensively. In the meantime, we will describe the following four redirection procedures that are provided by InOut:

- OpenInput(DefaultExtension)
- OpenOutput(DefaultExtension)
- CloseInput
- CloseOutput

OpenInput(DefaultExtension)

This procedure allows the programmer to identify and open a new input source. If the statement OpenInput(DefaultExtension) is executed in a program, a prompt will appear at the terminal that requests the name of the new input source. If the name entered by the user in response to the prompt ends in a period, the character string DefaultExtension is added to the end of the name entered by the user.

A typical use of this option would occur in an operating system that uses standard suffixes in its file naming convention. For example, a system might use the suffix TEXT in the name of a text file. Therefore, if we want to use a file whose name is MYFILE.TEXT as our input source, we could respond to the prompt with either MYFILE. or MYFILE.TEXT (if DefaultExtension had been assigned the value TEXT).

If the file, which must exist and be on-line, is successfully opened, the InOut variable Done is set to TRUE. This variable can be checked by a program to determine the status of the operation. Once the file is opened, all subsequent input is taken from this file.

OpenOutput(DefaultExtension)

This procedure allows the programmer to identify and open a new output source. Its use and operation are identical to OpenInput.

CloseInput and CloseOutput

These two procedures close the files that were opened using OpenInput and OpenOutput. After they are executed, input/output returns to the system default device, or terminal.

The chief benefit of input/output redirection is program flexibility. This capability allows the same program to be used to read and write data regardless of the source or destination of the data from one execution to another. Changing data sources and destinations is accomplished by the appropriate answer to the OpenInput and OpenOutput prompt and not by modifying program read/write statements and procedures.

Some care should be used when using these redirection procedures. Text data residing on a disk file that is being used for input must be formatted properly, or unexpected results will occur. Also, if the standard output unit is redefined to be a disk file, guess where any screen prompts from your program for cueing your inputs are sent? You guessed it—to the disk file, and if you cannot run your program (or worse yet—cannot stop your program) without visual prompts, then you have a problem. Our recommendation would be to use the approaches that appear in later chapters.

Another point to guard against when using these procedures is the possible dependency of the InOut module on other modules that also play a role in the process of reading and writing data. For example, in the Volition Systems implementation, InOut depends on a module named Texts. If your program uses the library module Texts in addition to InOut, program actions that modify variables in Texts may also affect the operation of InOut.

5.2.2 The Module RealInOut

The module InOut provides the capability to read and write integer and cardinal numbers as well as characters and character strings. A separate standard library module, RealInOut, is used to read and write real numbers. Module RealInOut contains the following procedures:

- ReadReal(RealInput)
- WriteReal(RealOutput, FieldWidth)
- WriteRealOct(RealOutput)

The recommended standard for REAL implementation calls for *at most* seven significant digits with a maximum exponent of 38. That is, a precision of seven digits with a range of plus or minus 38.

ReadReal and WriteReal operate exactly the same as their numeric input/output counterparts in the InOut module. Refer to that section for details. WriteRealOct displays real numbers in octal form.

The detailed description in section 5.2.1 of the InOut procedures provides all of the information that is needed to use the RealInOut procedures. However, you must be aware that RealInOut uses procedures from the module InOut to access the input/output text streams prior to real conversion. This means that if OpenInput or OpenOutput from InOut are used to redirect the standard input/output, then the source/destination for ReadReal and WriteReal are likewise redirected. This is an effect similar to that of the Texts module on InOut that was mentioned at the end of the last section.

The recommended standard implementation for RealInOut accesses the text streams through the use of InOut's Read and Write procedures. The Volition Systems documentation states that the streams are accessed by means of ReadString and WriteString. This difference should have no impact on any programs.

As a final note related to RealInOut, the BOOLEAN variable Done, which is used to indicate valid/invalid Read operations in both RealInOut and InOut, is actually two separate variables. That is, each module has its own Done variable. In Chapter 8, when we consider modules in depth, we will describe how to differentiate between multiple occurrences of the same variable name.

SUMMARY

We see that although Modula-2 has no language-defined input and output statements, complete input/output capability is provided by means of standard system libraries. The use of these library routines will not appear any different to the programmer than the predefined procedures of a language such as Pascal. The library procedures described in this chapter are at the highest level of the input/output hierarchy. They should be available in every implementation, and programs that rely on these procedures should be completely portable across all computer types. These input and output procedures provide the capability to read and write all of the standard Modula-2 data types. More advanced and potentially less portable input/output procedures will be explained in Chapter 9.

QUESTIONS AND PROBLEMS

1. Given the declaration

   ```
   VAR i : INTEGER;
       c : CARDINAL;
       r : REAL;
       chr : CHAR;
   ```

   write the input and output statements to read and write these variables.

2. How would you determine that the input/output above was performed properly (i.e., no input/output errors)?

3. How would you change the source of your input and output in Problem 1 to read from a disk file named DiskFile and write to Printer:?

SUPPLEMENTAL PROBLEMS

In Chapter 3, you were asked to consider ways to implement the calculator that would allow integer and cardinal values of any size regardless of actual implementation constraints. In Chapter 4, you were asked questions regarding the distinction between numeric inputs and command inputs for purposes of processing user inputs.

One way to address both of these issues is to avoid the Modula-2 integer and cardinal types and to use a string of characters instead. Rather than deal with the number 123, we'll work with the string "123."

This leads to some good news and bad news. The good news is that although 65535 is the largest cardinal value for a typical implementation, there is nothing to preclude "1234567890987654321" as a valid string. More good news is that the first element of this string, "1" in this example, is the same data type as our commands such as "+", "−", etc.—they're all characters.

The PROCEDURE ProcessInput in Appendix E shows how the character type is used in a CASE statement to control input processing for both "numeric" data and commands in a single control structure.

Problem 1

The bad news is that we can't say that

```
Sum := "456" + "789";
```

since + is not a legal string operator. So how are we to perform mathematical operations on these "numbers"?

Consider ways to "add" two strings so that "456" plus "789" results in "1245." Listing 5.3 gives a partial clue. The remainder of the clue involves remembering how you add with pencil and paper. In the next chapter, after covering arrays, we'll ask you to develop algorithms to accomplish this task. In the meantime, think about how you would add two single character digits such as "4" + "7".

Problem 2

Write a simple program to read the user's input to the calculator for use by the calculator process control loop.

CHAPTER 6

DATA STRUCTURES— ARRAYS AND SCALARS

NEW CONCEPTS: Arrays, Subscripts, Subranges, Sets, Enumerated Scalars, User-Defined Types
ISSUES: Memory Allocation, Range Checking

INTRODUCTION

Chapter 4 introduced Modula-2's basic data types. This chapter introduces some of the more advanced Modula-2 types. All of these types can be combined to define complex data structures (user-defined data types) that are custom-tailored to meet a program's unique needs.

The new data types are arrays, subranges, enumerations, and sets. Each of these types contribute to programming efficiency. They offer a range of data structures corresponding to data types that occur frequently in programs, thus providing a more natural approach to problems. The programmer is not required to force data of one type into some alternate form simply because the one that is needed is not available. Arrays are common to most languages. The other three types are less common.

As we have stated before, Modula-2 is a strongly typed language. This means that every data element must have an explicitly declared data type, and that type compatibility is enforced. Modula-2 allows extremely complex data types to be created by the programmer. These data types contribute to the development of very readable, reliable, and maintainable programs. An appreciation for this capability will grow as you become more familiar with the language. Conversely, it is difficult to appreciate this capability by just reading about it (unless you have experience with a language such as Pascal), because it is difficult to draw parallels.

At the end of this chapter, we will return to the subject of strings, which was introduced in Chapter 3.

6.1 ARRAYS

6.1.1 Overview of Array Concepts

Suppose that you were hired by the United States Weather Bureau to keep track of the temperatures in your home town. The Weather Bureau wants a record of the temperature for each hour of the day. At first, the VAR (variable) block in Listing 6.1 might appear to be a good start.

LISTING 6.1

```
(* Listing 6.1 Weather Bureau data declaration without array. *)

VAR MidNiteTemp, OneAM, TwoAM, ThreeAM,
    FourAM, FiveAM, SixAM, SevenAM,
    EightAM, NineAM, TenAM, ElevenAM,
    Noon, OnePM, TwoPM, ThreePM, FourPM,
    FivePM, SixPM, SevenPM, EightPM,
    NinePM, TenPM, ElevenPM : INTEGER;

BEGIN
  Max := MidNiteTemp;
  IF OneAM > Max THEN Max := OneAM END;
  IF TwoAM > Max THEN Max := TwoAM END;
  ...
```

This approach becomes tedious, however, when faced with the task of finding the high temperature for the day. The dilemma arises from the need to deal with data both as individual elements (i.e., the hourly temperature) and as a group (i.e., the highest of *all* the hourly temperatures for a day). With the data as declared in Listing 6.1, one or more statements *for each* individual element must be written. For a group of data that involves more than a handful of elements, this quickly leads to large, non-maintainable programs.

Because this need arises frequently in programming, most programming languages include an ARRAY data structure to group together a number of individual data elements which have a common underlying data type. This chapter covers how to declare array variables, how to assign values to them, and how to refer to their values in expressions. Later in this chapter we will discuss how STRINGS are really a special form of an ARRAY.

Rather than create a separate name for each value to be stored in our example, a better approach is to realize that all of these data elements have a common type, i.e., a temperature. The hour that each temperature is taken can uniquely identify a particular data element, much in the same way that a post office box number can uniquely identify a post office box.

In such a situation, an ARRAY can be used in place of declaring separate variables for each value. An identifier is required to refer to the entire group. The name of the entire group is called the array name. Individual members of the group, elements, can be referenced by use of a subscript, which is unique for each element of the array. In order to refer to an element of the array, both the array name and its subscript must be given. For example, if the array name was Temperature, the temperature for 6 A.M. could be referenced by:

    Temperature[6],

where the number enclosed in square brackets is the subscript.

A range of subscript values is required in order to reference all of the elements of the array. The number of different values the subscript can have will determine the number of items in the array. In the weather example, if subscript values of 0 through 23 are used to refer to the 24 hours from midnight to 11 P.M. (so-called military time), 24 different temperatures can be stored. Using this convention, a single array will replace 24 separate variables in the sample program. Listing 6.2 shows how an array can simplify finding the highest temperature during the day. The details of Listing 6.2 will be explained in the remainder of this section.

6.1.2 Referencing an Element of an Array—Subscripts

Figure 6.1 represents the 24 elements of the temperature array (Temp array). Each element holds one integer value. Each element is referenced by a different subscript. The subscript values are not chosen at random. They are logically related to the nature of the problem and must be declared—including their type and range—as part of the array declaration. Any reference to a subscript outside of the defined range is illegal, and will result in an error message and termination of the program.

A few simple rules govern referencing array elements. Both the array name and a subscript are required in order to refer to an element of an array. Obviously, the array name must have been previously declared to be of type

LISTING 6.2

```
(* Listing 6.2 Weather Bureau data with array. *)

MODULE Weather;
  FROM InOut IMPORT
       WriteInt, WriteString;
  VAR
       Temp : ARRAY [0..23] OF INTEGER;
       hr,
       Max,                (* The high temperature *)
       Time : INTEGER; (* The time for the high *)
BEGIN  (*Weather*)
  (*Routine for reading in weather data goes here*)
  Max := -999; (* start with an impossibly low temp *)
  FOR hr := 0 TO 23 DO
    IF Temp[hr] > Max THEN  (*found a new high*)
      Max := Temp[hr];
      Time := hr;
    END  (* IF *)
  END;  (* FOR *)
  WriteString("High temperature was ");
  WriteInt(Max, 1);
  WriteString(" at ");
  WriteInt(Time, 1);
END Weather.
```

ARRAY. The subscript must follow the array name and be enclosed by square brackets. In Figure 6.1 and the above discussions, we have used integer constants as subscripts. However, a subscript can be any expression, and need not be an integer. As discussed in Section 6.3.3 below, this provides a programmer with great flexibility in designing arrays.

Because any expression can be used in a subscript, this means that variables can appear in subscripts. This is the essence of the power of arrays. A single array statement can be written with a variable subscript, instead of a separate statement for each element. Any element of the array can be referenced through this *single* statement simply by assigning the appropriate value to the subscript variable.

The array structure allows the sample program in Listing 6.2 to be kept short. Instead of a separate expression for each temperature variable, as in

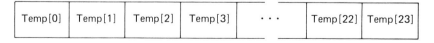

FIGURE 6.1 Temperature Array

Listing 6.1, Listing 6.2 uses the single expression Temp[hr] to refer to any element of the array. As the value of hr changes during the execution of the program, the element of the array that is referenced also changes. For example, the first time through the FOR loop, hr will have the value 0 (representing midnight). The loop will have the effect of comparing Temp[0], which is the midnight temperature, to Max and storing Temp[0] in Max (assuming that the midnight temperature is higher than − 999), and assigning 0 to Time. The next time through the loop, hr will have the value 1, and the 1 A.M. temperature, Temp[1], will be compared to Max. If Temp[1] is greater than Max, its value will be assigned to Max, and 1 will be stored in the variable Time. This process will be repeated until Temp[23] is compared to Max on the final pass through the loop. Thus, by using a variable for an array subscript, and placing a single IF statement within a loop, the need to program 23 separate IF statements has been eliminated.

Another rule governing subscripts concerns the data type of the expression that is used as a subscript. In general, subscripts can be of any type, except REAL. The data type of the expression used as a subscript must match the subscript data type used to delare the array. In Listing 6.2, the array Temp is declared to have INTEGER subscripts with values in the range of 0 to 23. Hence, all the subscripts that refer to Temp must also have integer subscripts. That is in fact the case, since hr is an integer variable. Note that we did *not* say that the array data type and the array subscript type had to be the same. In fact, the array type and the subscript type are, most often, different. For example, an array storing REAL numbers could have INTEGER subscripts (and certainly could not have real subscripts).

6.1.3 Declaring an Array

Arrays can be declared in a VAR (variable) block by following all of the same rules that apply to declaring non-array variables. An array declaration consists of:

1. the word ARRAY;
2. a description of the subscript type, usually stated as a range of values enclosed in brackets;
3. the word OF; and
4. the base data type of the individual elements of the array.

For example, in Listing 6.2, the Temp array was declared:

```
VAR Temp: ARRAY [0..23] OF INTEGER;
```

The base data type is INTEGER, and any subscript used to refer to an element of Temp must be an integer (or cardinal) with a value between 0 and 23. The Modula-2 compiler will reserve memory to store 24 integer values in the Temp array.

Other subscript options exist. These depend on types defined by the programmer prior to the array declaration. These options will be obvious once type declarations are explained later in this chapter. As an example, if the subscript [0..23] had been defined as a type with the identifier HoursOfTheDay, then the Temp declaration could have been written as

```
VAR Temp: ARRAY HoursOfTheDay OF INTEGER;
```

6.1.4 Multidimensional Arrays

Listing 6.2 served the Weather Bureau's needs for processing one day's worth of data. But what about data for an entire month or year? Just as an array for each hour in a day allowed a single IF statement placed within a loop to process all of the data for a day, an array holding a month's worth of daily data would allow a single IF statement to find the highest temperature for an entire month. Similarly, an array holding a year's worth of monthly data will simplify the search for the highest temperature during the year. What we do not want, however, is a single array containing 8760 elements, i.e., one element for each of the 24*365 hours of a year, which is declared as:

```
VAR Temp: ARRAY [1..8760] OF INTEGER;
```

or alternatively as

```
VAR Temp: ARRAY [1..(24*365)] OF INTEGER;
```

Note the expression in the second version of the declaration. This is legal in Modula-2 but not in Pascal.

If we have a single array for all of the hours of a year, and the highest temperature occurred at hour 4793, how do we determine the hour, day, and month? Clearly, some additional computation would be required. We can do better, however, because Modula-2 provides multidimensional arrays. Temp was a single-dimension array.

A multidimensional array is an array whose base data type is another array. An array MonthTemp can be declared to hold 31 days of individual daily arrays:

```
VAR MonthTemp : ARRAY [1..31] OF
                ARRAY [0..23] OF INTEGER;
```

where the second line merely duplicates the declaration of Temp from Listing 6.2. Similarly, an array YearTemp can also be declared as twelve MonthTemp arrays:

```
VAR YearTemp : ARRAY [1..12] OF
               ARRAY [1..31] OF
               ARRAY [0..23] OF INTEGER;
```

A shorthand way of declaring the same structure would be:

```
VAR YearTemp: ARRAY [1..12], [1..31], [0..23] OF INTEGER;
```

Arrays of other arrays are called multidimensional arrays. In order to uniquely identify an individual element in a multidimensional array, a subscript value must be designated for each dimension of the array. Hence, although one subscript could specify a unique element of the Temp array (by indicating the hour), two subscripts are needed to specify a unique element of the MonthTemp array (the day and the hour), and three subscripts are needed to specify a unique element of the YearTemp array (the month, day, and hour). When more than one subscript is required, Modula-2's syntax allows the subscripts to be stated in one of two formats:

```
YearTemp[3,6,4] or YearTemp[3][6][4]
```

Both forms refer to the temperature for 4 A.M. on March 6. Note that the subscript order corresponds to the declaration order of first the month, then the day, and then the hour. Listing 6.3 is a modification of the program in Listing 6.2 to find the highest temperature for the entire year.

Note that a separate expression, separated by commas, must appear for each dimension of the array. In Listing 6.3, the INTEGER variables month, day, and hr serve as the subscript expressions to access individual elements of the array. Because the FOR loops step through every value in the range of all three subscripts, every element of the array will be compared against Max. This requires the IF statement in the innermost loop to be executed 8928

LISTING 6.3

```
(* Listing 6.3 Weather Bureau data with multidimensional array. *)

MODULE Weather;
  FROM InOut IMPORT
        WriteInt, WriteString;
  VAR
        Temp : ARRAY [1..12], [1..31], [0..23] OF INTEGER;
        hr, day, month,
        Max,                (* The high temperature *)
        Time,               (* The time for the high *)
        HotDay,             (* The day of the month with hottest hr *)
        HotMonth : INTEGER; (* The month with the hottest day *)
BEGIN
  (*Routine for reading in weather data goes here*)
  Max := -999; (* start with an impossibly low temp *)
  FOR month := 1 TO 12 DO
    FOR day := 1 TO 31 DO
      FOR hr := 0 TO 23 DO
        IF Temp[month, day, hr] > Max THEN
          Max := Temp[month, day, hr];
          Time := hr;
          HotDay := day;
          HotMonth := month;
        END  (*if*)
      END (*for hr*)
    END (*for day*)
  END; (*for month*)
  WriteString("High temperature was ");
  WriteInt(Max, 1);
  WriteString(" at ");
  WriteInt(Time, 1);
  WriteString(" on ");
  WriteInt(HotMonth, 1);
  WriteString(" / ");
  WriteInt(HotDay, 1);
END Weather.
```

times (24 × 31 × 12). Every time a new highest temperature is found, the month, day, and hour are saved in variables HotMonth, HotDay, and Time. At the end of the program, these three variables will have the date and time of the hottest hour of the year.

Note that although the inner loop of Listing 6.3 is executed 8928 times, there are only 8760 hours in a non-leap year. What is the problem? The extra hours are caused by our definition of a month (i.e., ARRAY [1..31] OF Temp). The program treats every month as if it had 31 days. This problem can be cured by a number of techniques. The simplest, not safest, solution is to store impossibly low values as the temperatures for nonexistent days. A better solution is to control the month loop values by using a variable that reflects the actual number of days in each month. This will be demonstrated later in the chapter in Listing 6.4.

Array Bounds

Each dimension of an array is declared to have a range for its subscripts. The declared ranges will determine the number of individual array elements that are stored in the computer's memory. When an element of an array is referenced in a statement, each subscript must have a value that falls within the range for that subscript. For example, the third subscript of the YearTemp array may only have values from 0 to 23, even though the second subscript (that represents the day) can have values of 0 to 31. The valid ranges of each subscript are referred to as the upper and lower bounds of the array.

The total memory requirements for an array are driven by the product of the bounds for each dimension. For example, Temp requires storage for 12*31*24 (8928) integers. Storage can be exhausted quickly when using multidimensional arrays.

As a program is developed, changes in the program may require the array bounds to change. The upper and lower bounds of a subscript usually appear in a number of places in the program and may be hard to locate. The use of constants simplifies this problem. Array bounds should be assigned to a constant, as discussed in Chapter 3. In this way, if the bounds must be changed, they can be modified throughout the program simply by changing the constant declaration.

The syntax rules for an array are shown in Figure A.27. The SimpleType and type portions of this syntax diagram are covered in the remaining sections of this chapter.

6.2 CREATING NEW DATA TYPES

Until now, we have assigned names (identifiers) and data types to variables and constants by using VAR (variable) and CONST (constant) blocks. The choice of data types, thus far, have been predefined by Modula-2. However, Modula-2 also permits programmers to define their own data types. A TYPE block serves this purpose. The TYPE block can be intermingled with VAR and CONST blocks in the declaration portions of a MODULE or procedure. Identifiers are assigned to TYPEs, just as they are to variables and constants. The TYPE declaration must appear prior to the first use of the new type in the program.

6.2.1 TYPE Block Syntax

For an example of a TYPE block, consider the Weather Bureau problem. The new problem is to handle data from several different cities. If a multidimensional YearTemp array were to be declared for each city, the VAR block could look like:

```
VAR
    Chicago : ARRAY [1..12], [1..31], [0..23] OF INTEGER;
    Detroit  : ARRAY [1..12], [1..31], [0..23] OF INTEGER;
```

or we could write,

```
VAR
    Chicago, Detroit : ARRAY [1..12], [1..31], [0..23] OF INTEGER;
```

By Modula-2's rules of type compatibility, in the first example, Chicago and Detroit have *different* data types. In the second example, they are considered to have the same data type. This is *very* important (as well as confusing). For both cases, an assignment such as

```
Chicago[1, 10, 12] := Detroit[2, 15, 10];
```

would be legal because both elements of this assignment statement are of type INTEGER (i.e., they are elements of the array's base type, which is INTEGER). However, for the first example declaration, the assignment statement

```
Chicago := Detroit; (*entire "compatible" arrays can be assigned*)
```

is *illegal* because Modula-2 considers the types to be different (even though their declarations are identical). However, Chicago:=Detroit is legal if we use the second version of the declaration. Failure to recognize these differences can cause problems in the assignment of entire arrays, and with actual and formal procedure parameters (see Chapter 8).

As an alternative to defining a complex data type as part of the variable declaration, Modula-2 provides the TYPE declaration. The city weather example becomes:

```
TYPE
    YearOfTemp = ARRAY [1..12], [1..31], [0..23] OF INTEGER;
```

```
VAR
    Chicago : YearOfTemp;
    Detroit  : YearOfTemp;
```

The syntax of a TYPE block (shown in Figure A.21) is very similar to a VAR block (which we covered previously in Figure A.38). The only syntactic differences are:

- TYPE uses = where VAR uses : .
- Only a single identifier can precede the = in a type declaration. A list of identifiers separated by commas can appear prior to VAR's : .

After the word TYPE, one or more declarations (Figure A.61) may appear, each ending with a semicolon. If one type identifier is used in the definition of a second one, the declaration of the first must precede the second. For example:

```
TYPE
    Temp = ARRAY [0..23] OF INTEGER;
    MonthTemp = ARRAY [0..31] OF Temp;
    YearTemp = ARRAY [0..12] OF MonthTemp;
```

The new data type Temp must be declared before MonthTemp. Otherwise, the compiler will generate an "undeclared identifier" error message when it finds Temp in the MonthTemp declaration.

Let's return to the issue of type compatibility once more by considering the following example.

```
MODULE TypeTest;
TYPE
    type1 = ARRAY [1..10] OF INTEGER;
    type2 = ARRAY [1..10] OF INTEGER;
    type3 = type1;
VAR
    Array1 : type1;
    Array2 : type2; (*NOT compatible with 1*)
    Array3 : type3; (*Compatible with 1*)
    Array4 : type1; (*Compatible with 1*)
BEGIN
    Array1[1] := 1;              (*ok*)
    Array2[1] := Array1[1];      (*This is ok, TOO*)
```

```
      Array1 := Array3;          (*ok*)
      Array1 := Array4;          (*ok*)
      Array1 := Array2;      (*Incompatible types*)
   END TypeTest.
```

This example illustrates type and variable declarations as well as type compatibility rules. Make certain that you understand what makes the various parts of this example legal and illegal. The final assignment statement will cause a compiler error of "incompatible types."

6.3 SUBRANGE TYPES

In both Listings 6.2 and 6.3, a number of variables, such as hr, are used to store only a limited range of values. Modula-2 provides a notation to indicate a selected portion of all possible values of a given data type. Such selections are called subranges. The advantage of using a subrange is that it makes a program easier to read, and allows the system to test that values assigned to the variable never exceed the expected range. The test can occur during both compilation and execution.

We have already seen the notation for describing a subrange as a part of the syntax rules for declaring arrays. A subrange is declared by stating the lower and upper values separated by two dots, and enclosing them in square brackets. The upper and lower values can be any valid constant expression. For example, [0..23] indicates a subrange of integer or cardinal values beginning with 0 and ending with 23. Just as arrays have a base type, so do subranges. The base type of a subrange is the data type of the two constant expressions used to describe the subrange's lower and upper bounds. The syntax diagram for a subrange type is shown in Figure A.26.

Subrange notations can be used as a data type description in declaring variables, or in describing the range of an array subscript. Also, new data types can be defined in terms of subranges. For example, the VAR block in Listing 6.2 could be written as:

```
TYPE
   Hours = [0..23]; (* Subrange type *)
VAR
   hr : Hours; (* Values from 0 to 23 *)
   Temp : ARRAY Hours OF INTEGER;
```

By using a newly declared data type, Hours, to declare both the hr variable and the Temp array, the program becomes easier to modify. For example, suppose that the Weather Bureau wants to store temperatures for every half hour. Changing the declaration of Hours to [0..47] will be easier to modify than changing two different variable declarations.

Note that subranges need not be integers. They can be *any* constant expression (see Figure A.12), but they must be a contiguous range of values. For example, ["A".."C"] is a legal subrange of type CHAR that has three possible values: A, B, and C. But subrange notation cannot be used to represent all of the letters that are vowels because the vowels are not a contiguous range in the alphabet. (A set, presented in Section 6.5, is better suited for this purpose.)

One final feature in declaring a subrange provides for greater flexibility. The lower and upper bounds of the subrange can be any constant expression. This includes identifiers that the programmer had declared in a CONST block. Using this option, the data structures from Listing 6.2 could be written:

```
CONST
   FirstHr = 0;
   LastHr = 23;
TYPE Hours = [FirstHr..LastHr];
(* How about Hours = [FirstHr..(FirstHr + 23)]?
   Try it out on your computer *)
VAR
   hr : Hours; (* Values from 0 to 23 *)
   Temp : ARRAY Hours OF INTEGER;
```

Of course, the constants FirstHr and LastHr could also be used in the body of the program, in statements such as:

```
FOR hr := FirstHr TO LastHr DO
```

In this manner, the program becomes easy to read, modify, and maintain.

Any operation that is legal for the base type of the subrange is likewise legal for the subrange itself. For example, if the subrange was [0..23], all of the normal operations for integer and cardinal types apply.

6.4 ENUMERATION TYPES

Suppose that Modula-2 did not include a standard definition for the BOOLEAN data type. How could BOOLEAN be declared by a programmer so that it had the same features as the standard definition? That is,

1. Every Boolean variable could have only one of two possible values.
2. Those two possible values are the predefined constants TRUE and FALSE.
3. The constants have the order FALSE < TRUE.

Modula-2 permits a programmer to define special data types that consist of a finite number of possible values, where each value is assigned a name. For example, if Modula-2 did not have a predefined Boolean data type, it could be added to the language with the following TYPE declaration:

```
TYPE
   BOOLEAN = (FALSE, TRUE);
```

The name of the type and the set of values belonging to the type must obey the normal rules for identifier names. Once declared, the new data type name can be used just like any other data type, and the names of the type's values are treated as constants of the new data type. Data types that are declared by listing all possible values are called *enumerations*. The only operations that can be performed on enumeration type variables are assignments and comparisons. If other operations are required, they must be provided by the programmer by means of procedures (see Chapter 8).

The following are typical enumerations:

```
TYPE
   Color = (red, orange, yellow, green, blue, indigo, violet);
   Weekday = (Monday, Tuesday, Wednesday, Thursday, Friday, Saturday,
             Sunday);
```

Note that enumerations can be used in subranges. For example,

```
TYPE
   Workday = [Monday..Friday];
```

is a legal and useful declaration. Weekday must have been declared first.

6.4.1 Why Use Enumerations?

Programs frequently have variables that represent one of a group of possible values. As just noted, the days of the week are an example. In most programming languages that do not allow for enumerations, the programmer arbitrarily assigns a code number to each possible value. We used this approach in Listings 6.2 and 6.3 where the numbers 0 to 23 were arbitrarily assigned to the times from midnight to 11 P.M. Similarly, we assigned the numbers 1 to 12 to the months of the year. Such coding schemes make a program difficult to read and provide no protection against mistakes such as assigning erroneous values to the "coded representation." Enumerations avoid these problems. All possible values are spelled out (literally) in the declaration. The system will not accept values that are not included in the type's constants. Last but not least, the values assigned to an enumeration variable can have natural names, thus adding to program readability and maintainability:

```
VAR ScreenColor : Color;
:
:
ScreenColor := violet;
```

Enumerations have one other important property, a built-in order. Just as whole numbers have a numerical order, an enumerated type's constants also have a defined order. The order of the constants in an enumerated type is the order in which they are listed in the type declaration. As a result, in the above examples, Monday is the predecessor to Tuesday, and Saturday is the successor to Friday. The Boolean expression Monday < Sunday is TRUE, and Thursday > Saturday is FALSE. Items should be listed with care in an enumeration declaration because the order can be important.

Although enumerations have an order, they are different from subranges. A subrange has an underlying base data type—for example, INTEGER in the case of the subrange [0..23]. But enumerations do not have a base data type and can represent any arbitrary collection of named items.

6.4.2 Declaring an Enumerated Type

An enumeration can appear anywhere a type description can appear—after the colon in a VAR block or after an equal sign in a TYPE block. The declaration consists of a list of identifiers separated by commas and enclosed in parentheses. Each identifier must be unique. The uniqueness of identifiers extends beyond the enumeration constants. Identifiers in the same program scope cannot have the same value (see Chapter 3). Therefore, the following will result in a compiler error of "identifier declared twice" because a appears both as an enumeration constant and as a type identifier.

```
TYPE
  EnumerationType = (a, b, c);
  a = ARRAY [1..5] OF CARDINAL;
```

The syntax diagram for an enumeration is shown in Figure A.24.

6.4.3 Enumerations as Subscripts

Enumeration data can be used anywhere that predefined types can be used. This includes assignment statements, expressions, FOR-loop control variable values, and array subscripts. To be used as an array subscript, an array must be declared to have subscripts of the particular enumeration. All operations affecting the array's subscript must be compatible with the enumeration. In most cases, this approach results in easier-to-read programs.

The program in Listing 6.3 to find the hottest temperature of the year assigned integers to the values of month, day, and hour of the day. Listing 6.4 is a revision of that program using enumerations as subscripts for the month values. This version of the program also solves the problem of assuming every month has 31 days. Notice the use of an array element with enumerated subscripts as the final value of the control variable for the day FOR loop.

Note that because HotMonth is a variable of an enumerated data type and not an INTEGER, it cannot be displayed with WriteInt. Instead, the ORD (ordinal) standard procedure is called to return the internal code number for these values, which is displayed with WriteCard. (See Section 6.4.5 below.)

6.4.4 Enumerations in Case Statements

Chapter 4 introduced the case statement, which provides a multiple branch control structure. Recall that the syntax of a case statement requires that the expression following the word CASE and each list of values that precede the alternative branches must be of the same type. Those items can be of any type, except type REAL. Therefore, the expression and values controlling a CASE statement can have an enumerated type.

For example, in Listing 6.4 we had a problem in displaying the month of the highest temperature. Because the variable HotMonth was of enumerated type Months, we could not say WriteInt(HotMonth, 1). Instead, we used the ORD (ordinal) standard procedure to return the internal code of HotMonth

LISTING 6.4

```
(* Listing 6.4 Weather Bureau data with Enumerated subscripts. *)
MODULE Weather;
  FROM InOut IMPORT
       WriteString, WriteInt, WriteCard;
  TYPE
       Months = (Jan, Feb, Mar, Apr, May, Jun, Jul,
                 Aug, Sep, Oct, Nov, Dec); (*enumerated type*)
       Hours = [0..23]; (*subrange of cardinals*)
       Days  = [0..31]; (*another subrange*)
  VAR
       Temp : ARRAY Months, Days, Hours OF INTEGER;
       hr   : Hours;
       day  : Days;
       month : Months;
       Max  : INTEGER; (* The high temperature *)
       Time : Hours; (* The time for the high *)
       HotDay : Days; (* The day of the month with hottest hr *)
       HotMonth : Months; (* The month with the hottest day *)
       MonthLength : ARRAY Months OF Days;  (*Store each mo's length*)
BEGIN
  (*Routine for reading in weather data goes here.*)
  FOR month := Jan TO Jul BY 2 DO  (*BY 2 skips every other month*)
    MonthLength[month] := 31
  END;
  FOR month := Aug TO Dec BY 2 DO
    MonthLength[month] := 31
  END;
  FOR month := Apr TO Jun BY 2 DO
    MonthLength[month] := 30
  END;
  FOR month := Sep TO Nov BY 2 DO
    MonthLength[month] := 30
  END;
  MonthLength[Feb] := 28; (*forget about leap year*)
  Max := -999; (* start with an impossibly low temp *)
  FOR month := Jan TO Dec DO (*enumerated type index*)
    FOR day := 1 TO MonthLength[month] DO  (*array element loop bound*)
      FOR hr := 0 TO 23 DO
        IF Temp[month, day, hr] > Max THEN
          Max := Temp[month, day, hr];
          Time := hr;
          HotDay := day;
          HotMonth := month;
        END (*if*)
      END (*for hr*)
    END (*for day*)
  END;  (*for month*)
  WriteString("High temperature was ");
  WriteInt(Max, 1);
  WriteString(" at ");
  WriteCard(Time ,1);
  WriteString(" hrs on ");
  WriteCard(ORD(HotMonth) + 1, 1);
  WriteString(" / ");
  WriteCard(HotDay, 1);
END Weather.
```

(expressed as type CARDINAL) and added 1 to it since the ordinal value of the first element of an enumerated list is 0 and not 1. The statement

```
WriteCard(ORD(HotMonth)+1,3);
```

displays a number, but the name of the month would be easier to understand. The following CASE statement will do the job when substituted for the WriteCard statement:

```
CASE HotMonth OF
    Jan: WriteString("Jan")|
    Feb: WriteString("Feb")|
    Mar: WriteString("Mar")|
    Apr: WriteString("Apr")|
    May: WriteString("May")|
    Jun: WriteString("Jun")|
    Jul: WriteString("Jul")|
    Aug: WriteString("Aug")|
    Sep: WriteString("Sep")|
    Oct: WriteString("Oct")|
    Nov: WriteString("Nov")|
    Dec: WriteString("Dec")
END;
```

Note that since all possible values of the enumerated type Months are present in the list of alternatives, there is no reason to include an ELSE clause.

6.4.5 Standard Procedures ORD, CHR, and VAL

Listing 6.4 illustrates the need to convert between the different Modula-2 data types. The ORD procedure used in Listing 6.4 is one example of a standard language procedure for performing such conversions.

ORD returns the value (CARDINAL) of the internal code that the system assigns to an enumeration, BOOLEAN, CHAR, INTEGER, or CARDINAL expression. With respect to CHAR variables, Modula-2 uses the ASCII international standard coding scheme to assign numbers to various character symbols. A table of ASCII codes appears in Appendix B. The ordering sequence of variables is important because it determines the result of any comparison between variables. For example, the BOOLEAN expression "A" < "B" is TRUE because A has the ASCII code value 65 and B has the value 66.

Programs can utilize the coding scheme sequence. The following assignment statement will convert a CHAR variable, DigitChar, which has a value from "0" to "9" into its corresponding numeric value of 0 to 9.

```
CardValue := ORD(DigitChar) − ORD("0");
```

Because the ASCII values for "1", "2", "3" . . . have ASCII codes that are 1, 2, 3 . . . greater than that of "0", the difference between ASCII code values gives the correct numeric value for these character symbols.

ORD also works with enumerations. Each identifier in an enumeration is assigned a value, beginning with 0, in the order that it appears in the declaration. For example, if CursorDirection is declared by

```
TYPE CursorDirection = (up, down, left, right);
```

then ORD(up) is 0; ORD(down) is 1; ORD(left) is 2; and ORD(right) is 3.

Two other standard procedures perform the reverse of ORD's function. That is, they take an internal code number and return the item that code number represents. CHR returns the character with a particular ordinal value. Both of the following assignment statements store the letter "A" in CHAR variable c:

```
c := CHR(65); (* "A" has ASCII code 65 *)
c := CHR(ORD("B") − 1); (* "B" has ASCII code 66 *)
```

The latter statement demonstrates the relationship between ORD and CHR. ORD returns the ordinal value of its argument. CHR returns the character that corresponds to the specified ordinal value. Note carefully that statements such as these rely on a specific character set representation—specifically, ASCII. They probably will not work properly in a non-ASCII environment.

CHR only returns a CHAR value. VAL performs the same function for enumeration data types. Applying the previous declaration for TYPE CursorDirection, VAL(CursorDirection,0) is up, VAL(CursorDirection,1) is down, and so on. Note that two expressions must follow VAL—an enumeration data type identifier and a ORD value for that type. The value returned is of that type. If cd is a variable of type CursorDirection,

```
cd := VAL(CursorDirection,3);
cd := right;
```

both of the above statements have the same effect.

Note that because ORD, CHR, and VAL are built into the Modula-2 language, they are automatically defined in every program.

6.5 SETS

Subranges and enumerations provide useful tools for representing objects other than numbers and characters. However, both have their limitations. The values of a subrange must be consecutive. For example, a group of characters with consecutive ASCII codes can be represented by a subrange,

```
TYPE
   FirstHalfOfAlphabet = ["A".."M"];
```

but nonconsecutive characters, such as the vowels, cannot be represented by a subrange. Another drawback of enumerations and subranges is that their variables can store only one value at a time. For example,

```
VAR
   Letters : FirstHalfOfAlphabet;
   :
   :
   Letters := "F";
```

is obviously legal. But,

```
   Letters := "F" and "K";
```

is impossible. If we want to store more than a single letter, an array is required, such as

```
VAR
   Letters = ARRAY [1..10] OF CHAR;
   :
   :
   Letters[1] := "F";
   Letters[2] := "K";
```

Modula-2 has a data structure to overcome both of these problems. A SET can represent a group of items (for example, the vowels). These items must be constants. Variables declared to be of the SET data type can hold any possible combination of those items. If a SET type named VowelType were declared to consist of the lower-case vowels, and Vowels were declared to be a variable of type VowelType, Vowels could store any of the possible vowel combinations (32 of them; why 32?):

{ }, {a}, {e}, {i}, {o}, {u}, {a,e}, {a,i}, {a,o}, {a,u}, {e,i}, {e,o}, {e,u}, {i,o}, {i,u}, {o,u}, {a,e,i}, {a,e,o}, {a,e,u}, {a,i,o}, {a,i,u}, {a,o,u}, {e,i,o}, {e,i,u}, {e,o,u}, {i,o,u}, {a,e,i,o}, {a,e,i,u}, {a,e,o,u}, {a,i,o,u}, {e,i,o,u}, {a,e,i,o,u}

6.5.1 Declaring Sets

As with arrays and subranges, sets have an underlying base type. This type can be either an enumeration or a subrange. (Subranges, in turn, can be of any type except REAL.) For example, given vowels as the enumeration, a set of vowels could be defined with

```
TYPE
    vowels = (a, e, i, o, u);
    SetOfVowels = SET OF vowels;
VAR
    Vowels : SetOfVowels;
```

An alternative, and totally different, form of the vowel set is

```
TYPE
    SetOfCharacters = SET OF CHAR;
CONST
    aeiou = SetOfCharacters{'a', 'e', 'i', 'o', 'u'};
VAR
    VowelSet : SetOfCharacters;
```

We will explain these two different approaches later in this section.

The set is defined by preceding the base type with the words SET OF. Such a data type description can appear in either a variable or type declaration. The SET syntax diagram is shown in Figure A.19.

With one exception, all sets must be declared. The one standard SET data type that requires no declaration is called BITSET and is defined as:

```
TYPE
    BITSET = SET OF [0..W];
```

where W depends on the particular Modula-2 implementation, e.g. $[0..15]$ on the Apple. The number of elements in BITSET—16 for the Apple—reflect the length of the system's "word". Recall that the Apple and all other Volition Systems implementations emulate a 16-bit computer.

Before demonstrating the power of sets, a few other restrictions are worth noting. First, in the Volition Systems implementation, sets are limited to 4080 elements (255 words), and sets of negative integers are not allowed. The maximum number of elements in a set is implementation dependent, and can cause portability problems. Some implementations allow as few as 16 elements in a set. Appendix D provides an example of a technique to expand the effective maximum set size when this is a problem. Second, when defining a set in terms of a subrange, the starting and ending bounds of the range must be constant expressions. Finally, in the absence of any other data type name, all sets are assumed to be of type BITSET.

6.5.2 Using Sets

Because a set represents a group of items, set constants are slightly more elaborate than constants for simple data types. The items present in the set are listed—either one by one or as subranges or both—and then enclosed in curly brackets to indicate that they are a set constant. Since a program can have many different types of sets, the name of the data type should precede the brackets. If no type name is included, type BITSET is assumed. Consider the following examples with CharSet defined as SET OF CHAR and Vowels defined to be SET OF (a, e, i, o, u):

```
{1,4,6}—assumed to be of type BITSET
CharSet{"A".."Z"}—set of all the capital letters
CharSet{"a", "1..5", "Z", 101C}—mixed notation
CharSet{OC..37C}—set of non-printable characters
CharSet{"a", "e", "i", "o", "u"}—set of lower case vowels
Vowels{a, e, i, o, u}—totally different from above item
Vowels{i, a, u, e, o}—same as above; order independent
Vowels{ }—empty set (this was one of the 32 combinations)
```

Modula-2 defines the four set operators listed in Table 6.1. Each operator takes two set values of a given type and returns a new set of the same type. In addition, Modula-2 defines the five relations that apply to sets. These relations, which are listed in Table 6.2, return BOOLEAN results.

TABLE 6.1

OPERATOR	NAME	EXAMPLE	RESULT
		Set Operators	
+	Union	A + B	Set whose members belong to A or B or both
-	Difference	A - B	Set whose members are in A but not in B
*	Intersection	A * B	Set whose members belong to both A and B
/	Symmetric difference	A / B	Set whose members belong to A or B, but not to both

In order to demonstrate the use of set operators, assume that variables A, B, and C of type CharSet have been assigned the following values:

A := CharSet{'a', 'b', 'c', 'd'};
B := CharSet{'b'};
C := CharSet{'c'..'e'};

Using the above values, the following examples illustrate the use of the set operators:

A + C is {'a'..'e'}—i.e., all elements in either A OR C
A - B is {'a','c','d'}—i.e., elements in A but not in B
A * C is {'c','d'}—i.e., all elements in both A AND C
A / C is {'a','b','e'}—i.e., elements in A OR C, but not in both
B <= A is TRUE—read this as B is included in A (which is true)
A >= B—interpreted identically to the above
C <= A is FALSE—because 'e' is in C and not in A
(A / C) + (A * C) = (A + CharSet{'e'}) is TRUE
'a' IN A is TRUE—IN is "set membership"; 'a' IS a member of A
'a' IN C is FALSE, 'a' IS NOT a member of C

TABLE 6.2

OPERATOR	NAME	EXAMPLE	RESULT
		Set Relations	
=	Equal	A = B	TRUE, if sets A and B are equal
#	Unequal	A # B	TRUE, if sets A and B are not equal
<=	Inclusion	A <= B	TRUE, if set A is included in set B
>=	Inclusion	A >= B	TRUE, if set B is included in set A
IN	Membershi	x IN S	TRUE, if set element x is contained in set S

As you can see from these examples, the rules for creating set expressions are the same as those for other data types.

A program will help illustrate the use of sets. This example is taken from a library of screen handling routines presented in Chapter 9. It has been modified (and simplified) to address the following special task.

Suppose that a program is to stop for keyboard input and is not to continue until the user types a vowel. Furthermore, nothing that the user types should appear on the screen. The program in Listing 6.5 performs this task. (The listing in Appendix D illustrates an alternative implementation of this same program for systems that allow only a small number of elements in a set.)

In Listing 6.5, there are two different variables of type CharSet. One controls what letters will permit the program to proceed (Okset). The second identifies the characters to be erased from the screen (Printables). Only capital letters are assigned to Okset because the assignment statement Ch := CAP(Ch) converts lower-case letters to upper case. (CAP is a Modula-2 standard procedure.) This basic character input routine will be seen again in

LISTING 6.5

```
(* Listing 6.5 - Example using set of characters *)

  MODULE VowelTester;
    FROM InOut IMPORT
        Read, Write, WriteString;
    CONST
        bs = 10C;
    TYPE
        CharSet = SET OF CHAR;
    VAR
        Ch : CHAR;
        okset : CharSet; (* set of allowed letters *)
        Printables: CharSet; (* set of letters that display on screen *)
  BEGIN
    (* initialize variables *)
    Printables := CharSet{' '..'}'};
    okset := CharSet{'A','E','I','O','U'};
    WriteString("Please type a vowel to continue: ");
    REPEAT (*UserInput rtn *)
      Read(Ch);
      (* if typed character showed up on screen, erase it. *)
      IF Ch IN Printables THEN
        Write(bs); Write(' '); Write(bs);
      END (*if*);
      Ch := CAP(Ch);
    UNTIL Ch IN okset;
    WriteString("Thank you.");
  END VowelTester.
```

Chapter 8 when procedures are covered. Note in Listing 6.5 that the relation IN is used in the IF and REPEAT..UNTIL statements to test for set membership.

6.5.3 INCL and EXCL

There are two Modula-2 standard procedures that operate on sets. INCL will add a member to a set. For example, in the following procedure, the last two statements have the same effect:

```
TYPE
   CharSet = SET OF CHAR;
VAR
   CharacterSet : CharSet;
:
:

   CharacterSet := CharacterSet + CharSet{'a'};
   INCL(CharacterSet, 'a');
```

In the next-to-the-last line, the + operator results in the union of two sets. CharSet was written as a set constant with one member, 'a'. In the last line, 'a' was not enclosed in brackets. This is because the INCL procedure calls for the identification of a set member and not a set.

Set exclusion means removing an element from a set. The following two statements illustrate, by way of comparison, the use of the standard procedure EXCL.

```
   CharacterSet := CharacterSet − CharSet{'a'};
   EXCL(CharacterSet, 'a');
```

Both statements will eliminate 'a' from the set variable CharacterSet if 'a' is currently a member of that set. If it is not a member, neither statement will have any effect.

6.6 USING STRINGS

Chapter 3 presented CHAR and STRING as two distinct data types, and many of the sample programs have used character and string constants. In Chapter 3 we deferred the question of what operations could be performed with strings. We address that issue now.

STRINGs provide a useful way to test our newly acquired knowledge of arrays because a string is a type of array. In the Volition Systems implementation of Modula-2, the following definition appears in a library module named Strings:

```
TYPE STRING = ARRAY[0..80] OF CHAR;
```

Note that the subscript bounds of arrays of type STRING are 0 and 80. Does this mean that every string will be 81 characters long? No. In fact, the length of a STRING can change during a program. But this declaration does impose a limitation on the maximum length of the string—81 characters. Of course, if storing longer strings are necessary, a new data type can be easily defined to handle strings of any size. For example,

```
TYPE BIGSTR = ARRAY [0..500] OF CHAR;
```

If the following appeared in a program,

```
VAR S : STRING;
:
S := "Hello";
```

the contents of the string array, S, would contain the following:

```
S[0] S[1] S[2] S[3] S[4] S[5] S[6] . . .
"H"  "e"  "1"  "1"  "o"  0C   undefined . . .
```

The first letter, a capital H, is assigned to S[0]. Each subsequent letter is placed in a separate element of the S array, and the last letter, a lower case "o," is assigned to S[4]. A special character called a NULL, which has the ASCII code of 0, is placed in S[5] by the system to mark the end of the string. In Modula-2, the end of the string is always marked by 0C (null) unless the string is filled to its maximum length.

Because each character stored in a string is actually an element of an array, the values of each position of the string can be accessed separately. For example, the statement:

```
S[0] := 'J';
```

will change the contents of the string to "Jello." Note that the value to be assigned is of type CHAR because it replaces a single element of the string (which is a character) and not the entire string. Care is required when using array subscripts to refer to the individual positions in a string. The first character in the string has the subscript [0], not [1]. Therefore, if we wanted to change the fifth character of the S array to "y" (in order to turn Jello into Jelly), the following statement is *wrong*:

```
S[5] := "y";
```

It is S[4] that is the fifth character of the string, not S[5].

6.6.1 Rules for Using Strings

The above examples illustrate the assignment of character values with a string array. What about assignments with string values? The following rules apply when dealing with assignments to variables declared as ARRAY OF CHAR:

1. A string constant may be assigned to any string variable declared with a dimension greater than or equal to the length of the constant. For example:

    ```
    VAR S, T, U : ARRAY [0..5] OF CHAR;

    S := 'Hello';
    T := 'Hello!';
    U := 'a real big hello';
    ```

    S[5] is the null character. T[5] contains "!". There is not a null character to mark the end of T because this string is at its maximum length. The final example will result in an error because the constant will not fit into U.

2. A string variable may not be assigned to a second variable using the assignment arrow (:=). Instead, the Assign procedure from the Strings module (presented in Section 6.6.2) should be used.

3. String constants are not explicitly typed. A string constant is assumed to have type ARRAY[0..N-1] OF CHAR, where N is the number of characters in the constant. Therefore, "Hi" is assumed to be of type ARRAY [0..1] OF CHAR.

4. A string constant of a given length is assignment compatible with any string variable with a dimension equal to or greater than its length.

6.6.2 Strings Module Procedures

The library module named Strings provides procedures for operating on strings. Although Strings is not an official part of the Modula-2 language, the Volition Systems implementation, presented here, is reasonable to expect in a system implementation. To illustrate the use of these procedures, assume that S1, S2, and S3 are all declared to be type STRING, and that S1 has been assigned the value "Walla ". (Note the space at the end.) Then the statement

    Assign(S1, S2)

will move a copy of the characters stored in S1 (including the null character that marks the end of the string) into S2. S1 is unchanged. (Remember, saying S2 := S1 will not work.) The statement

    Concat(S1, S2, S3);

will merge S1 and S2 and place the value "Walla Walla " into S3 without changing the values stored in S1 or S2.

Frequently programs need to determine the current length of a string. The Strings module includes a procedure for returning a CARDINAL value equal to the number of characters currently in the string (excluding the null character). In our "Walla " example, Length(S1) is 6 (counting the final blank, but not counting the null at the end of the string), and C := Length(S3) would assign the value 12 to the CARDINAL variable "C".

The Assign statement will replicate an entire string into a second string variable. But what if only a part of a string should be copied? The Copy procedure serves this purpose. For example,

    Copy(S3, 1, 3, S2);

will assign the value 'all' to S2. The format of Copy is: Copy(Source,Start,Length,Destination). Source and Destination are both strings. Source[Start] is the first character to be copied. A total of Length characters will be copied into Destination.

Strings procedures are provided to add or remove characters from a string. For example,

    Delete(S3, 1, 6);

will remove the six letters 'alla W', starting at S3[1] and leaving S3 equal to "Walla ". This change can be reversed with the statement

```
Insert('alla W', S3, 1);
```

which restores the value 'Walla Walla ' to S3.

A procedure that is useful in searching through strings to determine the starting point for insertions and deletions is Pos. Pos returns a CARDINAL number indicating the starting location of the first occurrence of a particular pattern in a string. If the pattern is not found in the string, Pos returns a value equal to HIGH(string)+1. HIGH is a Modula-2 standard procedure that returns the number of elements in an array. In this case, Pos returns a value that is one greater than the number of elements in the string, thus indicating an impossible value—or no match found. For example,

```
WriteCard(Pos('ll',S3),7);
```

will display a 2, because the first double l in S3 begins at S3[2].

Finally, CompareStr can be used to compare two strings. For example,

```
CompareStr(S1,S2);
```

returns an integer value that is equal to −1 if S1 < S2, 0 if S1 = S2, or 1 if S1 > S2. S1 < S2, S1 = S2, and S1 > S3 are not legal expressions. We must use CompareStr instead.

SUMMARY

This chapter has introduced a number of powerful data types—arrays, subranges, sets, and enumerations. In addition, user-defined types were described. All of the fundamental concepts of Modula-2 have now been presented.

The material covered thus far will account for the vast majority of lines of code that you will write in Modula-2. The parts that remain to be covered are more advanced features. Everything from here on builds on the material covered to this point. A solid grounding in this material is essential to successful programming in Modula-2.

QUESTIONS AND PROBLEMS

1. If the same high temperature occurred more than once in the program of Listing 6.1, what result would be returned?

2. If we wanted to initialize all of the temperature arrays for 10 different cites (see the Chicago/Detroit example) to −999, could we do it for one of the cities and then set the other nine arrays equal to this first array? If so, which way is quicker? (Try it.)

3. If you needed a three-dimensional array, say

ThreeD : ARRAY [1..x], [1..x], [1..x] OF INTEGER

how large could you make the upper bound, x, before all of the memory of your computer had been used?

4. What is the output which results from the following program?

(*This demonstrates "lots of stuff"—sets, enumerations, type transfers, for loops, ifs, and operations *)

```
MODULE TEST;
  IMPORT InOut;
  TYPE
    (*Using enumerations and set together*)
    DaysOfTheWeek = (Mon, Tue, Wed, Thur, Fri, Sat, Sun);
    WeekDays = SET OF DaysOfTheWeek;
  VAR
    DaySet : WeekDays;
    DayEnumeration : DaysOfTheWeek;
    i : CARDINAL;
  CONST
    GoodTimes = WeekDays{Sat..Sun};
    HardTimes = WeekDays{Mon..Fri};
    ShortWeek = WeekDays{Tue..Fri};
    FullWeek = WeekDays{Mon..Sun};
  BEGIN (*TEST*)
    DaySet := FullWeek − HardTimes;
    FOR DayEnumeration := Mon TO Sun DO (*One way*)
      IF DayEnumeration IN DaySet THEN
        InOut.WriteCard(ORD(DayEnumeration), 1); InOut.WriteLn;
      END (*if*);
    END (*for*);

    DaySet := FullWeek * ShortWeek;
    FOR DayEnumeration := Mon TO Sun DO (*Two ways*)
      IF ORD(DayEnumeration) IN BITSET(DaySet) THEN
        InOut.WriteCard(ORD(DayEnumeration), 1); InOut.WriteLn;
      END (*if*);
    END (*for*);
```

```
      DaySet := GoodTimes + HardTimes - WeekDays{Mon, Wed, Fri};
      FOR i := ORD(Mon) TO ORD(Sun) DO (*3 ways to skin a cat*)
         IF i IN BITSET(DaySet) THEN
            InOut.WriteCard(i, 1); InOut.WriteLn;
         END (*if*);
      END (*for*);
   END TEST.
```

SUPPLEMENTAL PROBLEMS

With the exception of RECORDS (Chapter 7) and PROCEDURES (Chapter 8), we've now covered every part of Modula-2 that appears in the Appendix E program.

Problem 1

Before we can add two numbers "the old fashioned way" (i.e., the way that you do it with pencil and paper), we must make certain that they are lined up properly. Write a program that right justifies a string of digits within an array of characters and fills in the spaces to the left with the character "0." Assign the maximum string length to a constant. You will have to determine when you've reached the end of a legal string (either the string terminator or a non-digit character). Use a set type variable (this chapter) to define and check for string characters that are "digits."

Problem 2

Assuming that you are given two strings of digits that have been justified by the process from Problem 1, write a program to "add" these strings in the manner discussed in Problem 1 of Chapter 5.

   Algorithms for −, *, and DIV will also be required. Appendix E covers + and −.

Problem 3

Although the approach of using strings rather than integer or cardinal types allows us to handle large numbers, even this approach has a limit. The limit is determined by the size of the constant that you selected in Problem 1. How do you determine that this limit is exceeded in performing the operations defined by Problem 2? In computer parlance, we're talking about things like overflow. Does the problem exist for all four mathematical operations (or just two of them)?

Problem 4

Go back and finish the stack implementation problem of Chapter 4 (Clear, Pop, and Push) using an array structure for the stack (if you haven't already done so).

Problem 5

Write a small program to exchange the order of the top two items on the stack. When might this be useful?

Problem 6

Write a small program to clear (i.e., empty) the stack. When would this be used?

Problem 7

Write a small program to discard the top element of the stack. You guessed it—why would you need this?

CHAPTER 7

RECORDS AND DYNAMIC DATA STRUCTURES

NEW CONCEPTS: Records; Variant Records; Pointers; Dynamic Data Type; Linked Lists, Trees, and Complex Structures
ISSUES: Role of an Operating System

INTRODUCTION

In this chapter we introduce two very powerful data types—records and pointers. These data types are not available in all languages, particularly the older languages such as FORTRAN and BASIC. They do exist in the more modern languages such as Pascal and Ada. The Modula-2 implementation differs from Pascal primarily in syntax.

Chapter 6 presented the array-structured data type. The basic characteristic of an array is that it is a collection of data elements in which all of the elements of the array must be of the same type. Many real world applications require collections of elements that are made up of many different types. For example, consider a personnel file. The data that might be contained in such a file could include

- Person's name—this is an ARRAY OF CHAR
- Hourly wage—this is a REAL number
- Birth date—how would you do this one?
- Marital status—this could be BOOLEAN or an enumerated type
- Other pertinent data . . .

137

This collection of data cannot be kept in a single array because it violates the basic rule governing array elements—they must all be of the same type. In this chapter we introduce a new structured data type called a record. The record type will allow us to handle, as a single entity, collections of data elements made up of diverse types.

Another new data type, the pointer, will also be introduced in this chapter. The pointer allows data objects to be created dynamically during program execution. All of the data types that have been introduced thus far are referred to as static data elements. This means that they must be known to the system at compilation time, and their quantity and structure is fixed (static) for the life of the program.

Static data types are not flexible enough to address issues in which the requirements for the number and exact composition of a given variable are unknown prior to execution of the program. For example, if we are developing a personnel file made up of a record for every employee, how many records should we plan for? Pointer types and dynamic data structures provide one way to deal with issues such as this. During the execution of the program, the size and shape of the personnel file can expand and contract as needed.

We have grouped record and pointer types together for two reasons. First, as we have already mentioned, they are both in the category of "advanced" data types. Secondly, and more importantly, the actual implementation of dynamic data structures through the use of pointers involves the use of records.

7.1 RECORDS

We regularly encounter the requirement to collect and represent data related to objects or people. Examples include personnel records, library card catalogs, and parts supply records.

In dealing with collections of data such as these, there is usually a need to access the data by either one of two basic methods. In one case, we will want to refer to all of the data related to an individual in its aggregate form. The second situation calls for the ability to access any single element of this collection. For example, we might ask for John Smith's entire personnel record, or we might inquire only about his date of birth.

Modula-2 provides the record type to address these requirements. That is,

- collections of potentially dissimilar data types can be treated as a single entity, and

- the data elements in this entity can be accessed collectively or individually.

A sample declaration for record types is given in Listing 7.1. This listing describes records that will be used in examples throughout the chapter. A detailed explanation of record types and variables follows in the subsequent sections.

Listing 7.1 illustrates some of the power of the record type in constructing extremely complex, composite data structures. We see from examining the record for an Individual that the record itself can be composed of other structured data types such as an array (LastName), an enumeration (Sex), other records (Date), and the simple data types such as BOOLEAN (TuitionPaid).

LISTING 7.1

```
MODULE RecordDemo;

TYPE
  DayType = [0..31];
  MonthType = (Jan, Feb, Mar, Apr, May, Jun, Jul, Aug, Sep,
               Oct, Nov, Dec);
  YearType = [1850..2000];
  NameType = ARRAY [0..20] OF CHAR;
  SexType = (Male, Female);

  Date = RECORD
           Day   : DayType;
           Month : MonthType;
           Year  : YearType;
         END;

  Individual = RECORD
                 LastName,
                 FirstName : NameType;
                 Sex : SexType;
                 BirthDate : Date;
                 TuitionPaid : BOOLEAN;
               END;

VAR
  Student : Individual;
  ClassMembers : ARRAY [1..40] OF Individual;
  LastDayOfClass : Date;


BEGIN (*RecordDemo*)
END RecordDemo.
```

Furthermore, we see that the record type can be a part of other data structures. For example, the variable ClassMembers is an array of records.

This versatility in defining single data entities that are comprised of a number of complex and diverse data types is extremely useful. We can process entire records (e.g., ClassMembers[27]) as well as particular data elements from a specific record (e.g., ClassMembers[27].LastName). This capability is an important ingredient for writing understandable and reliable programs that can handle complex data structures.

7.1.1 Record Elements

Before getting into the details of records, let's define some terms. First of all, the record type is made up of a sequence of *fields*. From Listing 7.1, the statements

```
Day : DayType;
TuitionPaid : BOOLEAN;
```

are examples of record fields in the record types of Date and Individual, respectively.

The fields, in turn, are made up of field *identifiers* and field *types*. Day and TuitionPaid are field identifiers. DayType and BOOLEAN are the corresponding field types.

Examination of Listing 7.1 shows that the syntax for the declaration of the sequence of fields which make up the record is the same as the syntax for the declaration of variables that was described in Chapter 3 for simple variables and in Chapter 6 for structured data types. Specifically, consider the fields of Date, which are written as

```
Day    : DayType;
Month : MonthType;
Year   : YearType;
```

There is nothing new here. This is precisely how these same elements would be declared if they were regular variables instead of elements of a record. If we know how to declare variables, we also know how to declare record elements.

We should note that record field identifiers will not conflict with other variable identifiers that may have the same name. Therefore, we could have a variable called Day in our program of Listing 7.1 without fear of a conflict with the Date record field of the same name.

The syntax diagram for records is shown in Figure A.28.

7.1.2 Processing Records

Now that you have seen how to declare record types and variables, the next step is learning how they are processed.

First of all, let's consider the allowable options for accessing the data in a record. We said earlier that the record can be accessed as an entity. For example, we can read or write the complete record for a student. In addition, any element of a particular record can be accessed. For example, a student's year of birth can be obtained.

If student records are added to the list of ClassMembers in the order that each student enrolls, the record of the third student to enroll will be identified as

```
ClassMembers[3]
```

We could use a language facility such as the FOR loop to cycle through the entire class as illustrated in the following pseudocode:

```
FOR i := 1 TO ClassSize DO
      Get the data for ClassMembers[i];
      Process the data for ClassMembers[i];
END;
```

If we wanted the last name of the third member of the class, we must write

```
ClassMembers[3].LastName
```

To determine the year that the third student was born requires

```
ClassMembers[3].BirthDate.Year
```

to be written as the record variable designator.

The term just used, variable designator, is the name given to the individual record variable element identifiers. The syntax diagram for a designator is shown in Figure A.39. The "up arrow" portion of the syntax diagram will be covered in the dynamic variable section later in this chapter.

As can be seen from the example, designators can get to be fairly long. When possible, we would like to avoid having to write

```
Student.LastName := 'Knepley';
Student.FirstName := 'Joey';
Student.Sex := Male;
Student.BirthDate.Day := 29;
Student.BirthDate.Month := Jul;
Student.BirthDate.Year := 1963;
Student.TuitionPaid := TRUE;
```

particularly in complex records made up of more records (made of more records (made of more records . . . see Chapter 10, this is a recursion)). The WITH clause and WITH statement make a shorter notation possible in these cases. Using WITH, the above lines are written as

```
WITH Student DO
    LastName := 'Knepley';
    FirstName := 'Joey';
    Sex := Male;
    BirthDate.Day := 29;
    BirthDate.Month := Jul;
    BirthDate.Year := 1963;
    TuitionPaid := TRUE;
END;
```

We can also nest the WITH statements. Nesting is illustrated in Listing 7.2. The program segment illustrated here assumes that the declarations in our example shown in Listing 7.1 have been made. Notice that the WITH statements have been nested to remove the need to qualify references to the student's birthdate. The input/output procedures of Chapter 5 are used to display some record data elements.

Note that it is not necessary to explicitly list every record field element in order to assign the contents of one record variable to another. In Listing 7.2, the assignment

```
ClassMembers[i] := Student;
```

is a much shorter way to accomplish the same thing.

The syntax diagram for the WITH statement is shown in Figure A.57. Care must be taken in use of the WITH statement if the record designator uses array indices, as is the case with ClassMembers. If we used the form

LISTING 7.2

```
(* Record declarations of listing 7.1 go here*)

VAR
  i : CARDINAL;

  BEGIN (*RecordDemo*)
      i := 3;
      WITH Student DO
        WITH BirthDate DO
          LastName := 'Knepley';
          FirstName := 'Joey';
          Sex := Male;
          Day := 29;
          Month := Jul;
          Year := 1963;
          TuitionPaid := TRUE;
        END (*birthdate*);
      END (*student*);

      ClassMembers[i] := Student;
                      (*NOTE this assignment option; the
                      record is assigned as a whole, as
                      opposed to an element at a time.
                      We could have done
                      ClassMembers[i].LastName := Student.LastName;
                      etc, etc, but that's a lot more work.*)

      (*This next part assume IMPORT InOut was declared, per Ch 5*)
      InOut.WriteString(ClassMembers[3].FirstName);
      InOut.Write(' ');
      InOut.WriteString(ClassMembers[3].LastName);
  END RecordDemo.

      (*Program execution results in "Joey Knepley" being written to
  the terminal.*)
```

```
WITH ClassMembers[i] DO
    . . . Processing . . .
END;
```

and in the course of processing we change the value of the array index i, unpredictable things will happen, as is the case when we tamper with a FOR loop index. Guarding against this problem is up to the programmer and not the compiler or the operating system.

There are advantages to using the WITH form when indices are involved. The indices are computed once at the top of the statement, rather than once for each record element that occurs in the WITH statement.

7.1.3 Variant Records

Although records are obviously very useful data structures, there is still more to them. Thus far, each record of a given type has had a fixed structure. However, this is not a necessary constraint since in Modula-2 the structure of a record is allowed to vary (variant records). To illustrate, look again at the example in Listing 7.1. We will consider how to handle a record when different information is required depending on whether the individual is a male or female or whether the tuition has been paid or not. The structure of the record will vary depending on the value of the field elements Sex and TuitionPaid.

Suppose that for males we have to include whether or not each has registered for the draft, and for females no special information is required. In addition, if the tuition has not been paid, we need the name of the parent responsible for the bill, and if it has been paid, we want the date of the payment. One alternative is to include these fields in every record, and only use the ones that are appropriate. The fields under consideration are

```
Registered : BOOLEAN;      (*Males only*)
ParentName : NameType;     (*Unpaid tuition only*)
PaymentDate : DateType;    (*Paid tuition only*)
```

As you have probably already guessed, it is not necessary to include every possible field in every record. Modula-2 provides the variant record to handle cases such as this. In the case of our example of Listing 7.1, use of the variant structure results in

```
Individual = RECORD
   LastName,
   FirstName : NameType;
   CASE Sex : SexType OF
      Male : Registered : BOOLEAN|
      Female : (*null statement*)
   END (*case sex*);
   BirthDate : Date;
   CASE TuitionPaid : BOOLEAN OF
      TRUE : PaymentDate : Date|
      FALSE : ParentName : NameType;
   END (*case tuition*);
END;
```

Pascal programmers will notice differences between the variant records of Pascal and Modula-2. A minor difference is the use of the vertical bar, |, to separate variant declarations rather than Pascal's use of parentheses. A significant difference is that Modula-2 permits several variant parts.

The syntax diagram for variant record structures is given in Figure A.31.

7.2 DYNAMIC DATA STRUCTURES

There are a number of practical programming problems that are difficult to solve using only the data types that we have introduced thus far. One problem is caused by the fact that our current collection of data structures are fixed at program execution time. By this we mean that if we declare the following variables

```
VAR
    I1 : INTEGER;
    B1, B2 : BOOLEAN;
    C1 : ARRAY [1..100] OF CARDINAL;
```

the number of data elements available during the execution of the program is the group of 103 elements shown above that are specified when the program is compiled. Furthermore, the memory space is fixed at the amount required to store these variables regardless of whether we actually need more or less. This is not a problem as long as we know our data storage requirements ahead of time. Unfortunately, this information is not always available.

Another problem area arises when we use arrays for processes such as sorting. In such operations, it is common to have to move large numbers of array elements in order to make room for new items that must be inserted between two existing elements. If the array is large and this operation is repeated often, the execution of the program becomes very slow. The computer spends most of its time just moving data back and forth.

Listing 7.3 is a program that reads numbers from the terminal and inserts them in a list in ascending order as they are entered. This is not provided as an example of a good method to perform this operation, but merely to illustrate the problems that can be encountered. The data movements that result from entering the sequence of numbers 50, 40, 10, 20, 30 are shown in Figure 7.1.

In this section, we introduce the pointer type. This data type makes dynamic data structures possible. Through the use of dynamic data structures, we can create data which expand and compress to meet our demands as the program is running. In the case of the program in Listing 7.3, we have a static array of dimension 100 to hold our list. This array size is fixed regardless of whether we actually need 5 or 5000 elements.

LISTING 7.3

```
MODULE PointerDemo;

IMPORT InOut;

CONST
  MaxItem = 100;

VAR
  Number : INTEGER;
  i, j,
  NumberOfItems : CARDINAL;
  Item : ARRAY [1..MaxItem] OF INTEGER; (*fixed data structure*)
  Found : BOOLEAN;


BEGIN
  NumberOfItems := 0;
  InOut.WriteString('Enter a number, (0 to stop): ');
  InOut.ReadInt(Number);

  WHILE Number # 0 DO        (*Read numbers & put in ascending order*)
    Found := FALSE;
    INC(NumberOfItems);
    i := 1;
    WHILE (NOT Found) & (i < NumberOfItems) DO
      Found := Number < Item[i];    (* Look at this; understand it? *)
      INC(i);
    END (*while*);
    IF NOT Found THEN
      Item[i] := Number;   (*Add at high end of list*)
    ELSE
      FOR j := NumberOfItems TO i BY -1 DO  (*Insertion*)
        Item[j] := Item[j - 1];    (*Lots of data being moved*)
      END (*for*);
      Item[i - 1] := Number;
    END (*if*);
  InOut.WriteString('Enter a number, (0 to stop): ');
  InOut.ReadInt(Number);
  END (*while*);

  FOR i := 1 TO NumberOfItems DO
    InOut.WriteInt(Item[i], 6);    InOut.WriteLn;
  END (*for*);
END PointerDemo.
```

We can also use the pointer type to solve the problem of array data element movement depicted in Figure 7.1. Rather than work with a fixed array, we can use a *linked list*. In a linked list, when a data element is inserted, there is no need to move existing data elements in order to make room for the new data, as we will see later.

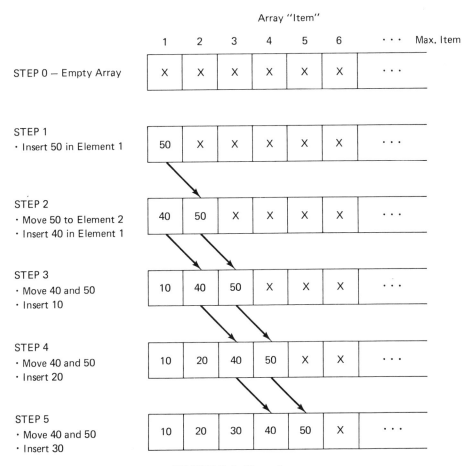

FIGURE 7.1 Item Array

7.2.1 Pointer Types

The pointer type itself is not a data structure. Pointers are used to establish relationships among the otherwise static data structures that we have encountered thus far. The relationships are established by using the pointers to link
data structures together. These linkages can be made very complex.

Figure 7.2 illustrates the use of pointers to create a linked list structure as
an alternative to the fixed array that appeared in the program of Listing 7.3
and that was depicted in Figure 7.1. Note that the list is composed of nodes
that are made up of two parts. The first is the data part, which in this case is a
single number. In general, the data part could be any data structure. For ex-

ample, the student record of Listing 7.1. The node's second part is a pointer that "points" to the next node in the list.

In general, the node can contain many pointers (at which time the data structure is referred to as a tree rather than a list). Also, any node can be pointed at by any number of pointers. It is easy to see how very complicated data structures can be formed through the use of the pointer type.

We still have not said what the pointer type is. Its value is a memory address. This memory address is the location of the data object that is pointed to by the pointer variable. When a data object is created, the address of the new data object is assigned to the pointer variable. As we shall see in the next section, variables pointed to by the pointer types are dynamic; i.e., they can be created (and destroyed) while the program is running.

Modula-2 contains a system constant that belongs to every pointer type. This is the constant NIL. If we assign NIL to a pointer type, that pointer type points to NOTHING.

For example, when using pointer types to implement lists, the NIL pointer value is used to indicate the end of a list. Therefore, we can test to see if we are at the end of a list by checking to see if the value of the pointer to the next node in the list is equal to NIL. This will be illustrated later.

The difference between a pointer and the data object that is referenced (pointed to) by the pointer is very important to understand. This is the subject of the next section.

7.2.2 Dynamic Variables

A pointer cannot be used to point at just any data type. Each specific pointer type must be associated with a specific data object type. This is illustrated in the type declaration shown in Listing 7.4.

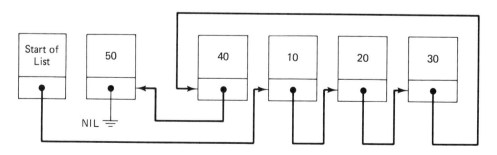

FIGURE 7.2 Linked List

LISTING 7.4

```
TYPE
   PointerType = POINTER TO DataNode;

   DataNode = RECORD
               Number : INTEGER;
               Pointer : PointerType;
            END;

VAR
   Item,
   HeadOfList : PointerType;
```

The pointer type PointerType is said to be "bound to" objects of the type DataNode. Pointers of type PointerType, therefore, can be used only to reference variables whose type is DataNode.

You should have noted an apparent paradox in Listing 7.4. The declaration of PointerType referred to DataNode before DataNode was declared. However, DataNode refers to PointerType, so reversing the order of the declarations does nothing to solve the problem. In the instance of a pointer type declaration, this is a legal declaration. There is no alternative.

The fact that we have declared DataNode to be a dynamic data structure and have further declared that the variables Item and HeadOfList should be bound to DataNode types does not result in the creation of any dynamic variables. Everything up to this point of the program is simply made available to the compiler in the same manner as a program that contains only static structures.

The actual creation of a dynamic variable does not occur at compilation time. Dynamic variables are created by the operating system as a result of statements that are executed while the program is running. If none of these special statements are ever executed during a particular run of the program, the number of dynamic variables created is zero. This is an important feature of the dynamic data type. We only create as many variables as the particular task requires.

Dynamic variables are created by execution of the statement NEW. For example, NEW(Item) results in a variable of type DataNode being created. In addition to creating the new variable, the address (pointer) of this new variable is assigned to the pointer variable Item. The dynamic variable itself has *no name*. Its name is *not* Item. Examine Listing 7.4 again. Item is of type PointerType, and PointerType is a POINTER TO DataNode. Therefore, Item is a POINTER TO the dynamic variable of the type DataNode and is not the variable. Recall that we said an address was assigned to the pointer type and that this is the address in which the variable can be found in the computer's memory.

Very mysterious. If the dynamic variable has no name, then how can it be accessed? The answer is that the dynamic variable is accessed through the pointer. An element of the language called the dereferencing operator, ↑, is used to accomplish this. Recall that the pointer type references (refers to, points to) the actual dynamic variable. So what would be more natural (?) than a dereferencing operator to get at the variable itself. For example, the dynamic variable that was created by NEW(Item) can be accessed by the designator Item↑. Item is the address (pointer) of the object, and Item↑ is the object itself. The relationship between the pointer type and the dynamic variable that is referenced by the pointer is displayed graphically in Figure 7.3.

The syntax diagram for the pointer type is shown in Figure A.35.

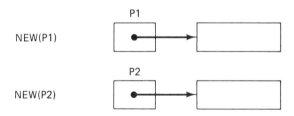

FIGURE 7.3a Creating Pointer Variables

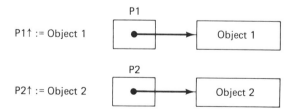

FIGURE 7.3b Assigning Data Objects to Pointer Variables

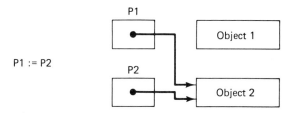

FIGURE 7.3c Effect on 7.3b of Assignment P1:=P2

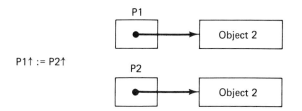

FIGURE 7.3d Effect on 7.3b of Assignment P1↑:=P2↑

7.2.3 Creation and Disposal of Dynamic Variables

We have already stated that variables are created through the use of the standard procedure NEW(Item). Similarly, elements can be deleted by means of the standard procedure DISPOSE(Item). Program examples that illustrate the use of these statements will be given in the next section.

NEW(Item) causes storage space to be allocated in memory. The variable Item↑ is stored in this space. The memory address of the storage space is stored in Item. DISPOSE(Item) causes the space that was allocated in memory for Item↑ to be returned to the system.

Every Modula-2 language implementation is expected to have a standard library module (see Chapter 8) named Storage to handle storage allocation and deallocation for the system. The use of the standard Modula-2 procedures NEW and DISPOSE depends on the availability of Storage. In particular, the statement

    FROM Storage IMPORT ALLOCATE, DEALLOCATE;

must appear in your program if NEW or DISPOSE are used (see Chapter 8). (Because NEW and DISPOSE are standard procedures, they may be used without being declared or imported.)

7.2.4 Dynamic Structures: Lists and Trees

Lists are very useful data structures for solving a variety of practical problems. A pictorial representation of a list was shown in Figure 7.2. A list can be viewed as a collection of nodes that are linked together. Every node has two parts—a data element and a single pointer. The data element can be as complex as desired. The example in Figure 7.2 used a single number for simplicity only. The corresponding data declaration for the structure depicted in Figure 7.2 was given in Listing 7.4. In this section we will show how a list, implemented with dynamic data elements, is used to solve the problem posed by the program of Listing 7.3.

A fixed-array approach to problems involving the insertion and deletion of new data elements within an existing array is too slow. Too much time is spent (wasted) moving the old elements in order to make room for the new data. Consider the situation shown in Figure 7.4.

In this figure, the array is being used to store a sorted list of numbers. If a new number must be added to the list, every old number that is greater than the new one must be moved to make room. This is shown in going from Figure 7.4a to 7.4b. (This difficulty is in addition to the problem that occurs if the array fills up and overflows.)

Now consider how this same situation is handled through the use of a linked list. Figure 7.5a shows the linked list formulation of the fixed-array sorted list shown in Figure 7.4a. Figure 7.5b shows that when the new number

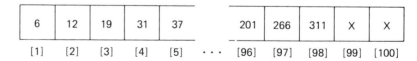

FIGURE 7.4a 100-Element Integer Array

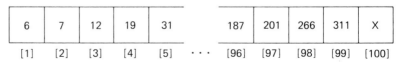

Adding "7" to sorted list – 97 numbers must be moved

FIGURE 7.4b Impact of Adding New Entry

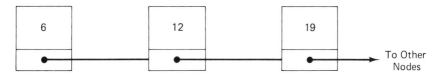

FIGURE 7.5a Linked List Sort Formulation

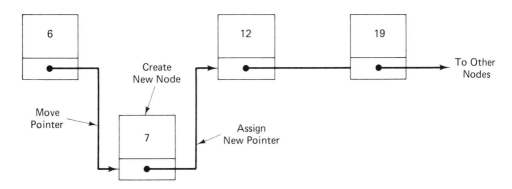

FIGURE 7.5b Impact of Adding 7 to Sorted List

is added, no data is moved. Instead, a new node is created, and this new node is inserted in the list simply by *moving pointers.* Similarly, a node is removed (deleted) from the list by rearranging pointers. It is easy to see that a lot of time can be saved by using a linked list instead of an array in situations such as these.

Several fundamental operations are needed in order to perform linked-list operations. These operations are used to

- add new elements to the list,
- delete elements from the list, and
- search the list for an element.

In the remainder of this section, we will examine how these operations are performed using dynamic data elements. Once our bag of tricks is complete, we will apply these techniques to reformulate the array sorting program of Listing 7.3 as a linked list. The pointer type data declaration of Listing 7.4 will be used here, and is repeated in Listing 7.5 for convenience.

LISTING 7.5

```
TYPE
   PointerType = POINTER TO DataNode;

   DataNode = RECORD
               Number : INTEGER;
               Pointer : PointerType;
             END;

VAR
   Item,
   HeadOfList : PointerType;
```

Node Addition

A new node can be added to the end of the list (front or rear), or it can be inserted between two existing nodes. Let's first consider the case of adding a new node to the front of a list.

In order to add a node to the front of a list, you have to know where the front of the list is located. So where is it? When the construction of a list is initiated, the list is empty—nothing has been put in it yet. This is where the pointer constant NIL is needed. We start the list building process with the statement

    HeadOfList := NIL;

to indicate that there is nothing in the list. Notice that HeadOfList is a pointer variable, and recall that pointer types point to their associated dynamic variable (a node of type DataNode in this case). This statement says that the pointer variable that we are using to point to the front of our list, HeadOfList, is pointing at *nothing*, i.e., an empty list. So now the front of the list has been established.

The next step is to create a node and add it to the front of the list. A node is created with the statement

    NEW(Item);

This node has two elements. The first is the data part of the structure, and the second is a pointer. The first step that should be taken with this new node is to assign a value to the data part. The statement

    Item↑.Number := 50;

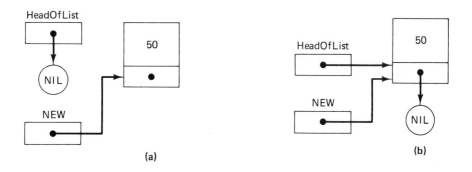

(a)

(b)

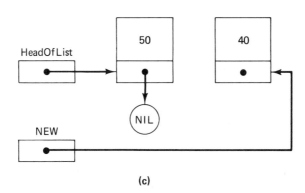

(c)

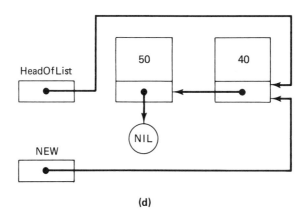

(d)

FIGURE 7.6

assigns the value 50 to the data part of the node. Figure 7.6a describes the situation at this point. The pointer HeadOfList is pointing at nothing, and the pointer Item is pointing at our newly created node, Item↑, which has a data value of 50. The next step is to add Item↑ to the front of the list—our original objective. This is done by

```
Item↑.Pointer := HeadOfList;
HeadOfList := Item;
```

which is a two-assignment statement sequence that results in Figure 7.6b. Observe what each of these two statements accomplishes. The first tells the pointer of the new node, Item↑.Pointer, to point at what had been the front of the list prior to the creation of the new node. The second tells the pointer to the front of the list, HeadOfList, to point at the newly created node that has just been added to the front of the list.

Disaster results if the order of these two statements is reversed. The address of the previous node that was at the front of the list will be lost forever. Why? Because HeadOfList was pointing at it, and we changed the value of HeadOfList before preserving its old value in Item↑.Pointer.

Figure 7.6c depicts the list after the creation of the second node and after a value of 40 has been assigned. The list, after this newest node has been added, appears in Figure 7.6d.

Listing 7.6 shows the program segment which performs the node addition operation that was just described.

LISTING 7.6

```
HeadOfList := NIL;

InOut.ReadInt(Value);   (*Assume IMPORT InOut, and Value : INTEGER*)

WHILE Value # 0 DO   (*Add nodes to front of list until Value = 0*)
  NEW(Item);
  WITH Item^ DO
    Number := Value;
    Pointer := HeadOfList;
  END (*with*);
  HeadOfList := Item;
  InOut.ReadInt(Value);
END (*while*);
```

In order to add nodes to the rear of the list, an additional pointer, RearOfList, is used. The start of the process is similar to the one we just finished.

```
HeadOfList := NIL;
RearOfList := NIL;
```

After creating the first node with NEW(Item) and assigning a value to the data portion as before, the next step is

```
Item↑.Pointer := NIL;
IF HeadOfList = NIL THEN (*list is empty*)
    HeadOfList := Item;
ELSE
    RearOfList↑.Pointer := Item;
END;
RearOfList := Item;
```

You have obviously noticed that even though we are adding to the rear, the pointer to the front is still being used. Why? First look at Figure 7.7a to see what the situation looks like before adjusting the HeadOfList pointer. Do you see any potential problems if HeadOfList is not there?

The problem occurs as more nodes are added. (Figure 7.7b shows the situation with two nodes in the list and the third being added.) RearOfList keeps pointing to the last node, and every node points to the one behind it (its successor). So how can any nodes except the last one be accessed if RearOfList is the only available pointer? They cannot be, and that is why HeadOfList must be kept. Notice in the program segment that HeadOfList is assigned a new value only if the new node is the first in the list.

Without any fanfare, two important data structures have just been introduced. The structure depicted in Figure 7.6, in which the list can be accessed from only *one end*, is known as a stack. The stack is used in so-called last-in–first-out (LIFO) situations. That is, the last element added to the list is the first element to be removed. (It is the only one we can reach.) The common analogy for a stack is the stack of trays in a cafeteria—trays are added and removed from the same end, the top. The structure of Figure 7.7, with access at *both ends* is known as a queue. The queue handles first-in–first-out (FIFO) cases. New elements are added at the rear and removed from the front. An analogy for a queue is the waiting line in a bank or supermarket—customers are served on a first-come, first-served basis. Stacks and queues are used in an extensive number of programming applications.

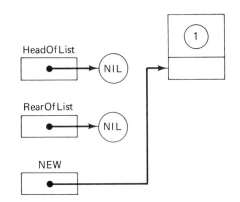

FIGURE 7.7a Creating First Node

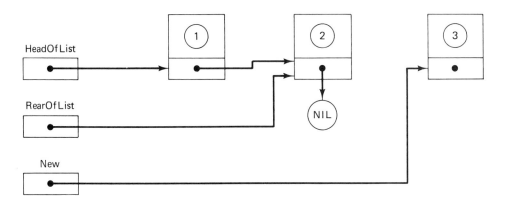

FIGURE 7.7b Adding Node 3 to Rear of List

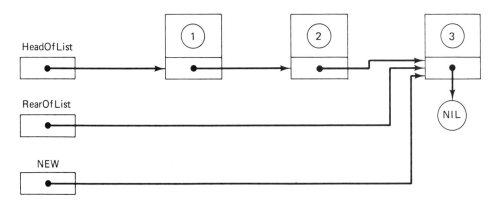

FIGURE 7.7c Node 3 Added to List

Node Deletion

Now that node addition has been covered, let's consider node deletion. As an example, we will use the queue structure of Figure 7.7. The new items were added to the rear, and, therefore, the older items are toward the front of the list. Under the queue's first-in–first-out (FIFO) rule, we will remove the nodes starting at the front of the queue.

One condition must be observed. If the queue is empty, we must not try to remove anything from it. When the list is not empty, we will remove a node, return the space it occupied to storage, and write the value of the node's data element. When the end of the queue is reached, the value of the pointer to the rear of the list must be set to NIL. This is necessary since the list is now empty, but RearOfList still contains the address of the last node added to the queue. This procedure is shown in Listing 7.7.

LISTING 7.7

```
WHILE HeadOfList # NIL DO   (*stop when queue is empty*)
   Item := HeadOfList;
   InOut.WriteInt(Item^.Number, 6);  (*"first out"*)
   HeadOfList := Item^.Pointer; (*next node to front*)
   IF HeadOfList = NIL THEN
      RearOfList := NIL;  (*in case queue is used again*)
   END (*if*);
   DISPOSE(Item);  (*return memory space to storage*)
END (*while*);
```

Building a Sorted List

The material on adding and deleting nodes covers almost all of the basics related to the use of pointers for applications that require dynamic data structures. Several topics that have not been explicitly addressed are

- adding a node between two other nodes (thus far we have only considered adding nodes at the front or rear of the list),
- searching a list, and
- list traversal, or moving through the list (needed for searching, among other things).

To cover these topics and to summarize what we have already learned, let's reconsider the program that was presented using an array data structure in Listing 7.3.

If you recall, the program of Listing 7.3 reads numbers from the terminal and inserts them into a list in ascending order. The following are two obvious problems with the program as it is now written:

- The array elements are moved too much due to the need to make room in the array for new elements.
- The array is fixed in size.

The program of Listing 7.8 is offered as an alternative to the program in Listing 7.3. It solves both of the problems cited above by using the pointer type to implement the list data structure. To allow ease of comparison, the basic structure of the program block in Listing 7.8 closely parallels that of the program in Listing 7.3. Both versions of the program contain the following pieces:

- The main control structure is the outer WHILE loop, which stops the sorting process when a zero has been entered.
- Within this loop, another WHILE loop is used to compare the new number against each old number until a number is found that is equal to or greater than the new number (or the end of the list is encountered).
- The new number is inserted at the proper place in the list through the use of an IF statement.

In Listing 7.8, since the list is empty when the program is started, HeadOfList is initialized to NIL. At the start of the main control loop, the

LISTING 7.8

```
MODULE Sort;

IMPORT InOut;

FROM Storage IMPORT ALLOCATE, DEALLOCATE;

TYPE
  PointerType = POINTER TO DataNode;

  DataNode = RECORD
             Number : INTEGER;
             Pointer : PointerType;
          END;
```

LISTING 7.8 (Continued)

```
VAR
  HeadOfList,
  Insert,
  Temp,
  Item : PointerType;
  Value : INTEGER;


BEGIN (*Sort*)
  HeadOfList := NIL;
  InOut.WriteString('Enter a number, (0 to stop): ');
  InOut.ReadInt(Value);

  WHILE Value # 0 DO
    Item := HeadOfList;
    IF (Value < Item^.Number) OR (Item = NIL) THEN (*insert at front*)
        NEW(Insert);
        Insert^.Number := Value;
        Insert^.Pointer := HeadOfList;
        HeadOfList := Insert;
    ELSE
        WHILE (Item # NIL) & (Value > Item^.Number) DO
            Temp := Item;  (*must "remember" the previous node*)
            Item := Item^.Pointer;
        END (*while*);
        NEW(Insert);
        Insert^.Number := Value;
        IF Item = NIL THEN  (*new item belongs at end of list*)
            Insert^.Pointer := NIL;
        ELSE  (*insert between 2 existing items*)
            Insert^.Pointer := Temp^.Pointer;
        END (*if item*);
        Temp^.Pointer := Insert;
    END (*if value*);
    InOut.WriteString('Enter a number, (0 to stop): ');
    InOut.ReadInt(Value);
  END (*while*);

  Item := HeadOfList;
  WHILE Item # NIL DO  (*traverse the list from front to rear*)
    InOut.WriteInt(Item^.Number, 6);  InOut.WriteLn;
    Item := Item^.Pointer;
  END (*while*);

END Sort.
```

pointer variable Item is initialized to begin at the front of the list in the search for the proper location to insert the new number.

An IF statement is encountered next. The IF checks for the special case in which the new number is smaller than the smallest number currently in the list. If this is the case, the THEN branch adds a new node at the front of the list precisely as was done in Listing 7.6. The ELSE branch of the IF statement handles all cases in which the new number is larger than the current smallest number.

In the ELSE branch, a WHILE Loop is used to *search* the list. The object of the search is to find the proper location to insert the new node. One of two cases is possible. In the first case, the end of the list is encountered, which means that the number is to be added at the rear. Otherwise, the number is to be inserted between two existing nodes. In order to handle either of these two cases, we must know the location of both the predecessor and the successor nodes. There are a number of ways that this can be done, including storing two pointers in each node instead of just one. The second pointer would point backward, toward the preceding node. In Listing 7.8 another approach was taken. Note the use of the pointer variable Temp and the associated comments in the program. A little study to see what is happening here will go a long way toward a better understanding of pointer types and dynamic data structures. With the exception of adding the variable Temp to provide a way back to the preceding node, the method depicted in the interior WHILE loop for traversing the list is fairly standard and straightforward.

Once the location has been determined, the new node is inserted. Regardless of whether the new location is at the end or in the middle, three of the four required steps are identical. Only the setting of the new node's pointer varies depending on whether or not the new node is added at the end.

SUMMARY

The record variable and dynamic variable represent two of the most powerful Modula-2 data structures. They provide the programmer with great flexibility while contributing to reliable and readable programs.

Although these two structures are not essential for writing programs, the programmer who plans to develop large software systems should definitely become familiar with them. The best way to develop and test your understanding of the pointer type is to write programs that utilize this data structure. It may go slow at first, but like anything else, practice makes perfect.

QUESTIONS AND PROBLEMS

1. Can a variant record contain nested variants, i.e., a variant record within a variant record?

2. If your answer to Problem 1 was yes, modify the record declaration in Section 7.1.3 to include Height and Weight for males who are on an athletic scholarship, IQ for males on an academic scholarship, and Hobby for all other males.

3. Draw a series of pictures similar to Figures 7.6 and 7.7 for the program shown in Listing 7.8.

4. Revise Listing 7.8 to reverse the sort order, i.e., largest first.

SUPPLEMENTAL PROBLEMS

Problem 1

The use of a string in place of a number leaves us with no direct way to indicate the sign of a number. There are a number of options but, since this is a textbook problem designed to explore Modula-2, let's pick one that may be considered as obscure as doing arithmetic with strings. Use an enumeration type (Chapter 6) for the sign and use the record type of this chapter to define our "Number" (i.e., a record that combines the string "number" and the enumeration "sign").

Problem 2

Write a small program to change the "sign" of the top number on the stack. While (or before) you're at it, modify your other calculator related programs that you've written thus far to work with "Number" from Problem 1. If you find that it's a lot of work to change the old code, examine your programming style in terms of use of constants, type declarations, modularity, etc.

Problem 3

After you've modified your code to work with "Number," rewrite the array based stack programs Pop, Push, and Clear to use pointers as we've illustrated in this chapter.

Problem 4

Write a small program to display the contents of the stack (including the unused parts). Do this with either the array or the pointer stack implementation.

CHAPTER 8

PROCEDURES AND MODULES

NEW CONCEPTS: Procedures, Modules, Locality, Visibility, Separate Compilation, Data Hiding
ISSUES: Program Reliability, Program Decomposition

INTRODUCTION

Large complex programs are difficult to develop, understand, and maintain. The road to better and more reliable software requires techniques that permit programs to be divided into smaller and more manageable pieces.

There are several issues related to the difficulties in developing large programs.

- An obvious issue is program size: How much information is an individual (programmer/designer) capable of handling before going into "overload"?

- An item related to size is detail: How much detail is necessary in order to define and solve a problem? Surely a large physical object can be defined without starting with its component atoms.

- A third related issue is the effect of actions in one part of the program on other parts of the program. These are commonly referred to as side effects and are usually unwanted and adverse. The greater the size and amount of detail, the greater the chance of unplanned side effects.

Corresponding to these three broad problem areas are three categories of solutions. In the case of size, it is desirable to decompose the program into a number of smaller and more manageable pieces—divide and conquer, so to speak. For the issue of how much detail is enough, the concept of data abstraction is used to omit unnecessary detail while retaining the essence of the problem. For example, do not read a byte if a record is what is needed. The problem of side effects can be controlled if the "visibility" of program elements can be controlled. That is, only allow program elements to be accessible to the parts of the program that absolutely need them.

Modula-2's strength lies in the features of the language that support the above capabilities. Among the most powerful of these features are the procedure and the module, which will be presented in this chapter. Program decomposition through the use of procedures and modules will be described and illustrated. An important feature of these powerful capabilities is their ability to control the visibility of program parameters. This is particularly true of the module.

8.1 MODULA-2 PROCEDURES

Consider the program shown in Listing 8.1. This program controls the reading of characters from the keyboard. The input character must be a lower-case letter before the program will accept it. When the program's Write(Character) statements are executed, we are guaranteed that nothing except one of the 26 lower-case letters will be printed.

A function of this kind is very useful for providing error-free data input. An interactive environment needs to restrict the set of allowable inputs that a user may enter. The system should accept only those input characters which have been deemed to be valid. In a real application, we want more flexibility in defining valid input than is demonstrated in Listing 8.1. We will improve this program as we develop the capabilities and roles of procedures throughout the chapter. The word processing program that is presented in Chapter 12 makes extensive use of a similar function.

If this keyboard input function were used in a large number of places within a program, we would get very tired of entering the same lines of code over and over. Also, the more often the code is entered, the more opportunity there is for an error to be made. Lastly, the memory requirements for the program will be adversely affected if the number of repetitions of the code gets large.

This is a case in which procedures are needed. The function can be written *once* as a small routine with a name. In the above example, maybe it would be called GetCharacter. Any time that the function is required within the program, instead of repeating all of the lines of code, we merely write GetCharacter. The procedure operates as a small subprogram. We have been

LISTING 8.1

```
MODULE ProcDemo;

IMPORT InOut;

TYPE
  CharSet = SET OF CHAR;

VAR
  GoodCharacterSet : CharSet;
  Character : CHAR;

BEGIN (*ProcDemo*)
  GoodCharacterSet := CharSet('a'..'z');
  REPEAT    (*keep reading input until character is in a-z*)
    InOut.Read(Character);
  UNTIL Character IN GoodCharacterSet;
  InOut.WriteString('The first character entered was ');
  InOut.Write(Character);  (*we're guaranteed this will be in a-z*)

  REPEAT    (*now do it again (& hope not again & again)*)
    InOut.Read(Character);
  UNTIL Character IN GoodCharacterSet;
  InOut.WriteString('The second character entered was ');
  InOut.Write(Character);
END ProcDemo.
```

using library procedures such as WriteString since the start of this book. The only difference between WriteString and GetCharacter is that the former is defined by the language implementer and the latter is defined by the programmer (us).

Procedures are a very important part of a programming language. They are one of the chief tools that allow us to develop a program in small, manageable pieces. Programming without procedures is an almost unthinkable process. Modula-2 procedures are exceptionally powerful. In subsequent sections, procedures will be described in detail.

8.1.1 Procedures

Modula-2 provides two types of procedures. One is simply called a procedure, and the second is called a function procedure. This section deals with the first type of procedure.

To proceed, let's return to the program of Listing 8.1 and see how it looks using a procedure (Listing 8.2). The initial description and discussion of pro-

LISTING 8.2

```
MODULE ProcDemo;

IMPORT InOut;

VAR
    Character : CHAR;

PROCEDURE GetCharacter;
  TYPE
      CharSet = SET OF CHAR;
  VAR
      GoodCharacterSet : CharSet;
  BEGIN (*GetCharacter*)
      GoodCharacterSet := CharSet{'a'..'z'};
      REPEAT    (*keep reading input until character is in a-z*)
          InOut.Read(Character);
      UNTIL Character IN GoodCharacterSet;
  END GetCharacter;


BEGIN (*ProcDemo*)
  GetCharacter;   (*call the procedure*)
  InOut.WriteString('The first character entered was ');
  InOut.Write(Character); (*we're guaranteed this will be in a-z*)

  GetCharacter;   (*call the procedure*)
  InOut.WriteString('The second character entered was ');
  InOut.Write(Character); (*we're guaranteed this will be in a-z*)
END ProcDemo.
```

cedures will be based on this example. In comparing Listings 8.1 and 8.2, we see that all of the elements of 8.1 have been carried over to 8.2, but with considerable rearrangement plus a few additions. The program is now in two main parts. There is the original program, ProcDemo, and there is a new program-like structure embedded within ProcDemo.

The new element of ProcDemo is a procedure. With only a few minor differences, the structure of the procedure is identical to that of a program. These differences are:

- The procedure begins with the word PROCEDURE instead of MODULE and ends with a semicolon rather than a period.
- A program can have a priority, and a procedure cannot (see Chapter 11).

- A program can import library routines (see modules in Chapter 8), but a procedure cannot.
- A procedure declaration can contain another procedure declaration. Therefore, procedures (but not programs) can be nested.
- In a subsequent section, we will see that a procedure can have a set of formal parameters. A program cannot.

Aside from these five differences, procedures and programs are constructed in the same way.

Some terminology needs to be defined. The portion of the example that begins with PROCEDURE and ends with END GetCharacter is called a procedure declaration. The two GetCharacter statements in the main block of ProcDemo are called procedure calls.

We can see from the example in Listing 8.2 how procedures can be helpful not only in cutting down on repetitive code but also in making programs easier to understand and follow. There is no doubt about what action is to be performed in the main block of ProcDemo. No detailed code needs to be deciphered. A character is gotten—twice—and printed. In larger and more complex programs, the benefit of more understandable code cannot be overstated.

We noted that procedures can be nested. Suppose that we wanted GetCharacter to sound a beep at the terminal whenever an invalid character was entered. We could do this as shown in the first half of Listing 8.3. Alternatively, we could take the approach shown in the second part of the listing, which uses a nested procedure.

This concludes the introductory section on procedures. If this was all that procedures had to offer, they would be valuable but limited. However, there are additional features of procedures that significantly enhance their capabilities. These features permit the procedure to perform its function on different data at the option of the calling statement. In our example, the valid set of characters can be varied from one call of the procedure to another. Also, the visibility of elements such as variables can be controlled. These features of procedures are the subject of the subsequent sections.

Time out for a brief note on programming style. You may have noticed that the BEGIN at the start of each program block in each of our examples is followed by the program identifier name in a comment statement. This is a small point of style but one that is useful in improving program readability, particularly in the case of nested routines such as in Listing 8.3. If the level of nesting gets fairly deep, it is sometimes difficult to determine just which procedure block you are in. If a consistent and logical indentation format, coupled with the identification of elements is used, the reader has a much easier time of it when digging through a program. For example,

LISTING 8.3

```
PROCEDURE GetCharacter;
  TYPE
      CharSet = SET OF CHAR;
  VAR
      GoodCharacterSet : CharSet;
  BEGIN (*GetCharacter*)
      GoodCharacterSet := CharSet('a'..'z');
      REPEAT   (*keep reading input until character is in a-z*)
          InOut.Read(Character);
          IF NOT(Character IN GoodCharacterSet) THEN
              InOut.Write(CHR(7));   (*ring them bells*)
          END (*if*);
      UNTIL Character IN GoodCharacterSet;
  END GetCharacter;

------------------------------------------------------------------

PROCEDURE GetCharacter;
  TYPE
      CharSet = SET OF CHAR;
  VAR
      GoodCharacterSet : CharSet;

  PROCEDURE RingTheBell;
      BEGIN (*RingThemBell*)
          InOut.Write(CHR(7));
      END RingTheBell;

  BEGIN (*GetCharacter*)
      GoodCharacterSet := CharSet('a'..'z');
      REPEAT   (*keep reading input until character is in a-z*)
          InOut.Read(Character);
          IF NOT(Character IN GoodCharacterSet) THEN
              RingTheBell;
          END (*if*);
      UNTIL Character IN GoodCharacterSet;
  END GetCharacter;
```

BEGIN (*Proc1*)
END (*for i . . .*),
END (*if test*), etc.
AND don't forget meaningful variable names.

And who knows, the reader digging through the program might be you, the original programmer. The syntax of Modula-2 is an improvement over Pascal in this area, but there are still good and bad techniques. Do everything possible to enhance the clarity of your programs. A structured language, used poorly, does not do much good.

8.1.2 Variable Visibility

We had stated that program side effects required control. As a practical matter, an adverse side effect is caused by changing the value of a variable in one part of a program without realizing that the same variable is used in another program location. Later on, the variable is used in the second location without realizing that its value has been altered—and who knows what happens then.

The ability to break a program into small pieces via procedures is one step in helping to guard against side effects. However, the real payoff in using procedures to alleviate these problems is in the ability to control the scope of variable visibility (validity). Modula-2 has rules that govern what variables are visible (valid) in what parts of a Modula-2 program.

The bottom line is this: If you cannot "see" a variable that you should not be changing, then you cannot change it. Therefore, one control against side effects is to restrict the scope of the program in which variables can be accessed. If you do not want location 2 to alter a variable from location 1, then do not let location 2 "see" location 1's variables. In a language such as BASIC this may not be possible. That is one of many reasons why languages such as BASIC are poorly suited for the development of reliable large programs.

A variable's visibility is governed by where the variable is declared. A variable exists only within the procedure in which it is declared. *This last statement cannot be overemphasized.* This procedure, in which the variable is declared, is called the variable's scope. The variable is said to be local to the procedure. Looking at the example in Listing 8.2, the variable GoodCharacterSet is a local variable. It is declared within the procedure GetCharacter. It cannot be seen outside of GetCharacter. The scope of GoodCharacterSet is GetCharacter.

In contrast to local variables, there are global variables. Global variables are declared in the outermost level of the program. The variable Character, in Listing 8.2, is a global variable.

Since the local variable exists only within the procedure in which it is declared, GoodCharacterSet has meaning only within the procedure GetCharacter. There is no chance that any part of the program, other than GetCharacter, can change the value of this local variable. The compiler will catch all invalid references to a local variable (all references outside of its scope). Therefore, we cannot even compile a program with this sort of error.

A global variable such as Character, on the other hand, is fair game throughout the program. Notice in Listing 8.2 that the value of Character is altered in the procedure by InOut.Read(Character) and is accessed (but not changed) in the main block. There is nothing to prevent us from accessing or modifying Character anywhere in the program. Unexpected changes to global variables such as Character, however, can cause adverse side effects.

As we will discuss, there are situations in which global variables are necessary and appropriate. However, as a matter of good and safe programming practice, local variables should be used when possible. If all variables were local, then adverse side effects could go no further than within a procedure. Small, well-debugged procedures would eliminate this latter problem from practical consideration.

There are several issues related to local identifiers and their scope that must be addressed. What are the rules related to identifier scope when procedures are nested? What happens if the same identifier name is declared in more than one part of the program? (Notice we have changed from variable to identifier because the issue is broader than just variables, and the same scope rules apply to all identifiers.)

Scope rules with nested procedures are illustrated in Listing 8.4. The scope of an identifier includes the procedure in which it is declared as well as all procedures nested within that procedure. To see this, notice that the variables a (CHAR) and x (INTEGER), which are declared in PROCEDURE Outer, are visible in PROCEDUREs Nested1 and Nested2. Conversely, the variable b (BOOLEAN), declared in Nested1, is not visible in Outer (nor Nested2) since Outer is not enclosed within Nested1.

There is no interaction among the local variables of totally separate procedures. This is true even if the local variables have the same names. This is demonstrated by comparing the variables that are visible within PROCEDURE Three to the variables visible in the Outer and Nested procedures. Only global variables are common.

The final point to be made has to do with the rules governing identically named identifiers. Redeclaring an identifier within a nested procedure redefines the scope of that identifier. The new (redeclared) version of the identifier has as its scope the procedure in which it is declared (as well as any procedures nested within this procedure). It is not visible to the enclosing procedure or to any other procedures nested within the enclosing procedure. Nested1's redeclaration of b (BOOLEAN) illustrates this point. The variable b (BOOLEAN) is not visible either to the enclosing procedure, Outer, or to other procedures nested within Outer (Nested2).

The same rules that apply to identical variable names also apply to other identifiers. For example, either the Nested1 or Nested2 procedure could have been named Three without any conflict with PROCEDURE Three shown in Listing 8.4. The scope of Nested1 is Outer and is therefore invisible to anything outside of Outer.

LISTING 8.4

```
MODULE GlobalPart;
    VAR
        a, b, c : CARDINAL;

PROCEDURE Outer;
    VAR
        a : CHAR;
        x : INTEGER;

    PROCEDURE Nested1;
        VAR
            b : BOOLEAN;
        BEGIN (*Nested1*)
            (*I see a : CHAR, b : BOOLEAN, c : CARDINAL, x : INTEGER*)
        END Nested1;

    PROCEDURE Nested2;
        BEGIN (*Nested2*)
            (*I see a : CHAR, b and c : CARDINAL, x : INTEGER*)
        END Nested2;

    BEGIN (*Outer*)
        (*I see a : CHAR, b and c : CARDINAL, x : INTEGER*)
    END Outer;

PROCEDURE Three;
    VAR
        z : CARDINAL;
    BEGIN (*Three*)
        (*I see a, b, c and z : CARDINAL*)
    END Three;

BEGIN
    (*I see a, b and c : CARDINAL*)
END GlobalProgram.
```

Before wrapping up this discussion on the scope of identifiers, it is necessary to give you some good news and some bad news. The good news is that since local variables exist only within the procedures that declare them, no storage space is required for a local variable except when its procedure is called. Therefore, storage space used for local variables can be returned to the system for other uses when the surrounding procedure is inactive. This results in efficient use of memory. The bad news is that since local variables do not exist except when their surrounding procedure exists, the value of a local variable disappears when the procedure is finished. This means that if you are depending on certain variables used within a procedure to retain their value from one call of the procedure to the next call, you cannot use a local variable. The only alternative, in this case, is to use a global variable. This puts us right back where we started in terms of susceptibility to side effects. Later, when we cover modules, we will return to this issue.

8.1.3 Parameters

Procedures can use parameters to greatly increase their flexibility and utility. The program shown in Listing 8.2 illustrates how parameters can improve a program. The procedure GetCharacter reads a character belonging to a predefined, valid set of characters. Having to predefine this character set limits the usefulness of GetCharacter. If a different set of characters is required, the procedure must be rewritten, or multiple procedures are required. Neither option is satisfactory.

The solution to this problem is the procedure parameter. Through the use of parameters, a single procedure can be used for all possible values of the parameter variables. The use of a parameter has the same generalizing effect as replacing a constant with a variable. In this case, instead of using a constant for the value of the sets of good characters, we will use a value assigned by the calling procedure. There are two types of parameters—the value parameter and the variable parameter. Each will be described and illustrated in turn.

Value Parameters

Listing 8.5 illustrates the use of value parameters in the program originally shown in Listing 8.2. There are a number of things to observe about this program.

First of all, the first line of the procedure, called its heading, is

```
PROCEDURE GetCharacter(GoodSet : CharSet);
```

This heading now includes a parameter list (GoodSet : CharSet), which is called the procedure's formal parameter. By way of contrast, the procedure call in the main block of the program has also changed from that in Listing 8.2 and is now

```
GetCharacter(GoodCharacterSet)
```

LISTING 8.5

```
MODULE ProcDemo;

IMPORT InOut;

TYPE
    CharSet = SET OF CHAR;

VAR
    Character : CHAR;
    GoodCharacterSet : CharSet;


PROCEDURE GetCharacter(GoodSet : CharSet);
  BEGIN (*GetCharacter*)
      REPEAT    (*keep reading until character is in goodset*)
          InOut.Read(Character);
      UNTIL Character IN GoodSet;
  END GetCharacter;


BEGIN (*ProcDemo*)
  GoodCharacterSet := CharSet('a'..'z');
  GetCharacter(GoodCharacterSet);    (*call the procedure*)
  InOut.WriteString('The first character entered was ');
  InOut.Write(Character);   (*we're guaranteed this will be in a-z*)

  GoodCharacterSet := CharSet('A'..'C', '?');
  GetCharacter(GoodCharacterSet);    (*call the procedure*)
  InOut.WriteString('The second character entered was ');
  InOut.Write(Character);   (*this will be either A, B, C or ?*)
END ProcDemo.
```

where GoodCharacterSet is known as the actual parameter. When the procedure call statement is executed, the contents of the actual parameter list are substituted for the formal parameter list.

The first procedure call "passes" the character set 'a..z' to GetCharacter. The second call passes a set with the four characters 'A', 'B', 'C', and '?'. The formal parameter, GoodSet, assumes the value of these character sets and responds appropriately. This ability to pass whatever data is required to the procedure greatly improves the effectiveness of a procedure.

Note the following points:

- The formal parameter list consists of a sequence of identifiers and their associated types. The type must be in the form of an identifier and not a type description. In Listing 8.5,

  (GoodSet : CharSet)

is the formal parameter list. It is important to note that

(GoodSet : SET OF CHAR)

is not allowed even though CharSet's type is SET OF CHAR. This is because SET OF CHAR is a type description and not an identifier.

- When the formal parameter is a value parameter, the associated actual parameter must be an expression of the matching type (i.e., assignment compatible). Note that variables and constants are special forms of expression. Therefore, rather than writing

GetCharacter(GoodCharacterSet);

we could have used

GetCharacter(CharSet{ 'a'..'z' })

or other equivalent forms. This is in contrast to the variable parameter type that will be described next. When using a variable parameter, the actual parameter must be a variable.

- The formal value parameter is local to the procedure in which it belongs. This implies that the actual and formal parameters, in the case of value parameters, utilize separate memory locations. This precludes any interaction (side effect) between the corresponding formal and actual pairs.

- The actual and formal parameter lists must agree in number, order, and type, and they must be assignment compatible. We cannot have a formal parameter list of

(x : REAL; y : INTEGER);

and a corresponding actual list of

(IntegerVariable, RealVariable).

- When the procedure is called, the expression in the actual parameter list is evaluated and the result is assigned to the corresonding formal parameter.

Variable Parameters

As with value parameters, variable parameters have both formal and actual parameters. The variable parameter's formal parameter is preceded by the symbol VAR. For example, the formal parameter list

    (VAR Chr : CHAR; GoodSet : CharSet)

is made up of the variable parameter, Chr, and the value parameter, GoodSet.

As was mentioned, although the actual parameter associated with a value parameter is an expression (which includes a variable as a special case), the actual parameter for a variable parameter *must be* a variable. This means that

    ('A', 'a'..'z')

is not a legal actual parameter list for the formal parameter list

    (VAR Chr : CHAR; GoodSet : CharSet)

since 'A' is a character constant and not a variable. Instead, it must be written in a form similar to

    (Character, 'a'..'z')   (*Character is type CHAR*)

in order to be valid.

One of the chief reasons for having the variable parameter is its ability to pass values *to and from* the procedure. The value parameter can pass data to the procedure from the calling program, but data cannot be passed back from the procedure via the value parameters. When using variable parameters, the flow is two-way.

The formal parameter in a variable parameter uses the same memory space as its corresponding actual component. Therefore, when the formal parameter's value is changed within the procedure, the corresponding actual component is also changed. (They are in the same location in memory.) This is the major distinction between variable and value parameters.

Let's see how this can be used in the Listing 8.5 program. In the sample program, the character that is read by the procedure is returned to the calling program via the global parameter, Character. Since global variables should be avoided when possible, here is a perfect spot for a variable parameter.

This latest version of the program is shown in Listing 8.6. A key point to notice is that, for the first time, the main program and the procedure are isolated from one another except through the parameter list. All of GetCharacter's variables are declared within the scope of the procedure. Its sole impact on the outside world is through the variable parameter, Chr. This makes the program very secure and reliable.

The second procedure call has been changed since the last version in order to illustrate, by comparison with the first call, two different versions of

LISTING 8.6

```
MODULE ProcDemo;

IMPORT InOut;

TYPE
    CharSet = SET OF CHAR;

VAR
    GoodCharacterSet : CharSet;


PROCEDURE GetCharacter(VAR Chr : CHAR; GoodSet : CharSet);
  BEGIN (*GetCharacter*)
      REPEAT    (*keep reading until character is in goodset*)
          InOut.Read(Chr);
      UNTIL Chr IN GoodSet;
  END GetCharacter;

VAR
    Character : CHAR;

BEGIN (*ProcDemo*)
  GoodCharacterSet := CharSet{'a'..'z'};
  GetCharacter(Character, GoodCharacterSet);    (*call the procedure*)
  InOut.WriteString('The first character entered was ');
  InOut.Write(Character);  (*we're guaranteed this will be in a-z*)

  GetCharacter(Character, CharSet{'A'..'C', '?'}); (*call the procedure*)
  InOut.WriteString('The second character entered was ');
  InOut.Write(Character);  (*this will be either A, B, C or ?*)
END ProcDemo.
```

the actual parameter. In the first call, the parameter is a variable. In the second, it is a constant expression.

One additional minor change since the last version is the location of the Character declaration. It now immediately precedes the main block to emphasize that it is not used throughout the program (as it was when it was required for global purposes).

This completes our general discussion of parameters. We now turn to some special cases in which parameters provide exceptional flexibility.

Open-Array Parameters

Since the declaration of an array cannot contain a variable subscript range, we are forced to dimension arrays at the largest size that can be anticipated. The problem of fixed-array dimensions is compounded when we write procedures that have arrays in their formal parameter list. Since actual and formal parameter lists must be assignment compatible, this all implies that the dimension of the array in the formal parameter list must be fixed at the same size as the array in the procedure's actual parameter list. This is a difficult situation to live with if the procedures are intended as general purpose utility programs such as matrix arithmetic routines. Do we need a separate procedure for every different size of matrix? It would seem so.

Fortunately, the open-array parameter is available in Modula-2. Using this technique allows us to write the formal parameter list as

    (CharString : ARRAY OF CHAR)

instead of

    (CharString : BigArray),

where BigArray might have been declared as

    TYPE BigArray = ARRAY [0..250] OF CHAR.

Now, instead of being able to pass only arrays whose type is BigArray, we can pass any array of characters regardless of dimension. The general form of the open array parameter is

    ARRAY OF ArrayType

where ArrayType is any valid array base type.

The only requirement for the use of open-array parameters is that the base types of the actual and formal parameters must be the same. There is no constraint on the array dimension except that only a single dimension can be "open."

In the open-array formal parameter list, the formal parameter is treated as an array having a subscript range equal to the range of the corresponding actual parameter but with a lower subscript bound of zero. This means that if the actual parameter is an array whose subscript range is $[x..y]$, the corresponding formal parameter's subscript range is $[0..y-x]$. For example, if a procedure heading is

    PROCEDURE OpenArrayDemo(OpenChar : ARRAY OF CHAR);

and the procedure call is

OpenArrayDemo(CharacterArray);

and CharacterArray was declared as ARRAY [40..60] OF CHAR, the formal parameter OpenChar is a 21-element character array equivalent to OpenChar[0..20].

The Modula-2 standard function HIGH(ArrayVariable) can be used within the procedure to determine the upper bound of the open array. HIGH(OpenChar) would return a value of 20 for the current example.

Listing 8.7 shows a simple program segment, based on the above discussion, which illustrates the use of the open-array type in a procedure.

A special application of the open-array parameter involves the use of the base type WORD, which is available from a standard library module named System. If the formal parameter is

ARRAY OF WORD

then the actual parameter can be of any type, since a variable of type WORD is *any* variable that is a single-word long. Therefore, an ARRAY OF WORD describes a sequence of unspecified length composed of an unspecified (any) single word variable; i.e., ARRAY OF WORD can represent *anything*. Use of this feature requires the functions SIZE and TSIZE, which are also part of the SYSTEM module. More will be said about this in the Chapter 11 discussion on low-level functions.

This completes the discussion of procedures and their parameters. Syntax diagrams for procedures are presented in Figure A.58.

LISTING 8.7

```
PROCEDURE OpenArrayDemo(OpenChar : ARRAY OF CHAR);
VAR
   ArrayIndex : CARDINAL;
BEGIN (*OpenArrayDemo*)
   FOR ArrayIndex := 0 TO HIGH(OpenChar) DO
       InOut.Write(OpenChar[ArrayIndex]);
   END (*for*);
END OpenArrayDemo;


This procedure is called by a procedure call such as

    OpenArrayDemo(CharacterArray);

where a representative declaration for CharacterArray is

    VAR CharacterArray : ARRAY [40..60] OF CHAR;
```

8.1.4 Function Procedures

In this section, the second of the two types of procedure, the function procedure, is described. The normal procedure was exemplified in our sample program by the procedure GetCharacter. The final version of GetCharacter, in Listing 8.6, was

```
PROCEDURE GetCharacter(VAR Chr : CHAR; GoodSet : CharSet);
   BEGIN (*GetCharacter*)
      REPEAT (*keep reading until character is in goodset*)
         InOut.Read(Chr);
      UNTIL Chr IN GoodSet;
   END GetCharacter;
```

and the corresponding calling program and procedure call was

```
.....Program Statements.....
GetCharacter(Character, CharSet{'a'..'z'});
InOut.WriteString('The second character entered was ');
InOut.Write(Character);
```

In this version of the procedure, the result is returned to the calling program by means of the variable parameter, Chr. The earlier version returned its result using a global variable. The function procedure provides a third method for returning results. The function procedure version of GetCharacter is

```
PROCEDURE GoodCharacter(GoodSet : CharSet) : CHAR;
   VAR
      Chr : CHAR;
   BEGIN (*GoodCharacter*)
      REPEAT (*keep reading until character is in goodset*)
         InOut.Read(Chr);
      UNTIL Chr IN GoodSet;
      RETURN Chr;
   END GoodCharacter;
```

and the corresponding calling program and procedure call is

```
.....Program Statements.....
InOut.WriteString('The second character entered was ');
InOut.Write(GoodCharacter(CharSet{'a'..'z'}));
```

There are three main points to be made about the function procedure version of GetCharacter (which has been renamed GoodCharacter).

- Look at the calling program, and notice that the function procedure is used as a term in an expression. In other words, a function can be used wherever a variable of the same type is legal in an expression. Compare this with the call for GetCharacter. In one case we have

    InOut.Write(GoodCharacter(CharSet{ 'a'..'z' }));

    and in the other

    GetCharacter(Character, CharSet{ 'a'..'z' });

    This shows us that the function procedure specifies a result, whereas the normal procedure specifies an action. This is the major difference between the two procedure types. The function procedure call is referred to as a function designator. The parameter list for a function procedure call *must be present*, even if it is empty. This is another difference between normal and function procedures.
- The formal parameter list for GoodCharacter is followed by the procedure's type (: CHAR). This is consistent with the use of the function designator (as if it were a variable) inside of an expression. In this particular instance, the procedure returns a character (CHAR) variable.
- A new statement, the RETURN statement, is present within the block of the procedure. The syntax is the word RETURN followed by an expression, which is the result to be returned to the calling program. RETURN statements may appear in multiple locations in the same function procedure. The execution of the procedure stops immediately following the execution of a return statement, and the result is returned to the calling program. RETURN statements can also be used in normal procedures, but without the expression that follows RETURN in a function procedure.

There is a fourth point to be made regarding function procedures that is not apparent in the program example. That is, a structured type (e.g., an array) cannot be returned as the result of a function procedure. This is not to say that a structured type cannot be returned as a variable parameter in the parameter list. It cannot be returned just as the actual function result. The function procedure result is a single, simple value.

Another comment on programming style and readability: Notice that the name of the procedure was changed from GetCharacter to GoodCharacter when the procedure was changed to a function procedure. This was done to be consistent with the nature of the roles played by these two facilities. The statement InOut.Write(GoodCharacter(...)) is much more indicative of the actual situation than the statement InOut.Write(GetCharacter). Comparing these to English sentence structure, in the first case we have verb(noun) as opposed to verb(verb). The closer the program is to English, the easier it will be to read and understand. Self-documenting programs should be a goal.

As has been mentioned, the role of the regular procedure is to specify the performance of some action whereas the function procedure is used as an argument in an expression. The following table illustrates name pairs that are appropriate depending on the type of procedure:

Regular Procedure	←action result→	Function Procedure
GetTheCharacter	←verb noun→	GoodCharacter
AddTheNumbers		Total
ReadTheSystemClock		CurrentTime

8.1.5 Standard Procedures

A number of standard procedures are defined for Modula-2 and are available to all programs. In alphabetical order they are:

ABS(x)   Absolute value of x. The result type matches the argument type.

CAP(x)   Upper-case version of character x. No action is taken unless x is a lower-case letter. It returns CHAR value.

CHR(x)   Character whose ordinal value is x. The Volition Systems implementation specifies x to be a CARDINAL.

DEC(x)   Decrement x by 1 (default) or by n (any expression compatible with
DEC(x, n)   x). x can be an INTEGER, CARDINAL, CHAR, or any enumeration type (including subranges). If x is a CHAR or enumeration data type, then the result is the predecessor.

DISPOSE(x) Returns to storage the memory space occupied by the dynamic variable referenced by pointer type x. This procedure depends on the availability of the system module procedures ALLOCATE and DEALLOCATE.

EXCL(s, x) Deletes the element x from the set s. x is an expression which matches s. (See Chapter 6.)

FLOAT(x)   Converts the CARDINAL type x to REAL.

HALT   Stops the program.

HIGH(x)   Returns the upper subscript of the index of array x. (See Chapter 6.)

INC(x)   Increment (successor) version of DEC above. INC(x, n)

INCL(s, x)   Element addition version of EXCL above. (See Chapter 6.)

NEW(x)   Creates dynamic variable of the type bound to pointer type x. Memory address of dynamic element is assigned to x. This procedure depends on the availability of the system module procedures ALLOCATE and DEALLOCATE.

ODD(x)   BOOLEAN result which tests if x MOD 2 is equal to 0. Returns FALSE if x is even (i.e., x MOD 2 equals 0).

ORD(x)   Returns ordinal value (CARDINAL) of x (element of type T). Type T is INTEGER, CARDINAL, CHAR, or any enumeration type. (See Chapter 6.)

TRUNC(x)   Returns the integral portion (CARDINAL) of the REAL argument x.

VAL(T, x)   Returns the value of the element of type T which has an ordinal value of x. Type T is INTEGER, CARDINAL, CHAR, or any enumeration type. The following relationship is true if y is of type T, VAL(T, ORD(y)) = y. (See Chapter 6.)

8.1.6 Procedure Types

All of the simple (or scalar) data types of Modula-2—INTEGER, CARDINAL, REAL, BOOLEAN, CHAR, and BITSET—have been introduced. The structured types—enumeration, subrange, set, array, record, and pointer—have also been described. All of these represent data (objects) and not activities (actions). Modula-2 also provides a Procedure type, which is the subject of this section.

Procedure types make procedure variables possible. Newcomers to strongly typed languages such as Modula-2, Pascal, and Ada find types and type declarations of variables to be a totally new concept. But once the creation of variable types is understood, the notion of types and variables that represent procedures is just a logical extension of this concept, although the application of this feature may appear to be fairly abstract.

In order to bridge the conceptual gap, let's first describe a hypothetical problem to which procedure types and variables can be applied. Then we will go back and look at these new facilities more thoroughly.

Suppose a list of positive integer numbers have to be printed, and the user needs the option of writing the output in either decimal, hexadecimal, or octal format. The following procedure will work for decimal output:

```
PROCEDURE WriteNumbers(NumberList : ARRAY OF CARDINAL);
  VAR
    ArrayIndex : CARDINAL;
  BEGIN (*WriteNumbers*)
    FOR ArrayIndex := 0 TO HIGH(NumberList) DO
    InOut.WriteLn; (*new line for each number*)
    InOut.WriteCard(NumberList[ArrayIndex], 6);
    END (*for*);
  END WriteNumbers;
```

The same procedure, with WriteHex or WriteOct (see Chapter 5) substituted for WriteCard, will meet the requirement for hexadecimal or octal
output. This suggests one of two programming alternatives.

- Three separate procedures could be written: PrintDec, PrintHex, and
  PrintOct. They would differ only in one line of code. The calling program would have to have three separate procedure calls, depending on
  which of the three options was required. This alternative is not very
  elegant.
- The basic procedure shown above could be expanded to include three
  separate write statements, one for each case. A formal parameter,
  added to the parameter list for WriteNumbers, would be used to indicate which of the three cases to use. The only change required to the
  calling program is the inclusion of the proper actual parameter in the
  procedure call. The formal parameter could be of the type CHAR,
  with a 'D' indicating decimal, 'H' hex, and 'O' octal. WriteNumbers
  would use an IF or CASE control structure in order to select the
  proper output format statement.

The second of the two alternatives would normally represent the best
choice available to us. Not many other feasible alternatives exist in most languages. This is an example of a problem that procedure types and procedure
variables simplify. The basic dilemma is the fact that the procedure (Write-
Card *is* a procedure) in WriteNumbers

```
InOut.WriteCard(NumberList[ArrayIndex], 6);
```

accounts for only one of the three optional output formats that are required.
    If the problem were how to print one of several different results in a fixed
format (instead of how to print a fixed list of numbers in several different formats), we would not have to think twice about how to do it. The answer would

be to pass the result to be printed as a variable in the parameter list, *or* make it a global variable. In either of these cases, the common answer is to make the result to be printed a variable for the procedure to process.

The conceptual block to the solution of the current problem, if there is one, is that although we are used to the idea of substituting variables for results (data objects), the notion of a variable that is an action is foreign. The use of a procedure variable is the solution to this problem. The procedure variable is not a common feature in programming languages. Just as there can be many different types of arrays with different dimensions and subscript ranges, so there can be many different types of procedure variables. A type declaration for a procedure variable describes the number and data types of the procedure's formal parameters. If the procedure variable represents a function procedure, then the type description should include the data type of the result.

Just as an INTEGER's type description can appear after the colon in a variable declaration or after the equal sign in a type declaration, so can the type description of a procedure variable. For example

```
VAR P, Q : PROCEDURE(BOOLEAN);
```

declares two procedure variables of the same type. Both P and Q can only represent procedures that have one formal BOOLEAN parameter. The procedure type declaration describes the number and type of formal parameters that the procedure variable is to have. If the procedure is a function procedure, then the declaration also specifies the result type.

In the example problem, the procedure type declaration would be

```
TYPE
   WriteProcType = PROCEDURE(CARDINAL, CARDINAL);
```

since WriteCard, WriteHex, and WriteOct are all normal procedures with two cardinal value parameters. The corresponding variable declaration would be

```
VAR
   WriteProc : WriteProcType;
```

in which any procedure that has two cardinal value parameters can be assigned to WriteProc. For example, the procedure InOut.WriteCard is a procedure with two cardinal value parameters, and therefore

```
WriteProc := InOut.WriteCard;
```

is a valid assignment statement.

Procedure types and variables can be used in the same manner as any other variable or type. The assignment statement just illustrated is one such use. If we followed this assignment statement with

```
WriteProc(123, 6);
```

this would be equivalent to having written

```
InOut.WriteCard(123, 6);
```

and would result in the number 123 being written in a 6-space field.

Since procedure variables can be used like any other variable, this suggests using them as parameters to be passed to a procedure for the solution of our example problem. The program of Listing 8.8 illustrates the use of procedure types and variables for the solution of this problem.

In this program an array, ListOfNumbers (artificially created), is passed to the WriteNumbers procedure. A procedure variable, to which the desired output format procedure has been assigned, is also included as the second parameter in the procedure call. This use of procedure variables is especially powerful, and represents one of main results of this section.

The formal parameter list of WriteNumbers was changed from the previous example to include a value parameter of the procedure type that had been defined to be compatible with WriteCard, WriteHex, and WriteOct. Also, the previous output statement,

```
InOut.WriteCard(NumberList[ArrayIndex], 6);
```

was changed to

```
WriteVariableFormat(NumberList[ArrayIndex], 6);
```

to correspond to the procedure variable in the formal parameter list.

A number of earlier examples from this chapter have been brought together in Listing 8.8:

- WriteNumbers uses an open-array parameter and the HIGH(x) standard procedure.
- The final version of the character input procedure with error trapping, GoodCharacter, is used as the argument within a CASE statement. The combination of the CASE statement and GoodCharacter make

LISTING 8.8

```
MODULE ProcVarDemo;

IMPORT InOut;

TYPE
    WriteProcType = PROCEDURE(CARDINAL, CARDINAL);

PROCEDURE WriteNumbers(NumberList : ARRAY OF CARDINAL;
                       WriteVariableFormat : WriteProcType);
    VAR
        ArrayIndex : CARDINAL;
    BEGIN (*WriteNumbers*)
        FOR ArrayIndex := 0 TO HIGH(NumberList) DO
            InOut.WriteLn;  (*new line for each number*)
            WriteVariableFormat(NumberList[ArrayIndex], 6);
        END (*for*);
    END WriteNumbers;


TYPE
    CharSet = SET OF CHAR;

PROCEDURE GoodCharacter(GoodSet : CharSet) : CHAR;
    VAR
        Chr : CHAR;
    BEGIN (*GoodCharacter*)
        REPEAT    (*keep reading until character is in goodset*)
            InOut.Read(Chr);
        UNTIL CAP(Chr) IN GoodSet;
        RETURN CAP(Chr);
    END GoodCharacter;


VAR
    WriteProc : WriteProcType;
    ListOfNumbers : ARRAY [1..5] OF CARDINAL;

BEGIN (*ProcVarDemo*)
    ListOfNumbers[1] := 10;
    ListOfNumbers[2] := 20;
    ListOfNumbers[3] := 30;
    ListOfNumbers[4] := 40;
    ListOfNumbers[5] := 50;
    InOut.WriteString('D(ecimal, H(ex or O(ctal output? ');
    CASE GoodCharacter(CharSet{'D', 'H', 'O'}) OF
        'D' :  WriteProc := InOut.WriteCard;
        'H' :  WriteProc := InOut.WriteHex;
        'O' :  WriteProc := InOut.WriteOct;
    END (*case*);
    WriteNumbers(ListOfNumbers, WriteProc);
END ProcVarDemo.
```

an excellent general purpose menu selection routine for interactive user prompts and responses, as demonstrated here.

- One of the standard procedures of the previous section, CAP, is used within GoodCharacter to allow both lower- and upper-case letters to be accepted (without the need to add 'd', 'h', and, 'o' to the list of valid characters).

The syntax diagrams for procedure types are shown in Figure A.36. The procedure type declaration is straightforward. It begins with the word PROCEDURE, and is followed by a list of formal parameter types. If the procedure is a function procedure, then the result type is included in the declaration. The following are examples of valid procedure type declarations:

```
TYPE
    PT1 = PROCEDURE(CHAR) : BOOLEAN;
    PT2 = PROCEDURE(ARRAY OF INTEGER) : INTEGER;
    PT3 = PROCEDURE(CARDINAL, CARDINAL);
    PT4 = PROCEDURE(VAR CHAR);
```

A procedure variable of type T can be assigned any procedure whose formal parameters match T in number and type. Assume that the following variable and procedure declarations are made:

```
VAR
    V1 : PT1;
    V2 : PT2;
    V3 : PT3;
    V4 : PT4;

PROCEDURE LetterIsVowel (Letter: CHAR) : BOOLEAN;
    BEGIN...procedure body...End LetterIsVowel;

PROCEDURE AddNumbers(List : ARRAY OF INTEGER;
                     VAR Sum : INTEGER);
    BEGIN...procedure body...End AddNumbers;

PROCEDURE WriteCard(CardVar : CARDINAL; Field : CARDINAL);
    BEGIN...procedure body...END WriteCard;

PROCEDURE WriteLetter (Letter : CHAR);
    BEGIN...procedure body...END WriteLetter;

PROCEDURE ReadLetter(VAR Letter : CHAR);
    BEGIN...procedure body...END ReadLetter;
```

Once these variable and procedure declarations are made, we have the following legal and illegal assignments:

Legal	*Illegal*
V1 := LetterIsVowel;	V1 := WriteLetter; PT1 is a function procedure and WriteLetter is not.
V2 := There are none!	NO procedures match type PT2.
V3 := WriteCard;	V3 := AddNumbers; Formal parameter types do not match.
V4 := ReadLetter;	V4 := WriteLetter; Formal parameter mismatch; variable vs. value.

Notice that the assignments do not include the parameter list of the procedure. That is, the correct form is

```
V3 := WriteCard;
```

and not

```
V3 := WriteCard(FirstParameter, SecondParameter);.
```

In this context, the name of the procedure without its parameter list represents a constant that may be assigned to a procedure variable.

A standard type named PROC is provided in Modula-2. PROC corresponds to a procedure with no parameter list. The declaration

```
VAR
   ProcVar : PROC;
```

is equivalent to

```
TYPE
   PROC = PROCEDURE;
VAR
   ProcVar : PROC;
```

and any procedure with no formal parameter list may be assigned to the procedure variable ProcVar.

There are two restrictions imposed on the use of procedure types:

- Standard procedures (see previous section for a listing) cannot be assigned to a procedure variable.
- Procedures assigned to a procedure variable cannot be declared local to another procedure.

The effect of the first restriction can be negated by enclosing the standard procedure within another procedure. Consider the following simple example:

```
TYPE
   Demo = PROCEDURE(CARDINAL);
VAR
   VarProc : Demo;
BEGIN
   :
   :
   VarProc: = INC; (*INC is a standard procedure*)
   :
```

This example violates the rule that states that standard procedures (INC in this case) cannot be assigned to a procedure variable. However, the following accomplishes the same objective, and is legal:

```
TYPE
   Demo = PROCEDURE(CARDINAL) : CARDINAL; (*1st change*)
VAR
   VarProc : Demo;
(*2nd change is the addition of this "shell" procedure*)
PROCEDURE BreakTheRule(Number : CARDINAL) : CARDINAL;
   BEGIN
      RETURN INC(Number);
   END BreakTheRule;

BEGIN
   :
   :
   VarProc: = BreakTheRule;
   :
```

8.2 MODULES

After seven plus chapters, we finally get to the feature of Modula-2 that gave the language its name—the module. Modules play an important role in the ability of Modula-2 to support the development of large, complex programs. At the start of this chapter, a number of difficulties related to the production of large programs were described. The following three problem areas were emphasized:

- Program size
- Level of detail
- Adverse side effects on program variables by actions in various parts of the program

Section 8.1 on procedures demonstrated at least partial solutions to these and related problems.

Program Size

An answer to the size problem was to divide the program into small, manageable pieces. Procedures certainly allow the program to be broken into small pieces. If each of these pieces performs a small and easily verifiable (manageable) subtask of the overall programming task, the programmer has an intellectually easier job to perform than is the case in dealing with the entire program en masse.

However, this is not the complete answer to the problem. Those pieces (procedures) are still contained within the body of the program, thus contributing to the overall program size. Since the procedure remains integral to the program, this also makes the partitioning of a programming assignment to several members of a team difficult. Furthermore, every change to any procedure requires both that procedure and every other part of the program to be recompiled. In general, procedures only help a little in solving problems related to efficiency of development and the reduction of requirements for compilation time, execution time, and memory/storage requirements.

Modules contribute to the solution of these remaining program size–related problems. Module features allow programs to be developed by programming teams with ease and safety. Modules allow program components to be kept in libraries and not duplicated in every program that uses these components. The library feature contributes significantly to the reduction of programming time and reduces the requirements for computer resources.

Detail

In the discussion on how to remove unnecessary detail that detracts from the understanding and reliability of programs, the concept of data abstraction was mentioned. Again, procedures help. The details of getting a valid character from the user's keyboard can be ignored through the use of the procedure GetCharacter that was described earlier in this chapter. Instead of the details, we use the procedure call GetCharacter(NewChar) as an abstraction. This definitely improves understanding and reliability. Unfortunately, we are still left with essentially the same residual problems that were discussed under the topic of program size.

Side Effects

The danger of adverse side effects is definitely reduced through the use of procedures, but it is not eliminated. Variables can be made local to a procedure, and therefore can be isolated from the effects of possible change by actions outside of the procedure, which represent the bounds of its scope.

However, any variable from the surrounding procedure can have its value altered by the nested procedure. We cannot prevent a procedure from "seeing" things that are in its surrounding outside environment. Furthermore, we saw that there were instances where these global variables, a major contributer to side effects, could not be eliminated even through the use of procedures.

Modules provide the capability to eliminate almost all factors that lead to side effects. Modules support the programming concept of information hiding, which is one step beyond data abstraction. Abstraction allows the programmer to ignore details. Hiding prevents the programmer, and his programs, from even knowing what the details are.

Modules can be built with the programming equivalent of a one-way mirror, in which you can see in but not out (or out, but not in). In contrast to the procedure, the module "sees" nothing external to itself unless explicitly stated.

The problem with procedures that necessitated the continued use of global variables arose from the fact that the life of a procedure's local variables was tied to the life of the procedure. The local variable, and its value, ceased to exist when its associated procedure terminated. In contrast, variables that are local to a module have an existence that is separate from the existence (execution) of the module. The existence of the module's local variables is tied to the existence of the environment that encloses the module. The environment may be a program, procedure, or another module.

In the remainder of this chapter, the details of modules and examples of their use will be presented. The module, and its related capabilities, together with the low-level machine access facilities to be covered in Chapter 11, are what really separates Modula-2 from its predecessor Pascal. The majority of the other differences between the languages are syntactical.

8.2.1 Module Concepts and Rules

Modules

There are three categories of modules:

- Program Modules. Every Modula-2 program is a program module.
- Library Modules, e.g., InOut, introduced in Chapter 5.
- Local Modules, which are nested within program or library modules.

In this section, we will concentrate on the program module. We will also describe those elements of syntax and semantics that are common to all three categories of modules. To get started, the shell of the simplest program module is depicted in Listing 8.9. It is so simple that it does nothing.

LISTING 8.9

```
MODULE ModuleName;          (*module heading*)

END ModuleName.             (*end of block & module termination*)
```

There are three main parts to the module in Listing 8.9:

- the module heading,
- the module block or body, and
- the module termination.

The program module begins with a heading, which is MODULE followed by the module identifier and a semicolon. The module block, in this example, is END. (BEGIN is not required if there are no statement sequences.) The block is followed by the same module name that appeared in the module heading and is terminated by a period. This module will compile without error.

LISTING 8.10

```
MODULE ModuleName;              (*module heading*)

CONST                          (*start of declarations*)
      AsciiBell = 7C;
TYPE
      TextLineType = ARRAY [0..80] OF CHAR;
VAR
      TextLine : TextLineType;

PROCEDURE WriteLine(line : TextLineType);
    END WriteLine;

MODULE LocalModule;
    END LocalModule;           (*end of declarations*)

END ModuleName.                (*end of block & module termination*)
```

Moving one step up in complexity, the program block of Listing 8.9 is expanded to include each of the allowable Modula-2 declarations. This is shown in Listing 8.10.

In terms of doing anything useful, the program in Listing 8.10 is no better than the one in Listing 8.9, but it is getting there. The module block now contains declarations. Notice that in addition to the CONST, TYPE, VAR, and PROCEDURE declarations that should be familiar by now, there is a MODULE declaration. This is a local module and will be discussed in a later section. It is included here for completeness. This program module will also compile without error. Remember that, unlike Pascal, there is no specific order in which the Modula-2 declarations must appear.

There are only three elements of a module not shown in Listing 8.10. They are

- the statement sequences that would normally appear in the body of the modules and procedures if we wanted any action to be taken.
- the (optional) module priority, which causes the program module heading to be rewritten as

MODULE ModuleName[PriorityConstantExpression];

where the [expr] is a constant expression, e.g., 10.
- the program module's "import" list (if any).

Of these three items, only the priority and import topics require additional explanation. Statement sequences have been the essence of the examples throughout the book to this point and require no further explanation. The subject of module priorities will be covered in Chapter 11 with low-level facilities. Priorities can be used with program and local modules, but not with library modules.

Imports and Exports

Program module examples with import lists have appeared earlier in the book. In Chapter 5, where basic input/output capabilities were introduced, the import list IMPORT InOut; was used with a request to trust us until Chapter 8. Well, here we are.

First of all, what is an import list? An import list is the mechanism by which a module can access (import) elements from other modules. The items that can be imported from other modules are constants, types, variables, and procedures. All three categories of modules—i.e., program, library, and local—are capable of importing.

Why would a module need to import elements from other modules? Recall that a procedure's rules for visibility of variables led to potential problems with side effects. The difficulty that we encountered with procedures was that they "saw" everything that was visible in the scope of the surrounding program environment, and there was no way to block out this view. Anything that a procedure sees it can alter, thus leading to potential adverse side effects.

By means of contrast, modules cannot see anything outside of the module unless they explicitly *import* it. Therefore, if a module requires access to elements of another module, it must import them. When one module imports something from another module, the importing module is said to be the "client" of the exporting module.

Before an item from one module can be imported by another module, the item to be imported must appear on the first module's *export* list. An export list contains the identification of the constants, types, variables, and procedures that are available for access by other modules. Program modules can import only. Library and local modules can export and import. More will be said about exports when library modules are described in the next section.

Imports are accomplished in one of two ways. These methods are illustrated in the following two examples:

1. FROM InOut IMPORT
   EOL,
   ReadInt,
   WriteInt;

2. IMPORT InOut;

In the first case, InOut—the source of the imported items—follows the word FROM. Following IMPORT is an explicit listing of the identifiers from InOut's export items that are to be imported. As a rule, only those items which are needed should be imported.

In the second case, the module's name, InOut, is imported. In this case every identifier on InOut's export list is implicitly imported. The InOut exports as as follows (see Chapter 5):

Done, EOL, termCH,
CloseInput, CloseOutput, OpenInput, OpenOutput,
Read, ReadCard, ReadInt, ReadString,
Write, WriteCard, WriteHex, WriteInt, WriteLn, WriteOct,
WriteString.

When the second import option is used, the identifier name must be qualified in a manner analogous to the qualification of record field identifiers (see Chapter 7). We, therefore, cannot just write EOL. InOut.EOL must be written instead. EOL alone is written when the first (FROM) option is used.

When the exporting module's name is not visible to the importing module, the qualified identifier name cannot be used. For example, if the import was

FROM InOut IMPORT Done;

then

IF Done...

is legal, and

IF InOut.Done...

is not legal because the module name, InOut, is unknown to the importing module. Why? Because the module name was not imported. Does this mean that we can import the module name along with the identifiers needed from the export list? No, because the module's name is not part of the export list and therefore cannot be imported. So we see that with imports from a library module, it is either one of the import conventions (and its associated identifier-naming convention) or the other. This is not the case with local modules, as we shall see.

One last note on export/import identifier names. What happens if two (or more) modules export an identifier with an identical name. In Chapter 5, we observed that InOut and RealInOut did precisely this. They both export an identifier, Done. How do we resolve the conflicts that will arise if a module imports both Dones? What we cannot do is

```
FROM InOut IMPORT Done;
FROM RealInOut IMPORT Done;
```

The second occurrence of Done causes a compile error. The compiler flags the variable as already existing. What must be done is either

```
FROM InOut IMPORT Done;
IMPORT RealInOut;
```

or

```
IMPORT InOut;
FROM RealInOut IMPORT Done;
```

or

```
IMPORT InOut;
IMPORT RealInOut;
```

which allows (forces) one or the other (or both) of the Dones to be qualified.

In Chapter 5, all of the example programs used IMPORT InOut. That is why every reference to InOut's elements in that chapter were qualified with InOut. Other chapters used the FROM InOut IMPORT . . . form, and did not qualify references to InOut procedures.

The discussion of imports and exports allows us to complete our picture of the program module that began in Listing 8.9. Listing 8.11 depicts a complete program module that contains one each of all program module elements (except the priority). Notice that there is no export list since this is not allowed in a program module.

The program of Listing 8.11 is intentionally oversimplified. Its purpose is to lay out in a clear, uncluttered fashion each of the allowable parts of a program module. There are only minor differences in the syntax of the three categories of modules. The larger differences are in how they are used. Between this program module and the module syntax diagrams shown in Figures A.65 to A.71, every aspect of the rules pertaining to modules of every category is covered.

LISTING 8.11

```
MODULE ModuleName;              (*module heading*)

FROM InOut IMPORT
      Write,
      WriteString;

CONST                          (*start of declarations*)
      AsciiBell = 7C;
TYPE
      TextLineType = ARRAY [0..80] OF CHAR;
VAR
      TextLine : TextLineType;

PROCEDURE WriteLine(line : TextLineType);
    BEGIN                      (*start of procedure body*)
        WriteString(line);
        Write(AsciiBell);
    END WriteLine;

MODULE LocalModule;
    END LocalModule;           (*end of declarations*)

    BEGIN                      (*beginning of module body*)
    TextLine := 'This is a sample program module';
    WriteLine(TextLine);
    END ModuleName.            (*end of block & module termination*)
```

Module Hierarchies

All three categories of modules can import elements from other modules. When an element is imported, it becomes a part of the importing program. Objects imported from library modules are linked to the importing program when the program is loaded into memory at execution time.

What we see developing is a hierarchy of modules, many or most of which may be transparent to the programmer doing the importing. For example, in the Volition System's implementation of Modula-2, the module RealInOut imports elements of InOut (and Reals). InOut, in turn, depends on two other modules—Conversions and Texts. Texts is dependent on Conversions, Files, Storage, and Program. Files requires the modules Storage and Program. Finally the module Storage depends on the module Program, and Program imports from Storage. (Sounds a little like passages from the Old Testament.)

This hierarchy of modules means that even if you have a very short import list, you may have imported a significant number of modules. For example, the simple import

FROM ReaIInOut IMPORT ReadReal;

causes every element of every module listed in the preceding paragraph to be loaded into our program. There is not anything inherently wrong with this as long as we are aware of what is happening, the possible implications, and the alternatives. Being aware of what is happening with regard to the module hierarchy depends on the documentation for your implementation as well as the hierarchy of modules that you have created yourself.

The higher level modules in the hierarchy offer convenience at the expense of computer resources. The possible implications are slower performance and increased memory requirements for the program at execution time.

The alternative is to enter further down in the hierarchy by importing lower level routines, and to perform some of the detailed functions yourself. Notice the phrase just used—"detailed functions." In the beginning of this section on modules, we observed that modules played a significant role in reducing the amount of detail needed in a program through data abstraction. We see that by building a module hierarchy, we can control the levels of abstraction (and thus detail). Each level of the hierarchy corresponds to a different level of detail and abstraction.

The next section introduces library modules. The library modules are the basic building blocks of Modula-2. They permit the advantages that we have attributed to modules throughout this section.

8.2.2 Library Modules

Separate Compilation

A major feature of library modules, and Modula-2, is the capability of storing separately compiled routines in library modules that can be accessed by program modules at execution time. Commonly used procedures and functions can be prepared and compiled one time. Thereafter, these routines can be used by any program module without the need for additional programming or compilation. This is a powerful capability and contributes to both the efficiency of the program development process and the reliability of the resulting code.

In the development of a Modula-2 program that utilizes library module elements, the library module comes into play at two different times.

- When a client program of the library routines is compiled, the compiler needs information related to the library routine's exported elements. The information that is required is neither the object nor source code of the library routines. The information that is needed by the compiler is the precompiled declarations for the exported items. When the client program is compiled, the export declarations are included in the client program just as if the client (programmer) had written them.

- When the client program is executed, the precompiled object code from the library module is linked to the object code of the client program. The imported code is a true part of the client program at execution. This is just as if the programmer had written this code as an integral part of the importing program.

Something *important* is implied in this description of the relationship between library modules and the programs that import routines from these libraries. Notice that we said that compilation of the client program *did not* require access to the library module's source or object code. Only the precompiled code for the export declarations are required. Therefore, the client program is totally decoupled and independent of the implementation details of the library routines.

This decoupling of library routines from importing programs means that the implementation details can be changed at will with absolutely no effect on the clients. This assumes that the library implementation provided the correct results to begin with, and subsequent changes are for purposes of efficiency or other good reason. This frees client programs from the necessity of changes and/or recompilation every time that the implementation of an imported library routine is changed.

Changes in the library module's declarations for exported items, however, will necessitate corresponding changes in every program using that module. At a minimum, the importing programs will require recompilation. In fact, a proper implementation of the language will enforce this by checking to ensure that all three pieces of the total program, i.e.,

- importing program,
- library module export object declarations, and
- library module procedure implementation code,

correspond with one another, i.e., all are the same version. More on this later.

This discussion leads to the topics of the next two sections—definition modules and implementation modules. Library modules, as it turns out, actually are made up of two parts. The first is the definition module. This is where the export list and export object identifiers are defined and declared.

The compiled definition module is what a client program must have available when it is being compiled. The second half of a library module is called the implementation module. The actual program code that implements the exported procedures and functions is contained in this module.

Definition Modules

As was described in the previous section, Modula-2 provides for the separate compilation of library modules. Furthermore, the method by which this separate compilation is accomplished results in a complete independence of a program that imports library routines from the implementation *details* of the routines. (Here is data abstraction and the hiding of details again.)

The mechanism that makes this decoupling of client and library possible is the fact that each library module is made up of two parts, a definition module and a implementation module. The definition module acts as a bridge between the client program and the library objects (i.e., procedures, constants, types, and variables). The definition module is made up of the list of exported objects and the declarations for these objects. The syntax diagram for a definition module is given in Figure A.69. A comparison of this figure with the syntax for program modules (Figure A.71) indicates the following differences between the definition module and the program module:

- The word DEFINITION precedes the definition module heading.
- A definition module cannot have a priority.
- A definition module can have export as well as import lists.
- The definition module has no statement sequence body.
- The definition module declarations are different in three ways:
  — Procedure declarations consist of the heading only.
  — Module declarations are not allowed.
  — Type declarations may consist of the type identifier only and not type descriptions.

More will be said regarding the specifics of the definition module syntax. To aid in this description, Listing 8.12 provides an example of a definition module. This example will be followed by the matching implementation module, and finally by a program module which utilizes its library routines.

Let's start by noting which of the allowable elements of a definition module are absent in Listing 8.12. First, there is no import list. For purposes of

LISTING 8.12

```
DEFINITION MODULE DefinitionDemo;

EXPORT QUALIFIED
        ReadCard, ReadString;

PROCEDURE ReadCard(VAR CardVar : CARDINAL) : BOOLEAN;
(*Returns cardinal number read from standard input;
  boolean value is false if no number was entered*)

PROCEDURE ReadString(VAR StringVar : ARRAY OF CHAR; VAR term : CHAR);
(*Returns string read from terminal; terminated by any blank or any
  control character, or when more than 80 characters are entered;
  parameter "term" is set to the value of the terminating character*)

END DefinitionDemo.
```

minimizing interdependencies among programs, and thus improving program reliability, the definition module should import only those objects that it needs. In our example, the definition module does not need access to the elements of any other module. This is not an unusual situation. Secondly, the declaration section does not include any constants, types, or variables—only procedures. This may not be very unusual if the primary purpose of the module is to perform functions as opposed to exporting data. Normally, however, some of these other objects will appear.

The elements of a definition module that *do* appear in the example of Listing 8.12 constitute the essential parts of any useful definition module—the export list and declarations. If the export list, which is optional, is missing, then the library serves no useful purpose. The purpose of the module is to provide access to objects from a library. Nothing can be accessed if it does not appear on an export list. A point to be noticed about export lists (see the syntax diagram of Figure A.65 and A.67) is that there can only be *one* export list in each module. This is in contrast to import lists, which can be as numerous as desired.

The declaration section of the definition module must, at a minimum, include a declaration for each object cited in the export list. If an exported identifier does not appear in a declaration, an error will result during the compilation of the definition module. No error results if the declaration includes elements that do not appear in the export list.

In the example of Listing 8.12, the exported items are ReadCard and ReadString. The definition module declaration shows ReadCard and ReadString to be procedures. ReadCard is a function procedure, and ReadString is a normal procedure.

The procedure headings, together with the associated comments, tell the user everything that is needed in order to use these two procedures in an importing program. In fact, in a normal system implementation, the definition module listings and documentation are all that is available to the user writing a client program. The details (there's that word again) belong to the developer and are not needed by the programmer of the client program.

A comparison of the export list syntax in Figure A.67 shows that the word QUALIFIED, which is used in our example, is optional. However, it is optional only in a local module. It *must* appear in the export list of a definition module.

The use of QUALIFIED provides a way to handle identifier name conflicts when more than one module exports an object with the same name. This conflict is possible with library modules that are developed by programmers who have no way of knowing what identifiers are likely to be used in other programmer's modules. Because of the likelihood of identifier clashes when using library modules, QUALIFIED exports are mandatory in a definition module.

If a module uses qualified exports, then any module that imports these qualified objects must use qualified identifiers when referring to them. That is, if we have

```
DEFINITION MODULE Q;
EXPORT QUALIFIED a, b, c;
:
:
```

and another module, Importer, which needs to access a, b, or c, then Importer must either use the input format

```
MODULE Importer;
IMPORT Q;
:
```

and refer to the imported objects as Q.a, Q.b, and Q.c, or else Importer must qualify the import by using the import list syntax

```
MODULE Importer;
FROM Q IMPORT a, b, c;
:
```

In this latter example, reference to simply a, b, and c is legal because they have been qualified by FROM. Note, however, that if a second module, P, also exported an item with the same name as one of Q's objects (b, for example) we could not write

```
MODULE Importer;
FROM Q IMPORT a, b, c;
FROM P IMPORT b;
    :
```

As was described in the first section on modules, in this latter situation either one or both of the import statements must import the module's name and not the list of identifiers.

Remember, library modules must use qualified exports. The reason is to avoid name clashes. Similarly, modules that import objects from library modules must use qualifying identifiers. The qualification can be either by means of the FROM import format or by use of the exporting module's name as a prefix in each reference in the client program.

There is one remaining unique feature of definition modules to be addressed. When we listed the differences between definition modules and program modules at the start of this section, it was noted that the definition module type declaration could consist of the type's name only, not its description. Normally, the type declaration will be in the normal declaration syntax that has been encountered thus far. That is,

```
TYPE
   TextType = ARRAY [0..80] OF CHAR;
   WeekEnd = (Sat, Sun);
   Date = RECORD
            Day : [1..31];
            Month : [1..12];
            Year : [1900..2000];
         END;
```

When types are declared in this way, the elements of the enumeration and the record fields (the details of structured types in general) are exported when types such as WeekEnd and Date are imported. As an example, the field Month, in the Date record, can be accessed and modified directly by an importing program. This is usually what is desired or required, but not always. For those cases in which it is undesirable to allow access to these details, the second form of the type declaration, which is unique to definition modules, can be used. That is, we could have

```
TYPE
  TransparentType = (One, Two, Three);
  OpaqueType;
```

where the details of OpaqueType's declaration are hidden from the user of this module, but the enumeration constants One, Two, and Three of TransparentType are visible. The details of the OpaqueType declaration are contained in the corresponding implementation module.

The practical use of this declaration syntax is limited to pointer types, although other limited (single word) uses are possible. Since pointers can be bound to virtually any data of any type, this is not a significant restriction. These special types are referred to as opaque or private.

This data type is used when it is desirable to restrict the client program from doing anything else with the data except declarations and assignments. Presumably, the library module that exports opaque data types also exports procedures that perform operations on the data.

The case of opaque data types with which most programmers are familiar is the FILE type, similar to the one that exists in Pascal. Together with FILE, the user is given procedures such as Close(FILE), Open(FILE, FileName), EOF(FILE), Seek(FILE, BlockNumber), and other file operations. In this case, we do not (and need not) know the details of FILE's declaration. In Modula-2 the details would be contained in the file operation library module's implementation section. Only the data type name, FILE, and the file operation procedures would be accessible to client programs.

Implementation Modules

The discussion of implementation modules is greatly simplified by the fact that program and definition modules have already been described. There is little, if anything, new in implementation modules.

It should be obvious that an implementation module is one half of an overall library module pair. It is identified as such in its declaration by using the same module identifier as the corresponding definition module, and the word MODULE is preceded by IMPLEMENTATION. Except for the word IMPLEMENTATION, the syntax for an implementation module is identical to the program module syntax that was covered earlier.

Every procedure heading that is in the definition module must appear in the implementation module. This includes repetition of the formal parameter list *exactly* as it appears in the definition module. This will be a change to Pascal programmers who have dealt with forward declarations, or who are familiar with the difference in procedure headings between the interface and implementation sections of units in some Pascal extensions. Conversely, *none* of the other definition module declarations are allowed to be repeated in the implementation module.

An important point regarding the relationships between the two halves of the library module is that the implementation module cannot be compiled unless a compiled version of the definition module exists. Now that the definition module has been described, the reason for this should be clear.

The reason is that the compilation process includes the definition module declarations in the implementation module. This is the first step in the compile operation. If declarations other than procedure declarations are repeated, the compiler will report an identifier name conflict and stop. The same is true for client programs. They must not repeat definition module declarations.

The implementation half of the library module, which was presented in Listing 8.12, is shown in Listing 8.13. The module builds on the program examples that are presented and described in Chapter 5. These earlier examples suggested alternative formulations for some of the InOut module's procedures. In the current example, the proposed alternatives for InOut.ReadString and InOut.ReadCard are used to build a new input/output library for these two procedures.

Refer to Chapter 5 for details on these procedures. Notice that ReadCard calls ReadString to read the data. ReadCard simply does the conversion from character string to CARDINAL format. Note that the conversion will fail if the input string does not represent a valid number in the range of CARDINAL numbers.

The solution of this range validity problem with ReadCard was left as an exercise in Chapter 5. There is a point to be made. If we did not realize that there was a problem with the implementation of ReadCard until after module DefinitionDemo had found its way into our collection of library routines, things are not as bad as they might be (although this is a terrible conversion routine). Once ReadCard is fixed, all that must be done is to recompile the implementation module—and *that's it.* Nothing else needs to be changed, and nothing else changes except the results, which are now correct. Try it.

The module ASCII is from the Volition Systems implementation and makes all of the ASCII control characters available. In this case, the CHAR constant bs (backspace) is imported for use in ReadString.

If the word IMPLEMENTATION were removed from the heading, this module could be compiled as a program module. The fact that the module body is empty causes a practical problem, but not a syntax problem. This illustrates that this implementation module, in fact, differs from the syntax of a program module only in the heading. (This implementation module could not

LISTING 8.13

```
IMPLEMENTATION MODULE DefinitionDemo;

FROM ASCII IMPORT bs;
FROM InOut IMPORT Read, Write;

PROCEDURE ReadString(VAR StringVar : ARRAY OF CHAR; VAR term : CHAR);
    CONST
        MaxString = 80;
    VAR
        Chr : CHAR;
        i : CARDINAL;

    BEGIN (*ReadString*)
        REPEAT                    (*suppress leading blanks*)
            Read(Chr);
        UNTIL Chr # ' ';

        i := 0;
        WHILE ((ORD(Chr) > ORD(' ')) OR (Chr = bs)) &
                                        (i <= MaxString) DO
            IF Chr # bs THEN
                StringVar[i] := Chr;
                INC(i);
            ELSIF i # 0 THEN
                DEC(i);
                Write(' ');
                Write(bs);
            END (*if*);
            Read(Chr);
        END (*while*);

       term := Chr;        (*set termCH*)
       IF i < MaxString THEN
            StringVar[i] := 0C;           (*null goes at end of string*)
       END;
    END ReadString;


PROCEDURE ReadCard(VAR CardVar : CARDINAL) : BOOLEAN;
    VAR
        Str : ARRAY [0..10] OF CHAR;
        i : CARDINAL;
        termch : CHAR;
    BEGIN (*ReadCard*)
        ReadString(Str, termch);
        CardVar := 0;
        i := 0;
        WHILE Str[i] # 0C DO  (*Null char. terminates string*)
            CardVar := 10 * CardVar + ORD(Str[i]) - ORD('0');
            INC(i);
        END (*while*);
        RETURN Str[0] # 0C;
    END ReadCard;

END DefinitionDemo.
```

be compiled in this manner if its definition module included declarations of CONST, TYPE, or VAR used by the implementation module.)

What about the module body? The function of the main body of the program module is fairly obvious. No body, no useful functions can be performed. The body of the definition module is equally clear—there is none. But how about the implementation module? Listing 8.13 shows that the example has no body (and the module does work properly). When and why are bodies used in a library implementation module?

The body of a module is executed when the program element (another module or procedure) that serves as its outside environment comes into existence. The module's variables come to life at the same time. Recall earlier discussions regarding the difference between modules and procedures. In terms of a module variable's existence, it might just as well belong to the outside environment. When the module's enclosing scope exists, the module's variables exist. Therefore, a typical and useful function for the body of a module is to initialize variables that are local to the module and its procedures, and that are required to exist even when none of the elements (procedures) of the module proper are active.

The word processor program described in Chapter 12 uses the output formatter module body to initialize output page format default values such as left and right margins, page length, and justification options. The output formatter module's surrounding environment is the word processing program, so these variables are set when the overall word processing program is executed. These variables exist for the life of the program even though the formatter is not always in use. Furthermore, if the option to change some of these values during the execution of the program is taken, the new values are retained even when the formatter use is ended. This is accomplished without the necessity of making these format parameter variables global to the overall word processor program. If more than one module shares the same outside environment, the enclosed modules' bodies are executed in the order of their appearance.

To wrap up the discussion of library modules, a program module which uses the example library module is presented in Listing 8.14. The following observations serve to point out either new facts or to reinforce previous examples:

- The library module ASCII, declared in the program module, has already been declared in DefinitionDemo's implementation part. However, this is not a problem for several reasons. First, there is no chance of variable name clash since the program module cannot "see" this part of the implementation module. Second, the elements of ASCII have been qualified on input (as opposed to importing the module

LISTING 8.14

```
MODULE LibDemo;

FROM ASCII IMPORT  cr;
FROM DefinitionDemo IMPORT ReadCard, ReadString;
IMPORT InOut;

VAR
    String : ARRAY [0..80] OF CHAR;
    termCH : CHAR;
    Card : CARDINAL;

BEGIN (*LibDemo*)
    InOut.WriteString('Enter string: ');
    ReadString(String, termCH);  (*InOut has ReadString & termCh also*)
    InOut.WriteLn  ;InOut.WriteString(String);  InOut.WriteLn;
    InOut.WriteString('String terminator was ');
    IF termCH # cr THEN
        InOut.WriteString('not ');
    END (*if*);
    InOut.WriteString('a carriage return');  InOut.WriteLn;

    InOut.WriteString('Enter cardinal number: ');
    IF ReadCard(Card) THEN
        InOut.WriteCard(Card, 6);
    ELSE
        InOut.WriteString('No number was entered');
    END (*if*);
END LibDemo.
```

name which brings the entire export list down on us). Each element imported in the two modules is different (bs and cr).

- The language and system implementation should be smart enough to know if the same library element was needed in two separate places, and not to load multiple copies of the same object. This is particularly true for large objects, or objects that are used in many places (input/output for example). The Volition System works in this preferred fashion. For example, if the implementation module required the same library module input procedure that the main program used, the system would detect this fact and load only one copy.

- DefinitionDemo and InOut both export objects named ReadString and ReadCard. The use of qualified identifiers in the client program resolves any potential conflicts.

8.2.3 Local Modules

Identifier Visibility Revisited

This section considers the last of the three different types of modules, the local module. We have discussed the issues related to visibility of identifiers several times already. It has been noted that modules offer advantages over procedures in controlling the visibility of program element identifiers.

The module's advantage is due to the fact that the existence of a module and its local elements is tied to the existence of the module's surrounding environment. Therefore if a module were nested within another module, such as the program module, its variables would exist for the life of the program.

The separation of the variable's existence from the existence of its scope is important in the case of procedures that depend on the value of a variable to be saved between several calls/terminations of the procedure. If the procedure is made local to the nested module and the variable is declared outside any of the procedures in the nested module, the value of the variable is saved even after the procedure terminates. The variable's continued existence is due to the fact that it belongs to the nested module. Otherwise, a global variable in the client program would be required. Repeated instances of this problem in a large program lead to the large global parameter sections in programs with their attendant potential for errors.

The reason for the existence of local modules is to deal with the identifier visibility problem within either program or library modules. The local module is simply a module that is nested within another module or within a procedure. The module can control visibility both into and out of the module. Outside items must be imported by the module before they can be seen inside the module. Similarly, inside objects must be exported before they can be seen outside of the module. Although procedures can perform the latter control function, they cannot keep out the external influences nor preserve data between executions of a procedure.

The program in Listing 8.15 serves to illustrate the effects of the module scope rules. In this example there is a program module, VisibilityTest, and three local modules, A, B, and C, are nested within it. The local module B is further nested within local module A. Additional nesting is possible, including procedures within local modules, and local modules within procedures to any level. Each local module has two local variables. The variable identifier z is used in each module, thus leading to potential name conflicts.

Recall from the discussion of export lists in the definition module section that QUALIFIED exports were mandatory for definition modules but were optional for local modules. The local module A uses the unqualified export

LISTING 8.15

```
MODULE VisibilityTest;

MODULE A;
    EXPORT a, z, B;
    VAR a, z : CARDINAL;
    MODULE B;
        EXPORT QUALIFIED b, z;
        VAR b, z : CHAR;
        END B;                (*b & local z visible in B*)
    END A;                    (*a, local z, B.b & B.z visible in A*)

MODULE C;
    EXPORT QUALIFIED c, z;
    VAR c, z : BOOLEAN;
    END C;                    (*c & local z visible in C*)

BEGIN (*VisibilityTest*)

    (*Routine for assigning values to variables goes here*)

    IF C.c THEN A.a := z      (*all variables are visible here*)
    ELSIF C.z THEN B.b := B.z
    ELSE END (*if*);
END VisibilityTest.
```

form to export both of its variables. (Ignore the B in the export list for the time being. Imagine that only a and z appeared in A's export list.)

At this point, the use of the optional, unqualified form is no longer available for module C if it wishes to export z also. Similarly, it was never an option for module B if B wanted to export its version of z. Both B and C must use qualified exports.

Let's look closer at module B since it is nested within A and wants to export both of its variables. It does this in the same manner as C, i.e., in a qualified export. So far, so good, but now there is a question to be answered. What is the range of visibility of B's variables? B can see them since they are local to B. A can also see them since an exported object is automatically visible in its surrounding scope, and module A is the surrounding scope of B.

Are module B's variables visible to the main program module? No! Remember, nothing from a module is visible outside the module unless it is exported, and B's variables have not been exported by A. (This is why we said to ignore the B in A's export list.) Notice that B's variables are exported from A by exporting B's module name. This is the only available method for making B's variables accessible to the main program module. This latter example demonstrates that before an object from a module at a low level of a group of nested modules can be seen outside of the nesting, it must be exported through *every level* of the nested modules.

The discussion thus far has focused on the ability of variables in a module to be seen outside the module. How about looking into a module from the outside? No module in this example can see any variables except its own since no imports were used. The exception is A. Module A can see B's exported objects since A constitutes B's surrounding environment. This is the same reason that the main program module is able to see everything that is exported from A and C.

A final observation has to do with the references to the variables within the program module's main body. References to the variables from B and C are qualified, as they must be. Variables from A can be referenced in either the qualified or unqualified representation, and one variable is shown each way.

SUMMARY

This chapter covered procedures and modules—the keys to the development of large, complex programs. The contents of this chapter are among the most important in the book. In order to write programs in Modula-2 it is essential that, at a minimum, you understand all aspects of procedures and program modules.

Library modules and separate compilation are important if you plan to develop large programs. These features are at the heart of the Modula-2 language. If you have no plans to use these capabilities, Modula-2 has relatively little new to offer you over and above what Pascal already offers.

It is important to understand the issues of the visibility of objects in a Modula-2 program and how visibility is affected by the various types of procedures, modules, and their parameters. Similarly, the concept of the existence of a variable and its related subprogram (procedure or module) is important to understand. The difference in this area between Modula-2 and Pascal shows a major improvement in Modula-2 over Pascal.

QUESTIONS AND PROBLEMS

1. Modify Listing 8.2 to accept only vowels (both upper and lower case).
2. Rewrite Listing 5.2 to include three procedures: blank suppression, string input, and setting termCH.

3. Rewrite Listing 8.5 to prompt the user to specify the GoodCharacter-Set interactively, and then pass this set to the GetCharacter procedure. Do this by means of one or more procedures.

4. How would you use the open-array parameter feature in conjunction with a multidimensional array?

5. Identify and implement an application that uses the procedure type.

6. Verify by means of the syntax diagrams of Appendix A that Listing 8.11 is a valid Modula-2 program.

7. Make the necessary modifications to Listing 8.13 to correct the problems identified in the text, i.e. range validity of the cardinal number.

8. Compile and run Listing 8.14 with the original version of the implementation module from Listing 8.13. Next, compile your new implementation module from Problem 7 above, and attempt to rerun Listing 8.14 without recompiling it. Did it work? (It should have.)

SUPPLEMENTAL PROBLEMS

At this stage you should have written small programs to:

- Read user input
- Control processing flow
- Right justify and pad string "numbers"
- Pop, Push, Clear, and Display a stack
- Exchange the order of the top two items on a stack
- Perform string "arithmetic" (+, −, *, DIV)
- Change signs

Problem 1

If you've written the programs called for in the earlier chapters, you've written all of the key pieces of the calculator program as implemented in Appendix E. Unfortunately, they are disjoint pieces and probably don't make use of the procedures discussed in this chapter. Combine these programs into a single calculator program comprised of a program module, procedures for each functional entity (e.g., Add, Subtract, ChangeSign), and a local module for the stack functions (Clear, Pop, Push, and Display). At this stage you should have a program that closely resembles the program shown in Appendix E.

Problem 2

Remove the stack local module from the program of Problem 1 and convert it into a library module that uses an array stack structure. After you've successfully compiled the definition module, implementation module, and program module and gotten everything to work, rewrite and recompile the implementation module using the pointer structure and convince yourself that nothing else needs to be changed or recompiled in order for the overall program to work.

PART III

ADVANCED TOPICS

CHAPTER 9

ADVANCED INPUT/OUPUT PROCEDURES

NEW CONCEPTS: Opening, Creating, and Closing Files; Sequential and Random Access Files

ISSUES: Language and Operating System Interactions

INTRODUCTION

It is difficult to present anything definitive or concrete on the subject of Modula-2 input/output when the language has no input/output statements. As was discussed in Chapter 5, Wirth decided not to include input/output statements in Modula-2 because input and output facilities are so dependent on specific computers and operating systems and because there is such a large number of diverse peripherals tied to these computers. Instead, input/output-related library modules are supposed to be supplied with each implementation of the language. Wirth recommended that certain basic "standard" modules be included as part of every system implementation. The standard input/output library modules InOut and RealInOut, which were described in detail in Chapter 5, are two such modules.

This chapter describes modules that perform general file input/output functions. The position of these files in the overall hierarchy of input/output operations is close enough to the machine and operating system level that it may not be realistic to expect that every system implementation will be the same.

In fact, most implementations are different from one another and from Wirth's recommendations. They differ in both the name of the modules and the functions that are provided. This lack of standardization of input/output modules, which are required by any serious programming effort, is a major deficiency. This is an area that requires a serious effort by a standards group. Such efforts are underway.

As it stands, programs probably will not be completely portable if they use modules below the level of InOut, RealInOut, and Terminal* in the module hierarchy. Unfortunately, most large programming tasks will require input/output functions at a level below InOut, RealInOut, and Terminal. This being the case, their portability is lost. The standard recommendation for this situation is to keep the number of system-unique statements to a minimum. This recommendation is difficult to follow with a function as ubiquitous as input/output. Unless you are very careful, input/output statements just have a tendency of being scattered throughout programs.

Having said all of this, what is this chapter all about? This chapter presents a set of input/output library modules that are part of a current Modula-2 implementation from Volition Systems. These modules are an excellent example of what should be provided as part of a system implementation.

The Volition Systems implementation of Modula-2 includes a large number of standard and utility library modules. (See Appendix C for a complete set of definition modules for these library units.) These include several modules that perform file input/output operations. These operations include reading and writing byte streams, records, and the basic data types. Sequential and random file access, and disk directory operations are also provided.

Examples of practical applications that use these modules will be developed and explained. These examples will serve to illustrate file input/output techniques. The example modules may not be directly transportable. However, changes to make them so should be relatively minor.

A second input/output topic dealing with general screen utilities is also covered in this section. A common requirement of most microcomputer programs is to interact with a user. The nature of the interaction is through screen displays to convey information and results and to elicit inputs from the user through prompts and menus. In general, the displays require more capability than InOut and the other standard modules provide. Specifically, displays require cursor positioning information and capabilities.

In addition to the display considerations, user interaction involves reading user inputs and trapping errors during the input process. A number of procedures, bound together in a module called CRT, are presented. Suggestions are made for the expansion of this module to include other important capabilities. Both the CRT module and a module of the file utilities called FileStuff are used in the word processing program that is developed in Chapter 12.

---

* The definition module for the module Terminal is included in Appendix C with the listings of the Volition Systems library modules. It provides procedures for reading data from the keyboard and writing it to the screen.

9.1 GENERAL FILE INPUT/OUTPUT OPERATIONS

This section describes general file handling functions such as opening and closing files and associating files with text streams. The file input/output operations based on the capabilities provided in the Volition Systems Files module are presented. Similarly, file operations using the Volition Systems library module Texts for reading and writing and standard data types—i.e., INTEGER, CARDINAL, CHAR, and STRING (actually a text line)—to and from a text stream are explained. Several program segments will be given to illustrate the use of the elements of the Files and Texts modules during the description of the procedures provided by these modules.

Procedures from Files and Texts will be combined with procedures of other standard modules to form a new module called FileStuff. FileStuff provides flexible options for opening and creating files and establishing file error handling capabilities. Opening of existing files and the creation of new files can be performed interactively or totally within the client program. FileStuff also performs input/output redirection functions. A subsequent section uses Files, Texts, and FileStuff in practical file handling application programs.

9.1.1 Data Files and File Operations

The Volition Systems implementation of Modula-2 provides a number of input/output modules. The modules Files and Texts are provided for data file operations and are presented in this section. We will describe the procedures that are provided in each module. Small program segments are provided to illustrate the operations of these procedures.

Module Files

The module Files provides a number of data file operations at what is nearly the lowest level of the input/output module hierarchy. In terms of input/output modules in the Volition Systems implementation, the hierarchy, from high to low, looks like

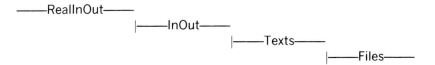

where each module depends on all of the modules below it (as well as others which are not shown) in the hierarchy.

The module Files provides a great deal of flexibility in comparison to modules above it in the hierarchy. The price is additional programming effort and some potential loss in program transportability.

Files provides a category of procedures to

- open existing files,
- create new files, and
- close open files, with options to retain the file or to delete it.

There is also a category of procedures to Read/Write

- a character,
- a record (see Chapter 7), and
- one or more bytes,

from a sequential file, which is assumed to be a stream of bytes.

In addition, Files handles random access to files, allows establishment of error handling procedures, and provides the capability to rename and delete closed files. The definition module for Files is shown in Appendix C.

We see that Files exports a type FILE. All input and output using Files is done by means of variables whose type is FILE. This is to say that if we want to read a character using the Read procedure from Files, i.e.,

```
Read(InputFile, Character);
```

a declaration of

```
VAR InputFile : FILE;
```

is necessary.

The example variable InputFile is a *logical* file, i.e., it exists only within the context of the program that contains it. It does not exist physically and has no meaning beyond the realm of the program. In contrast, the file that we want to read (write) from (to) is a *physical* file (e.g., disk file, keyboard, or modem). The physical file has meaning both in the real world and in the world of the program. Note that the word external is also used when we use physical, and internal is used for logical.

This concept of logical and physical devices is fundamental to the understanding of data file input/output operations. It is the basis for functions such as writing output to a printer—an operation that is an enigma to every beginning Pascal programmer. More importantly, it is the basis for using the same statement that wrote to the printer the last time the statement was executed to write to a disk file (or whatever) on its next execution.

If the language required us to explicitly identify a physical device with every input/output statement, the flexibility of the program would be severely limited. A particular write statement, for example, would always write to a printer and nothing but a printer.

Modula-2 and other reasonable languages provide the capability of associating any legal input/output device with any read/write statement. The important aspect of this association is that it is done while the input/output statements are being executed. It is not "hard-wired" at compile time, nor is the same statement forced to read/write to/from the same physical device on two successive executions of the statement. The user can redirect the input and output at will.

How is the relationship between the logical file and the physical file established? That is to say, how does the program determine from which input device to read when the Read(InputFile, Character) statement is executed? This is where the procedures Open and Create from the module Files are used.

The procedure Open is used to open an existing physical file. Opening the file means to associate the specified physical file with the logical file that is named in the parameter list of the Open procedure call. Although a programmer can select the name of the logical file by the identifier chosen for the FILE variable, physical file names are determined by the operating system at the time that the physical file is created. The procedure Open links the two files—physical and logical. For example, if we wanted the statement Read(InputFile, Character) to read from a disk (physical) file named #5:Data-File, we would write

```
IF Open(InputFile, '#5:DataFile') # FileOK THEN. . .
```

to make the association between the logical file, InputFile, and the physical disk file, #5:DataFile. Do not worry about the . . .# FileOK. . . just yet.

This example, although correct, is an example of hard-wiring a connection between the logical and physical elements. A much better arrangement would be

```
Open(InputFile, FileName);
```

where FileName is a variable that is compatible with the procedure Open's formal parameter, ARRAY OF CHAR. In this example, FileName can be whatever we desire and can be changed whenever required. When input from

LISTING 9.1

```
MODULE FileDemo;

FROM Files IMPORT
        FILE, FileState, Close, Open, Write, Read;

IMPORT InOut;

VAR
        LogicalFile1 : FILE;
        PhysicalFile1 : ARRAY [0..10] OF CHAR;
        Character : CHAR;

BEGIN (*FileDemo*)
  PhysicalFile1 := 'FILE1';
  Character := 'A';

  IF Open(LogicalFile1, PhysicalFile1) = FileOK THEN
    Write(LogicalFile1, Character);
  ELSE
    InOut.WriteString("1st file failed");  HALT;
  END (*if*);

  IF Open(LogicalFile1, PhysicalFile1) = FileOK THEN
    Read(LogicalFile1, Character);
    InOut.WriteString("The character read was ");
    InOut.Write(Character);
  ELSE
    InOut.WriteString("2nd file failed");  HALT;
  END (*if*);
  IF NOT (Close(LogicalFile1) = FileOK) THEN HALT END;
END FileDemo.
```

the keyboard is needed, FileName can be 'CONSOLE:', which is UCSD p-System terminology. To change from the keyboard to the earlier disk file, we simply change the value of FileName to '#5:DataFile' and execute the Open statement.

The operation of the File procedure, Create, is identical to Open with regard to logical/physical device assignments. However, Create opens new files (i.e. it creates a new physical file) whereas Open works with existing files.

Two Files procedures closely related to Open and Create are Close and Release. These procedures close an open (existing and new) file. This is a step that should be performed when the program no longer needs to access the file, including before the program terminates. (The Volition Systems implementation of Files will automatically close files that have been left open by a program. However, it is a good practice to close the files explicitly using either Close or Release.)

The procedure Close makes the physical file a permanent member of the operating system's file directory (disk files). Release frees the secondary storage space occupied by the physical file and removes its name from the directory. If a new file is Created, and the file is not Closed before the program terminates, the file and its contents disappear. If changes are made to an existing file, and the file is not closed before it is opened again, unexpected results can occur.

Note that the following sequence can lead to confusion and problems:

```
IF Open(InputFile1, FileName) THEN. . .
    :
    : . . . . Processing, but no close of InputFile1
    :
IF Open(InputFile2, FileName) THEN. . .
```

As a specific example of the potential problems that can crop up when files are not closed properly, consider the program shown in Listing 9.1. If the disk file 'FILE1' contained a single character, say 'X', when this program was run, the read/write statements in the second IF statement would read and write this 'X'. This is true in spite of the fact that the write statement in the first IF statement appears to have written an 'A' into the file in place of the 'X'.

To make things even more confusing, if the same program were *rerun*, the 'A' that was written to the file on the previous run would be read regardless of what was written the second time. The action of writing to the disk file and reading what was written are not in synchronization with one another, and it is doubtful that this would ever be the desired operation of the program.

This is an example of the problem that can occur if files are not opened and closed in the correct fashion. If the desired result from the program of Listing 9.1 was to have the Read statement find the character that had just been written, the file should have been closed first—in this case between the two IF statements.

Many actions related to file opening and closing will be implementation dependent. Check out your implementation carefully. Chances are that it may not even allow the situation depicted above in which a file that is already open is opened a second time without first being closed.

The module Files exports an enumerated type, FileState. The procedures Open, Create, Close, and Release are function procedures and each returns a result of type FileState. A result equal to the FileState constant, FileOK, indicates that the procedure outcome was normal. Five other constants indicate various error conditions such as "the specified file is not on line" or other file operation errors. In Listing 9.1 FileState is tested after each operation, and the program terminates if an abnormal result occurs.

FileState is not used solely with the four procedures just cited. Function procedure FileStatus of module Files can be used to check the result of every file operation performed by the elements of the Files module. FileStatus returns a FileState value to indicate the result of the most recent file operation as a FileState result.

Programs frequently are required to read the records of a file in a program loop until all of the records are processed. A mechanism for testing for the end of the file is needed in order to establish a terminating condition for such loops.

The module Files exports a BOOLEAN function procedure, EOF, which indicates whether or not the end of file has been encountered. At the same time that EOF is set to TRUE, the FileStatus would indicate a FileState constant equal to EndError. EndError is the FileState indicating that the end of file has been reached. It should be noted that a FileState of EndError is not the only way for EOF to be set to TRUE. EOF is also set to true any time that a file operation results in a FileState other than FileOK.

Thus far, the module Files capabilities for opening and closing files have been covered together with a procedure for determining the status of file operations as they are performed. Next we will cover the read and write procedures that are provided in Files.

The module Files provides three basic read and write options. You are able to read/write a single character, a sequence of bytes, or a word-oriented record. Reading and writing a character was illustrated in the previous example and is very straightforward. To illustrate reading and writing from a stream of bytes, consider the program segments in Listing 9.2. In order to use this capability, we use the special functions SIZE(x), TSIZE(x), and ADR(x) that are provided in the Volition Systems module named System. SIZE(x) returns the size of the variable x. TSIZE(x) returns the size of any variable whose type is x. ADR(x) returns the address of the variable x.

In the Listing 9.2 example, the function procedures WriteBytes and ReadBytes are used to write and read data to a file, and they return the number of bytes written or read. The context of the overall program for this particular program segment is a data-base application.

Data of type FieldDescription is used to record information regarding the name, length, and type of data to be stored in different fields of a data-base record. For example, we might state that the first field's name is Last Name, it is 20-bytes long, and its type is an array of characters. The second field's name is Department number with a length of 4 and a type of cardinal, etc. This information is obtained for each of an unspecified number of fields (<= Max-Field) and stored in the array, Field. Once all of the record field descriptors have been obtained in an early part of the program, they are written to a disk file for subsequent use in this or another program.

LISTING 9.2

```
TYPE
      FieldDescription = RECORD
                              Name : ARRAY [0..20] OF CHAR;
                              Length : CARDINAL;
                              Type : FieldType;   (*assume declared*)
                          END;
VAR
      OutputFile : FILE;
      BlkSize, NmbrOfFlds, DataLength : CARDINAL;
      Field = ARRAY [1..MaxField] OF FIeldDescription;

BEGIN
    :......appropriate file openings, etc. + processing which sets the
    :      values of variables NmbrOfFlds & Field
    :
    BlkSize := NmbrOfFlds * TSIZE(FieldDescription);
    DataLength := WriteBytes(OutFile,ADR(BlkSize),SIZE(BlkSize));
    DataLength := WriteBytes(OutFile,ADR(NmbrOfFlds),SIZE(NmbrOfFlds));
    DataLength := WriteBytes(OutFile,ADR(Field),BlkSize);
    :
    :......appropriate file closings, openings, etc. + processing
    :
    DataLength := ReadBytes(InFile,ADR(BlkSize),SIZE(BlkSize));
    DataLength := ReadBytes(InFile,ADR(NmbrOfFlds),SIZE(NmbrOfFlds));
    DataLength := ReadBytes(InFile,ADR(Field),BlkSize);
    :
    :...... more of whatever
```

Given the above scenario, we arrive at the first executable statement of Listing 9.2 with data in the array, Field, and with the variable NmbrOfFlds containing a count of the number of current entries in Field. Our objective is to write the valid part of Field to the disk file, i.e. rows 1..NmbrOfFields. The first step is to calculate the size of the portion of Field that contains valid data. This is equal to

```
BlkSize := NmbrOfFields * TSIZE(FieldDescription);
```

bytes, which is the first executable line in Listing 9.2.

The first output statement is

```
DataLength := WriteBytes(OutFile,ADR(BlkSize),SIZE(BlkSize));
```

which writes a number of bytes of data to the file OutFile. The number of bytes written is equal to the number of bytes in the variable BlkSize. The location of these bytes coincides with the address of the variable BlkSize. In other words, this statement writes the value of the variable BlkSize out to the file. Note that unlike WriteCard which produces a character representation of a CARDINAL value, this procedure places the value of BlkSize in the file using its internal representation. This saves the time involved in converting the value to a human-readable form.

Using the same convoluted technique, the second line

```
DataLength := WriteBytes(OutFile,ADR(NmbrOfFlds),SIZE(NmbrOfFlds));
```

writes the value of NmbrOfFlds to the file in its internal form. Lastly, the field description data in Field is written with

```
DataLength := WriteBytes(OutFile,ADR(Field),BlkSize);
```

since BlkSize bytes starting at the address of the array, Field, are written. BlkSize was the previously computed size of the data set that we wanted to store. The reason for storing BlkSize and NmbrOfFields is so that we can read this data and use it at a later time, which brings us to the final section of code.

The three final lines reverse the process that was just described to write the data to a disk file. After these statements are executed, the affected variables look just as they did before they were written. To describe the final read/write option that allows records to be handled, let's use the same example that was just finished. The change that will be made is to declare a record type describing the variables that were written using the byte-oriented procedure.

To do this we declare

```
TYPE
   FieldType = RECORD
                   BlkSize,
                   NmbrOfFlds : CARDINAL;
                   Field : ARRAY [1..MaxField] OF FieldDescription;
               END;

VAR
   FieldData : FieldType;
```

and it is now possible to use the single statements

```
WriteRec(OutFile, FieldData);
or
ReadRec(InFile, FieldData);
```

in place of the multiple WriteBytes and ReadBytes statements of Listing 9.2. Procedure WriteRec places an entire record variable in the file using the internal representation of that record. Procedure ReadRec performs the reverse process.

In this specific example, there is one difference in the result obtained by using each of the two different approaches. The difference is a problem of efficiency more than anything else. In our formulation of the byte-stream approach, we wrote and read a specific number of bytes. The number was equal to the portion of the Field array that had data in it. The record-oriented alternative just described writes the *entire* record to the file. The entire record includes all of the array elements of Field as determined by its array bounds regardless of what is in them, or more to the point, regardless of how many are empty. From an efficiency standpoint, the comparison is similar to the use of arrays and list structures. WriteRec forces a fixed length output. WriteByte allows flexibility in the amount written.

This wraps up the read/write capabilities of Files from the viewpoint of sequential files. The same operations can be performed using random access by means of the Files procedures GetPos, GetEOF, SetPos, SetEOF, CalcPos, and the data type FilePos.

Random access files can be accessed either sequentially or randomly. Random access requires knowledge of the position of records within the file. Such record positions are stored in variables of type FilePos. The procedure SetPos(MyFile, NewPos), in which NewPos is a variable of type FilePos, sets the current file position to the position NewPos. This will allow the next input/output operation to access the data at this position in the file.

CalcPos(RecordNumber, TSIZE(RecordType), NewPos) is a statement that would return, in the variable NewPos, the file position of the record indicated by RecordNumber, in a record whose elements are TSIZE(RecordType) bytes-long (or words-long, depending on the machine). Record numbers start with zero.

Using what we have seen so far, the fifth record (number 4) of MyFile can be read by

```
CalcPos(4, TSIZE(RecordType), NewPos);
SetPos(MyFile, NewPos);
ReadRec (MyFile, RecordData);
```

where the appropriate declarations are assumed.

GetPos(MyFile, NewPos) returns the value of the current file position in the variable NewPos. The end of file position is returned by GetEOF(MyFile, NewPos). The end of file position is set to NewPos by SetEOF(MyFile, NewPos).

Individual records or entire files can be overwritten. However, to append data to the file, the file must be positioned at its end before writing any records. This can be accomplished by

```
GetEOF(MyFile, NewPos);
SetPos(MyFile, NewPos);
WriteRec(....
```

The final capabilities of module Files relate to error handling and directory operations. Directory operations interact with an operating system to modify the system's data regarding the existence and names of files. The directory operations are minimal and straightforward. The procedure Rename(OldName, NewName) changes the name of the physical file OldName to NewName in the system's file directory. If a file with the name NewName already exists, the original NewName file is destroyed. OldName must not be open while its name is being changed. Procedure Delete(File-Name) deletes FileName from the system's file directory. FileName must be a closed file. Once deleted, the data in that file can no longer be accessed.

Error handling is facilitated by the procedure SetFileHandler and the data type FileHandler. An example of their use is:

```
PROCEDURE ErrorHandler(ErrorType : FileState);
   BEGIN (*ErrorHandler*)
      CASE ErrorType OF
         UseError : WriteString('UseError');
             :
            : etc for other FileState values
             :
      END (*case*);
   END ErrorHandler;

BEGIN (*main program*)
   :
   :
   IF Open(LogicalFile1, PhysicalFile1) = FileOK THEN
      SetFileHandler(LogicalFile1, ErrorHandler);
   ELSE
      InOut.WriteString("File opening failed"); HALT;
   END (*if*);
   :
   :
END Main.
```

In the example, if the file is successfully opened, the procedure SetFile-Handler ties the error handling procedure ErrorHandler to the operation of the file LogicalFile1. If any file operations related to this file result in a FileState other than FileOK, the ErrorHandler will be called by the routines in the module Files, and the associated FileState value is passed to ErrorHandler as a parameter. In the implementation of an error handler in this example, the name of the erroneous FileState is written to the terminal. Any other action that may be desired can be implemented.

Module Texts

The Volition Systems standard library module Texts provides the ability to read and write the standard data types using text streams (i.e., sequences of characters). Many aspects of this module are similar to the module Files, which will allow us to cover this section more quickly than the previous one.

The definition module for Texts is given in Appendix C. The objects defined in this module allow

- reading and writing of
    —characters,

—strings,
—integers, and
—cardinals

as well as the writing of an end-of-line terminator. They also allow a special read operation that causes the last character that was read to be read again by the next read operation.

- error handling similar to that in Files.

- text file variables to be connected (and disconnected) to an open (logical) file variable. Just as files in the module Files must be opened before they can be used, a text stream must be connected to a file before it can be used. Disconnecting a text stream is analogous to closing a file.

The Texts module reads and writes the standard data types—i.e., integer, cardinal, character and string—from text data streams. A text data stream is a sequence of characters whose sources or destinations can include any valid device that generates or receives data of this type. Often the text stream is divided into lines of text that are separated by a carriage return character. The keyboard, screen, printer, modem, and disk files are all examples of sources and destinations for text streams.

In the Volition Systems implementation, Texts does not access the physical file (e.g., disk file) directly. Instead, Texts is connected to a FILE type variable, as described in the previous section. Module Files performs the actual file access and data transport, that is, getting the data from the physical file to the program and vice versa. The situation is equivalent to the following

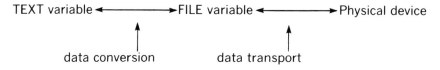

The read and write operations performed by Texts are similar in function to those provided by InOut, i.e., handling numbers, characters, and strings. The following compares the syntax of Texts and InOut for reading a character:

```
Texts.Read(TextFile, CharVar);   InOut.Read(CharVar);
```

The procedures for Texts include the source/destination identifier as part of the procedure parameter list (TextFile in the example). InOut procedures assume that the source or destination is the standard input/output device (normally the terminal), unless explicitly modified by means of the OpenInput and OpenOutput procedures, and therefore do not identify the source in the procedure parameter list. Texts provides a much greater flexibility in performing input/output redirection. Also, Texts allows multiple simultaneous text streams. InOut permits just one at a time.

Texts exports the standard variables input and output, which are the standard input and output text streams. Therefore,

```
ReadCard(input, CardValue);
```

in which input and ReadCard are imported from Texts, is identical in function to

```
ReadCard(CardValue);
```

in which ReadCard is imported from InOut.

In Chapter 5 we stated that the modification of variables in Texts could affect the operation of InOut by redirecting the standard input and output devices. The variables input and output are the variables in question. If they are connected to a device other than the system terminal, module InOut operations will be affected.

A text stream is connected to a file variable as follows:

```
VAR (*Assume all imports completed*)
    DataFile : FILE;
    TextFile : TEXT; (*The text stream*)
    PhysicalFile : ARRAY [0..30] OF CHAR; (*File name*)
                        :
                        :
IF Open (DataFile, PhysicalFile) = FileOK THEN
    SetFileHandler (DataFile, DataErrorHandler);
ELSE
    InOut.WriteString("DataFile opening failed"); HALT;
END (*if*);

IF Connect(TextFile, DataFile) = TextOK THEN
    SetTextHandler(TextFile, TextErrorHandler);
ELSE
    InOut.WriteString("TextFile opening failed"); HALT;
END (*if*);
                        :
```

9.1.2 File Utilities and Some Practical Applications

It should be apparent that a significant number of file openings and closings are required for most programs. Furthermore, more actions are required than simply writing Open(InputFile, FileName) if the job is to be done with any flexibility and reliability.

For example, numerous error conditions should be anticipated and handled. What do you do if the physical file is not found? Stop the program? Not very friendly! How are file names determined and passed to the file opening procedures? The answers to these questions are typically provided for in library module procedures and not by duplicating the same code in every program that performs file operations.

Module FileStuff

Handling common functions is a job for library modules. Listing 9.3 shows the definition part of a library module that handles the opening and closing of files. Part of the opening and closing function is the ability to redirect input and output.

In Listing 9.3, FileStuff combines the Files and Texts opening, closing, and error handling routines into a convenient, easy to use group of four procedures. FileOpen and TextFileOpen open files. FileClose and TextFileClose close files that were opened by FileOpen and TextFileOpen, respectively.

FileOpen is used to open new *or* old standard data files. TextFileOpen performs the same function for text files. Both are procedure functions whose value is TRUE if the requested operation was successful. Successful equates to a FileState of FileOK, or a TextState of TextOK.

The first parameter in each of the first two procedure's list is a procedure variable (see Chapter 8). The type of this procedure variable, FileProcedure, matches procedures Open and Create from Files (i.e., the formal parameter lists match). This allows us to use either Open or Create as the first parameter in our procedure calls to FileOpen and TextFileOpen. (Obviously, in order to use these procedures as parameters, they must be imported from Files into the client module.) TextFileOpen requires both a TEXT and a FILE variable in its parameter list. The second parameter for FileOpen is a FILE variable.

The last two parameters for each of the first two procedures are identical. The first of these two is a variable of StringType. This is a flag for the procedure. If the variable is equal to PromptIs, this tells the procedure that the next (last) parameter is a prompt to the user, and the user will be entering the name of the file to Open or Create in response to the prompt during program execu-

LISTING 9.3

```
DEFINITION MODULE FileStuff;

FROM Files IMPORT
        FILE,
        FileState;

FROM Texts IMPORT
        TEXT;

EXPORT QUALIFIED
        FileClose,
        FileOpen,
        FileProcedure,
        StringType,
        TextFileClose,
        TextFileOpen;

TYPE
  FileProcedure = PROCEDURE(VAR FILE, ARRAY OF CHAR): FileState;
  StringType = (PromptIs, FileName);

PROCEDURE FileOpen(fcall: FileProcedure; VAR f: FILE; strg : StringType;
                   s: ARRAY OF CHAR) : BOOLEAN;

PROCEDURE TextFileOpen(fcall: FileProcedure; VAR t : TEXT; VAR f: FILE;
                       strg : StringType; s: ARRAY OF CHAR) : BOOLEAN;

PROCEDURE FileClose(VAR f: FILE) : BOOLEAN;

PROCEDURE TextFileClose(VAR t: TEXT; VAR f: FILE) : BOOLEAN;


END FileStuff.
```

tion. If the flag equals FileName, then the next parameter *is* the name of the file to be opened. These two options cover the cases of interactive file redirection by the user, and the specification of a file by the program.

The final two procedures, FileClose and TextFileClose, are straightforward in terms of both form and function. Examine Listing 9.3 for the parameters of these procedures.

An example of the first procedure is FileOpen(Create, MyNewFile, PromptIs, 'Name of new file'), in which MyNewFile is a FILE variable. This statement will

- display the prompt 'Name of new file?' on the terminal,
- wait for the user to enter the name of the physical file to be opened,

- attempt to open the specified device,
- set up an error handler if the open is successful, and
- inform the user if unsuccessful and allow reattempts.

The implementation module for FileStuff is given in Listing 9.4.

LISTING 9.4

```
IMPLEMENTATION MODULE FileStuff;

FROM Files IMPORT
        Close,
        FILE,
        FileState,
        FileStatus,
        SetFileHandler;

FROM Terminal IMPORT
        Read,
        ReadLn,
        WriteLn,
        WriteString;

FROM Texts IMPORT
        Connect,
        Disconnect,
        SetTextHandler,
        TEXT,
        TextState;



PROCEDURE FileHandler(error : FileState);

  BEGIN
    WriteLn;
    CASE error OF
      NameError          : WriteString('Name') :
      UseError           : WriteString('Use') :
      StatusError        : WriteString('Status') :
      DeviceError        : WriteString('Device') :
      EndError           : WriteString('End')
    END (*case*);
    WriteString(' error (msg from filestuff filehandler)');
    HALT;
  END FileHandler;


TYPE
  CharSet = SET OF CHAR;
```

```
PROCEDURE FileOpen(fcall : FProc; VAR f : FILE; strg : StringType;
                   s : ARRAY OF CHAR) : BOOLEAN;

  VAR
    Name : ARRAY [0..50] OF CHAR;
    Ch : CHAR;
    i : CARDINAL;

  BEGIN
    LOOP
      IF strg = FileName THEN
        FOR i := 0 TO HIGH(s) DO
          Name[i] := s[i];
        END (*if*);

      ELSE
        WriteString(s);
        ReadLn(Name);
      END (*if*);

      IF fcall(f, Name) = FileOK THEN
        EXIT
      ELSE
        WriteString("Can't open ");
        WriteString(Name);
        WriteString('.    Continue?  Y(es or N(o ');
        Read(Ch);
        IF Ch IN CharSet{'N', 'n'} THEN
          EXIT
        ELSE
          WriteLn;
        END (*if ch*);
      END (*if fcall*)
    END (*loop*);

    IF FileStatus(f) = FileOK THEN
      SetFileHandler(f, FileHandler);
      RETURN TRUE
    ELSE
      RETURN FALSE
    END (*if*);
  END FileOpen;




PROCEDURE TextHandler (error : TextState);

  BEGIN
    WriteLn;
    CASE error OF
      FormatError       : WriteString('Format') |
      FileError         : WriteString('File') |
      ConnectError      : WriteString('ConnectStatus');
    END (*case*);
    WriteString(' error (msg from filestuff texthandler)');
    HALT;
  END TextHandler;
```

LISTING 9-4 (Continued)

```
PROCEDURE IOError(s : ARRAY OF CHAR);

  BEGIN
    WriteLn;
    WriteString('I/O error while ');
    WriteString(s);
    WriteString(' text file');
    HALT;
  END IOError;



PROCEDURE TextFileOpen(fcall : FProc; VAR t : TEXT; VAR f : FILE;
                       strg : StringType; s : ARRAY OF CHAR) : BOOLEAN;

VAR
  Name : ARRAY [0..50] OF CHAR;
  Ch : CHAR;
  i : CARDINAL;

BEGIN
  LOOP
    IF strg = FileName THEN
      FOR i := 0 TO HIGH(s) DO
        Name[i] := s[i];
      END (*if*);
    ELSE
      WriteString(s);
      ReadLn(Name);
    END (*if*);

    IF fcall(f, Name) = FileOK THEN
      EXIT
    ELSE
      WriteString("Can't open ");
      WriteString(Name);
      WriteString('.   Continue?  Y(es or N(o ');
      Read(Ch);
      IF Ch IN CharSet('N', 'n') THEN
        EXIT
      ELSE
        WriteLn;
      END (*if ch*);
    END (*if fcall*);
  END (*loop*);

  IF FileStatus(f) = FileOK THEN
    IF Connect(t, f) = TextOK THEN
      SetFileHandler(f, FileHandler);
      SetTextHandler(t, TextHandler);
      RETURN TRUE;
    ELSE
      IOError('connecting');
```

```
      END (*if con*);
   ELSE
     RETURN FALSE;
   END (*if Fil*);
END TextFileOpen;



PROCEDURE FileClose(VAR f : FILE) : BOOLEAN;

 BEGIN
   IF Close(f) # FileOK THEN
     WriteLn;
     WriteString('Error closing file');
     HALT;
   END;
   RETURN TRUE;
END FileClose;



PROCEDURE TextFileClose(VAR t : TEXT; VAR f : FILE) : BOOLEAN;



 BEGIN
   IF Disconnect(t) # TextOK THEN
     IOError('disconnecting')
   END;
   IF Close(f) # FileOK THEN
     WriteLn;
     WriteString('Error closing file');
     HALT;
   END;
   RETURN TRUE;
END TextFileClose;



BEGIN
END FileStuff.
```

File Transfers

Files frequently have to be transferred from one location to another—for example, from a disk file to a printer or from a disk to another disk. The procedures of Files and Texts, or of FileStuff, make setting up the files to be transferred a simple process. Assume that our file transfer program had the following two FileStuff elements:

- TextFileOpen(Open, InText, InFile, PromptIs, "Input file?")
- TextFileOpen(Create, OutText, OutFile, PromptIs, "Output file?")

The first of these will ask the user to specify a file in response to the prompt "Input file? " and will also connect this physical file, whatever it is, to the TEXT variable InText. Similarly, the user will be prompted to identify the output file. If the input response was #5:MEMO.TEXT and the output response was PRINTER: (UCSD p-System terminology), the memo on the designated input file would be listed at the printer by program segments similar to one of the following:

Read and Write a Character at a Time	Read and Write a Line at a Time
LOOP	LOOP
Read(InText, Chr);	ReadLn(InText, Line);
IF EOF(InText) THEN	IF EOT(InText) THEN
EXIT	EXIT
ELSIF EOL(InText) THEN	END (*if*);
WriteLn(OutText);	WriteString(OutText, Line);
ELSE	WriteLn(OutText);
Write(OutText, Chr);	END (*loop*);
END (*if*);	
END (*loop*);	

In the program segments above, all of the appropriate declarations are assumed to have been made. Other responses to the prompts are possible, and can be used to produce results such as the following examples, which use UCSD p-System terminology:

Input File?	Output File?	Effect
CONSOLE:	PRINTER:	Electric typewriter.
#5:MEMO.TEXT	CONSOLE:	List memo on screen.
#5:MEMO.TEXT	#4:LTR.TEXT	Creates new disk file on drive #4 named LTR.TEXT whose content is MEMO.TEXT.
CONSOLE:	#4:LTR.TEXT	Ditto above; content entered from keyboard.

The two file-open procedures cited, together with program loops similar to the above, are the basis for text file transfer operations in Modula-2. The ReadByte and WriteByte procedures, coupled with a large array of characters to act as a transfer buffer, provide a flexible and fast transfer construct for data files. See the byte-oriented read/write example in the Files module earlier in this chapter for more information.

9.2 SCREEN INPUT/OUTPUT OPERATIONS

One of the most common input/output requirements is for friendly, error-free interactive dialogues with computer users. The typical mechanism for this dialogue is CRT displays containing help panels (screens), input prompts, and menus. The user's response to this display should be idiot-proofed at least to the extent that invalid responses are trapped and identified to the user. The procedures and functions that are used to perform these tasks are extensive. They are usually very system implementation and hardware dependent.

9.2.1 General Functions

In order to illustrate the types of functions that are required, we present in Listing 9.5 a definition module for a small library module of CRT procedures. This set of functions is less than a bare minimum, but it is illustrative. These procedures were selected from a module that contains over 40 CRT operations. These procedures are used in the word processing program that is presented in Chapter 12. The module in Listing 9.5 is sufficiently commented to be self-explanatory.

LISTING 9.5

```
DEFINITION MODULE SimpleCRT;

EXPORT QUALIFIED
        (*These are VARIABLES*)
        CrtResult,
        False,
        True,

        (*These are TYPES*)
        CharSet,
        Result,
        UpperLower,
```

LISTING 9.5 (continued)

```
        (*These are PROCEDURES*)
        CenterLine,
        ClearEoln,
        ClearEos,
        ClearLine,
        ClearTheScreen,
        GoToxy,
        Prompt,
        UserInput;

TYPE
        CharSet = SET OF CHAR;
        Result = (CrtOk, CrtError);
        UpperLower = (Upper, Lower);  (*Upper & Lower are visible
                                        to client programs*)

VAR
        CrtResult : Result;        (*Set after after CRT operation*)
        False,                     (*False = ('F', 'f', 'N', 'n'}*)
        True         : CharSet;    (*True  = ('T', 't', 'Y', 'y'}*)


PROCEDURE CenterLine(line : CARDINAL; strg : ARRAY OF CHAR);
(*erase row "line" on the screen & center string "strg" on this row*)

PROCEDURE ClearEoln(column, line : CARDINAL);
(*erase row "line" starting at column "column"
 and continuing to end of row*)

PROCEDURE ClearEos(column, line : CARDINAL);
(*same as ClearEoln above, but continue to the end of the screen*)

PROCEDURE ClearLine(line : CARDINAL);
(*clears row "line" of the screen; equiv to ClearEoln where column = 0*)

PROCEDURE ClearTheScreen;
(*clears the entire screen; equiv to ClearEos with column and row = 0*)

PROCEDURE GoToxy(column, line: CARDINAL);
(*move the cursor to column, line*)

PROCEDURE Prompt(strg : ARRAY OF CHAR; response : CharSet) : CHAR;
(*display strg, centered at top of screen; wait for response in CharSet;
  return the response*)

PROCEDURE UserInput(okset : CharSet; case : UpperLower) : CHAR;



(*wait for user to enter a keystroke response which is in the "okset";
 if case = Upper then convert lower case to upper, otherwise treat upper
 & lower case separately*)

END SimpleCRT.
```

One of the important requirements for an interactive CRT display function is the ability to position the cursor to any desired screen location for the purpose of selectively adding or deleting characters on the screen. This is commonly referred to as full-screen terminal operations. The CRT module depends on the availability of a full-screen terminal capability.

9.2.2 Implementation of a CRT Module

The implementation part of the CRT library module is shown in Listing 9.6. There are several facets of this implementation to be noted, starting with the module main body.

The module body is executed when the module's surrounding environment, i.e., the client program which imports it, becomes active. In the case of the CRT module being used in Chapter 12's word processor, the module body is executed as soon as the word processor is executed.

LISTING 9.6

```
IMPLEMENTATION MODULE SimpleCRT;

FROM ASCII IMPORT
        bs;

FROM Globals IMPORT
        GlobalPtr,      (* ^ Globals, must be initialized *)
        GlobalRec,      (* the Globals themselves *)
        GetGlobalAddr;  (* function which returns ^ Globals, for init *)

FROM Screen IMPORT
        GotoXY;

FROM Strings IMPORT
        Length;

FROM Terminal IMPORT
        Read,
        Write,
        WriteString;

VAR
    GlobalVar : GlobalPtr;
    TermHeight,
    TermWidth : CARDINAL;
    ClEoln,
    ClEos : CHAR;
    Printables : CharSet;
```

LISTING 9.6 (continued)

```
PROCEDURE UserInput(okset : CharSet; case : UpperLower) : CHAR;

  VAR
    Ch : CHAR;

  BEGIN (*UserInput*)
    REPEAT
      Read(Ch);
      IF Ch IN Printables THEN
        Write(bs); Write(' '); Write(bs);
      END (*if*);
      IF case = Upper THEN Ch := CAP(Ch) END;
    UNTIL Ch IN okset;
    CrtResult := CrtOk;
    RETURN Ch;
  END UserInput;




PROCEDURE ClearEoln(column, line : CARDINAL);

  BEGIN (* ClearEoln *)
    IF (line > TermHeight) OR (line < 0) THEN
      CrtResult := CrtError;
      RETURN;
    END;
    IF (column > TermWidth) OR (column < 0) THEN
      CrtResult := CrtError;
      RETURN;

    END;
    GotoXY(column, line);
    Write(ClEoln);
    CrtResult := CrtOk;
  END ClearEoln;




PROCEDURE ClearEos(column, line : CARDINAL);

  BEGIN (* ClearEos *)
    IF (line > TermHeight) OR (line < 0) THEN
      CrtResult := CrtError;
      RETURN;
    END;
    IF (column > TermWidth) OR (column < 0) THEN
      CrtResult := CrtError;
      RETURN;
    END;
    GotoXY(column, line);
    Write(ClEos);
    CrtResult := CrtOk;
  END ClearEos;
```

```
PROCEDURE ClearLine(line : CARDINAL);

  BEGIN (* ClearLine *)
    IF (line > TermHeight) OR (line < 0) THEN
      CrtResult := CrtError;
      RETURN;
    END;
    GotoXY(0, line);
    Write(ClEoln);
    CrtResult := CrtOk;
  END ClearLine;




PROCEDURE CenterLine(line : CARDINAL; strg : ARRAY OF CHAR);

  VAR
    HCoord : CARDINAL;

  BEGIN (* CenterLine *)
    ClearLine(line);
    IF CrtResult = CrtError THEN
      RETURN
    END;
    IF Length(strg) > (TermWidth + 1) THEN
      CrtResult := CrtError;
      RETURN;
    END;
    HCoord := (TermWidth + 1 - Length(strg)) DIV 2;
    GotoXY(HCoord, line);
    WriteString(strg);
  END CenterLine;


PROCEDURE PutLine(column, line : CARDINAL; strg : ARRAY OF CHAR);

  BEGIN (*PutLine*)
    ClearEoln(column, line);
    IF CrtResult = CrtError THEN
      RETURN
    END;
    IF (Length(strg) + column) > (TermWidth + 1) THEN
      CrtResult := CrtError;
      RETURN;
    END;
    WriteString(strg);
  END PutLine;




PROCEDURE ClearTheScreen;

  BEGIN (* ClearTheScreen *)
    GotoXY(0, 0);
    Write(ClEos);
    CrtResult := CrtOk;
  END ClearTheScreen;
```

LISTING 9.6 (continued)

```
PROCEDURE GoToxy(column, line : CARDINAL);

  BEGIN (*GoToxy*)
    IF (line > TermHeight) OR (line < 0) THEN
      CrtResult := CrtError;
      RETURN;
    END;
    IF (column > TermWidth) OR (column < 0) THEN
      CrtResult := CrtError;
      RETURN;
    END;
    GotoXY(column, line);
    CrtResult := CrtOk;
  END GoToxy;



PROCEDURE Prompt(strg : ARRAY OF CHAR; response : CharSet) : CHAR;

  CONST
    PromptLine = 0;

  VAR
    Ch : CHAR;

  BEGIN (*Prompt*)
    IF Length(strg) < TermWidth THEN
      CenterLine(PromptLine, strg);
    ELSE
      CrtResult := CrtError;
      RETURN ' ';
    END;
    Ch := UserInput(response, Lower);

    ClearLine(PromptLine);
    RETURN Ch;
  END Prompt;



BEGIN (*CRT*)
  GlobalVar := GetGlobalAddr();
  TermHeight := GlobalVar^.SysCom^.CrtInfo.Height - 1;
  TermWidth := GlobalVar^.SysCom^.CrtInfo.Width - 1;
  ClEoln := GlobalVar^.SysCom^.CrtCtrl.EraseEol;
  ClEos := GlobalVar^.SysCom^.CrtCtrl.EraseEos;

  Printables := CharSet{' '..'}'};
  True  := CharSet{'T', 't', 'Y', 'y'};
  False := CharSet{'F', 'f', 'N', 'n'};
END SimpleCRT.
```

When the module body is executed, it initializes several variable values. Of particular interest are the first five assignment statements. These statements take advantage of a UCSD global variable module to access the operating system values for the variables

TermHeight (Terminal Height)
TermWidth (Terminal Width)
ClEoln (Clear to end of line character)
ClEos (Clear to end of screen character)

The variables ClEoln and ClEos are character variables. Writing ClEoln, e.g., InOut.Write(ClEoln), will cause the line that the cursor is positioned on to be erased starting at the cursor's location and continuing to the end of the line. Clear to the End Of the Line is what ClEoln stands for.

The alternative, which would be the normal method, is to set these values as global constants in the CRT module. The option shown here is used in a large CRT module that runs on two different makes of computers, both using the same operating system and language implementation. Although the values of these parameters are different for both systems—e.g., TermHeights of 24 and 25 and TermWidths of 40/80 vs. 80—this approach allows exactly the same code to be used on both machines. Otherwise, the global constant sections would each be different. In the original module, from which this is derived, the constant declaration differences would be substantial. There are 15 terminal parameters in that version. The approach shown here provides greater portability as long as the operating system conventions are the same for all implementations.

Each procedure performs rudimentary error tests to insure that screen boundaries are not being violated. An enumeration variable, CrtResult, is set by each procedure if the specified operation is completed successfully.

A single function, GotoXY, which is imported from the Volition Systems library module named Screen, is especially important. It positions the cursor to specified screen locations.

The procedure UserInput is a variant of the procedure GetCharacter that was developed in Chapter 8. The procedure Prompt, which in turn calls UserInput, is used extensively in Chapter 12's word processing program in order to elicit user inputs by displaying a prompt that provides a menu of choices to the user and forces a valid input in response to the prompt.

SUMMARY

This chapter presented a description of Modula-2 input/output operations that support reading (and writing) from (and to) a variety of peripheral devices. The Volition Systems library modules that support general text and file input/output were used as examples. In addition, two general purpose utility modules were introduced. The user can incorporate these routines directly in programs to achieve general purpose file redirection capabilities and a minimal CRT support package.

QUESTIONS AND PROBLEMS

1. Identify the input/output capabilities provided by your Modula-2 implementation.
2. Write a rudimentary data storage and retrieval system using the file input/output approach sketched in Listing 9.2.
3. Write a program that incorporates the FileStuff module (Listing 9.3), and experiment with using all possible combinations of input/output devices by means of interactive device specification. Incorporate a simple loop that asks for input source and output destination, reads a string, and writes the string to the destination.
4. Try Problem 3 using the InOut module procedures of Chapter 5.
5. Rewrite Problem 3 using the SimpleCRT module (Listing 9.5) to perform your user interface actions.

SUPPLEMENTAL PROBLEMS

Problem 1

Extend the CRT library module functions discussed in this chapter and in Chapter 12 to include all the CRT functions that are imported in the Appendix E program.

Problem 2

Modify the input/output portions of the calculator program to display a calculator on the screen. The calculator should have "keys" to match all allowable inputs and commands. The "calculator's" display should work exactly like a real calculator when "keys" are pressed by the user. (This includes numbers entering the display from the right side of the display.)

Problem 3

Modify the "math" procedures to allow the calculator to be used in binary, octal, decimal, and hex—as a user keyboard option. For the truly dedicated—include another option to convert data from one number base to another.

CHAPTER 10

RECURSION

NEW CONCEPTS: Recursive Definitions and Procedures
ISSUES: Programmer and Computer Efficiency

INTRODUCTION

This chapter is in no way critical to the understanding of Modula-2 and may be skipped. The purpose of this chapter is to illustrate the capabilities of Modula-2 in supporting recursive programming techniques.

If you are already familiar with recursion and recursive programming, there is little new for you in this chapter. If you are new to recursive problems, definitions, and programming techniques, this chapter will provide an introduction to the subject.

The topic of recursion can be difficult to grasp, although it is inherently very simple. For our purposes, recursion is first and foremost a way of describing something. A way of describing a mathematical object, a way of describing a data structure, a way of describing a solution to a puzzle, a way of *describing* something.

Given that something can be described recursively, it is eligible for solution by recursion. "Eligible for solution" does not imply that it *must* be solved by recursive techniques. Rather it *can be* solved recursively if the programming language supports recursion and if recursion is an appropriate technique for solving the specific problem ("appropriate" will be discussed later).

Conversely, if a recursive description is not possible, then neither is a recursive solution. To repeat, it all starts with the description. The solution by means of Modula-2 or other programming languages is a secondary consideration. In the remainder of this section, we will concentrate on providing illustrations of recursive definitions of things.

There are several categories of problems that lend themselves to recursive definitions and solutions. One such case is the category of mathematical formulae whose definitions are inherently recursive. By this we mean a mathematical expression whose definition of a general term in the expression is stated as a function of the preceding terms. Since this is not intended to be a book on mathematics, the explanation of mathematical recursion will be kept very simple. The purpose is to illustrate the application of Modula-2 recursive programming techniques and not to train mathematicians. With that apology, let's use the following as an example of mathematical recursion.

A formula is recursive if I can determine the answer for the case of x+1 (where x is meant to represent a number) after you tell me the answer for the case of x. A classical example of a mathematical function whose definition can be stated in a recursive form is the factorial, where N factorial, N!, is equal to

$$N! = N * (N-1) * (N-2) * (N-3) * \ldots * 3 * 2 * 1 \tag{1}$$

for all non-negative values of N and where 0! is defined to be equal to one. Another way (the recursive way) to write equation (1) is

$$N! = N * (N - 1)! \tag{2}$$

which fits the description of recursive mathematical functions given above. To see that it fits, if you tell me that 3! is equal to 6 (which it is since 3! = 3 * 2 * 1 = 6), then I can tell you the answer for 4!. It is 4! = 4 * 3! = 4 * 6 = 24.

It is easy to see in the example of the factorial that recursion is a handy thing to have around. Computing the value of 100! is considerably easier if the value of 99! (or any large number less than 100) is available. All that needs to be done is to multiply the known value of 99! by 100. That is far easier than multiplying 1*2*3* . . . *97*98*99*100.

We will discuss in a later section that recursive programming techniques are not the best way to handle the computation of factorials. This is an example of a case where the problem is eligible, but not appropriate, for recursive solution. Better ways exist.

Another case in which recursion is a useful solution technique is when the program data structure is (or can be) defined recursively. The classic examples here are related to the dynamic data structures that were addressed in Chapter 7. The tree, a version of the linked list used as an example of a dynamic data structure in Chapter 7, will serve as an example for a recursively defined data structure later in this chapter.

Basically, the logic for a recursive data structure proceeds as follows. What is a linked list (or stack, or queue, or tree, or . . .)? A linked list is a data structure consisting of a node with a data element (possibly empty) and a pointer element (possibly NIL, i.e., pointing at nothing) that points to a linked list.

That last sentence gave the recursive definition of a linked list data structure, in case you missed it. The definition of a linked list was given in terms of itself, just as the definition of a factorial was given in terms of a factorial.

The definition says that a linked list can be simply a NIL pointer, which points at nothing, or it can be a node pointing to a linked list. It also says that eventually the list will come to an end. That is, sooner or later a node (the last one) is going to point at the linked list, which is the nothing-linked list.

If this leaves you with an empty sort of feeling, it takes a while for the light to shine through. An example later in the chapter will help. The details of data structures are subjects of entire texts and courses that we cannot hope to duplicate here. We are trying to get back to Modula-2.

There are other categories of problems that can be defined, and thus solved, recursively. Included in this grouping are what might be classified as puzzles and games. A classic example is the Towers of Hanoi puzzle, which involves moving a series of disks of varying sizes from one tower (peg) to another. There are three towers (pegs) and any number of disks (rings) that are placed on the towers. At the start of the game, all of the disks are on one tower. The disks are arranged in order of size, with the largest disk at the bottom of the stack. The object of the game is to move all of the disks from the starting tower (say from tower 1) to one of the other towers (say tower 3). The rules state that only one disk can be moved at a time, and a larger disk can never be placed on a smaller disk.

Now you may be asking what this has to do with recursion. The relationship of this puzzle to recursive techniques lies in the way that the solution method can be described. To illustrate, suppose there are 5 disks to be moved (still one at a time). Then, instead of the original problem statement of

1. Move all (the top 5) disks from tower 1 to tower 3.

we can restate the problem as

1. First, move the top 4 disks from tower 1 to tower 2.
2. Then move the bottom disk from tower 1 to tower 3.

Notice what just happened. The alternative statement of the problem just reduced the problem from having to solve a 5-disk problem to one of 4 disks. In general, what is done is to state

SOLUTION FOR MOVING N DISKS FROM TOWER 1 → 3
- Solve for N-1 DISKS FROM 1 → 2
- Move bottom disk FROM 1 → 3

and then note that the first statement says to solve the same problem, except with one fewer disks and using a different tower combination. This is a recursive solution definition. The statement says to solve the problem by solving the problem, only each time the problem is a little smaller and easier, until the number of disks, N, is one. Since it seems that every programming book ever written that includes a section on recursion also includes a sample program for the Towers of Hanoi, please remember this book as "the one that didn't."

This introduction hopefully described at least one example of recursion to which you were able to relate. With this basis, the next section will describe the general programming approach used for the solution of these problems, followed by several sample Modula-2 programs.

10.1 RECURSION TECHNIQUES

The basis of recursion techniques is that the problem to be solved involves a recursive definition—(of a recursive definition of the problem to be solved (of a . . . you get the idea)). For example, "The way to compute 4 factorial is to first compute 3 factorial."

This answer, in and of itself, is useless unless it leads to an answer that stands alone—that is, no more recursion. In the case of the factorial example, here is how it happens:

" . . . and to compute 3!, first compute 2!; and to compute 2! first compute 1!; and to compute 1!, first compute 0!; and here's the end of the line."

The factorial eventually stops because factorials are not defined for negative numbers, and therefore we stop at zero. Furthermore, the answer for 0! is a *given* (it is defined to equal 1), and does not depend on the recursive definition of factorial.

So we see that problems that can be solved by recursion techniques require

- recursive definitions, *and*
- a terminating condition that has a known result or value.

Given that we have a problem that meets these criteria, and is therefore a candidate for solution by recursive methods, what is required from the problem-solving programming language? A language that allows procedures to call all visible procedures is required. (See Chapter 8 for program element visibility related to procedures.)

A specific example of what is required is the ability for a procedure to call itself (any procedure is visible to itself). With this capability, if we had a procedure that computed the value of N!, (where N was a formal parameter and N! was returned by the procedure), then the procedure could call itself to compute (N−1)!, and again for (N−2)! . . . until the value of the parameter is 0, since 0 is the terminating condition. Then the procedure would proceed to unwind itself.

Unwinding the factorial requires each procedure to

- wait for the result returned by the procedure that it called,
- multiply this result by the number that it received in its formal parameter list when it was called, and
- pass this new result on to its caller (who proceeds to repeat the process).

The only thing unique in unwinding the factorial, as compared to any other recursive function, is the second step. This step carries out the recursive definition for a factorial. This definition says that N! is equal to N (the procedure's formal parameter) multiplied by (N−1)! (the result returned by the procedure that was called by the current procedure). If the second step said "Perform whatever action the recursive definition calls for" then these three steps apply to every recursive procedure.

In many ways, recursive programming solutions make the programmer's code writing task shorter and easier. Often though, the programmer's time or convenience is being traded for computer resources. The use of recursive procedure calls adds time and memory overhead to the computer's normal operation.

As a general rule, if a repetitive step-by-step procedure can be developed as the solution to a problem, it will probably be more efficient than the corresponding recursive formulation. Recursive techniques are best for problems that would be difficult or impossible to handle any other way. This latter observation should be tempered by recognition of the fact that virtually any problem can be solved without having to rely on recursive procedures.

10.2 RECURSION IN MODULA-2

Modula-2 is well-suited to the task of recursive programming. Modula-2 procedures, both normal and function, can call themselves. A procedure calling itself is not the only form of recursive programming. Another case that results in recursion is when procedure A calls procedure B, which in turn calls A. In this instance, the recursive call is indirect, but nevertheless recursive.

In order to consider a specific example of recursion using Modula-2, let's continue with the factorial example. The program of Listing 10.1 computes and prints the value of N! for values of N from 0 to 8. The reason for limiting ourselves to this range is that 9! is 362880, which is larger than the largest allowable CARDINAL value on our system.

In Listing 10.1, we see that the following body of the recursive procedure, Factorial, is simple and straightforward. (And hopefully it is not a surprise if you started at the beginning of the chapter.)

```
IF n = 0 THEN
    RETURN 1
ELSE
```

LISTING 10.1

```
MODULE RecursionDemo;

FROM InOut IMPORT WriteCard, WriteLn;


PROCEDURE Factorial(n : CARDINAL) : CARDINAL;
    BEGIN (*Factorial*)
      IF n = 0 THEN
          RETURN 1
      ELSE
          RETURN n * Factorial(n - 1)
      END (*if*);
    END Factorial;


CONST
    MaxFact = 8;
VAR
    N : CARDINAL;

BEGIN (*RecursionDemo*)
    FOR N := 0 TO MaxFact DO
        WriteCard(N, 1);  WriteCard(Factorial(N), 8);  WriteLn;
    END (*for*);
END RecursionDemo.
```

        RETURN n * Factorial(n − 1)
    END (*if*);

The procedure first checks for the terminating condition. If the parameter value does not equal zero, then the recursive definition of factorial, i.e., n! = n * (n−1)!, is executed. The latter causes the procedure to call itself. Termination of the procedure is guaranteed since each time the statement

    RETURN n * Factorial(n − 1)

is executed, the value of the parameter is reduced by 1, and eventually will become zero.

We had mentioned that recursion should not be used if a simple repetitive procedure was available. A replacement for the recursive version of Factorial would appear similar to the procedure shown in Listing 10.2.

LISTING 10.2

```
PROCEDURE Factorial(n : CARDINAL) : CARDINAL;
    VAR
        fact : CARDINAL;
    BEGIN (*Factorial*)
        fact := 1;
        WHILE n > 1 DO
            fact := fact * n;
            DEC(n);
        END (*while*);
        RETURN fact;
    END (*Factorial*);
```

As a final observation regarding the two different Factorial procedures, note that neither checks to see if the value of the parameter is legal (e.g. is n negative?). This is not a good practice to mimic.

Trees

Chapter 7 covered dynamic data structures and gave a number of examples. Each of the examples had a common structure, which was that of a two-part node. One part was the data and the other was a pointer to another such node. All of the examples in Chapter 7 used a single pointer.

As a final example of recursion, we will use a data structure similar to that used in Chapter 7, except in this case the nodes will have two pointers, as shown in Figure 10.1a. One of the data structures that can be constructed from this basic element is called a tree. A binary tree is shown in Figure 10.1b. The data structure pointed to by the left pointer is called the left subtree, and that pointed to by the right pointer is the right subtree.

The binary tree is a very useful structure. It is used in applications such as maintaining lists of data. Lists kept in this manner can be searched for a specific member of the list very rapidly. Our example will demonstrate this application.

A binary tree can be used to maintain data in such a fashion that the data can be efficiently retrieved in sorted order. It is a trivial task to retrieve data in either ascending or descending order if the data is kept in a binary tree. Furthermore, a recursive search algorithm is an elegant data insertion and retrieval technique for use with binary trees. The applicability of recursion to binary trees stems from the fact that the definition of the tree data structure is inherently a recursive definition.

In order for a binary tree to be used for retrieval, the data must be inserted into the tree in a special way. The method requires that all data stored in nodes to the left of the current node (in the left subtree) must be less than the current node's data. Conversely, all data in the right subtree must be greater than the data in the current node. The data in the nodes of Figure 10.1b satisfy this requirement.

When data is stored as described, it is very easy to determine if a data element is in the tree. Furthermore, if the element is not in the tree, its correct location is determined at the same time that its absence is confirmed. The following sequence of steps, which will be translated into a Modula-2 procedure, illustrates an algorithm for searching/inserting data in a binary tree.

1. Start at the root (top node) of the tree.
2. If the tree is empty then insert the new item here.
3. Else if NewItem < NodeDataItem then search left subtree.
4. Else if NewItem > NodeDataItem then search right subtree.
5. Else item is already in the tree.

Each subtree that is pointed to by a node's left or right pointer is itself a binary tree. Therefore, steps 3 and 4 make the 5-step algorithm a recursive algorithm. Both step 3 and step 4 say to do this same procedure all over again, but use a new tree that is one level smaller (lower).

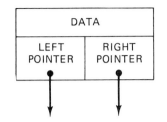

FIGURE 10.1a Binary Tree Node

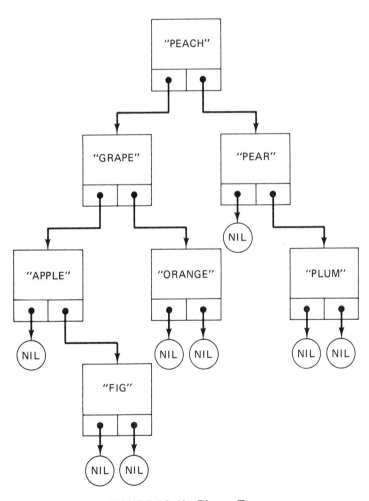

FIGURE 10.1b Binary Tree

The algorithm meets our previously stated criteria—its definition is recursive and eventually the procedure will terminate. Termination is guaranteed because each time step 3 or 4 is executed, the tree gets smaller and will eventually shrink to a height of zero. Termination will also occur at step 5 if the new item is found in the tree.

The implementation of a recursive binary tree algorithm is especially simple in Modula-2 through the use of pointer types, dynamic data elements, and recursive procedure calls. This program is shown in Listing 10.3.

The 5-step algorithm described above is implemented in a procedure called TreeSearch. Node data values, to be inserted into the tree, are passed to TreeSearch, along with a pointer to the root of the tree. When the data entry is complete, the list is printed by SortTheTree in either ascending or descending order.

This solution can be compared to earlier schemes for a similar problem in Chapter 7, in which we started with an array formulation of the solution to a sorting problem and then progressed to a linked list. With the recursive binary tree formulation, we have come to the end in terms of sophistication and elegance.

LISTING 10.3

```
MODULE BinaryTree;

FROM InOut IMPORT
    Done, Read, ReadInt, WriteInt, WriteLn, WriteString;

FROM Storage IMPORT            (*for dynamic data allocation*)
    ALLOCATE, DEALLOCATE;

TYPE
    TreePointer = POINTER TO Tree;
    Tree = RECORD
                Data : INTEGER;
                LeftPointer,
                RightPointer : TreePointer;
            END;
VAR
    TreeRoot : TreePointer;


PROCEDURE TreeSearch(key : INTEGER; VAR Root : TreePointer);
    BEGIN (*TreeSearch*)
        IF Root = NIL THEN (*the key is not in the tree; insert it*)
            NEW(Root);
            WITH Root^ DO
                Data := key;
                LeftPointer := NIL;
                RightPointer := NIL;
            END (*with*);
```

```
            ELSIF key < Root^.Data THEN
                  TreeSearch(key, Root^.LeftPointer);
            ELSIF key > Root^.Data THEN
                  TreeSearch(key, Root^.RightPointer);
            ELSE (*key is already in the tree, skip it*)
            END (*if root*)
      END TreeSearch;


PROCEDURE SortTheTree(Root : TreePointer; AscendingOrder : BOOLEAN);
    BEGIN (*SortTheTree*)
        IF Root # NIL THEN
            WITH Root^ DO
                IF AscendingOrder THEN
                    SortTheTree(LeftPointer, AscendingOrder);
                ELSE
                    SortTheTree(RightPointer, AscendingOrder);
                END (*if*);
                WriteLn; WriteInt(Data, 6);
                IF AscendingOrder THEN
                    SortTheTree(RightPointer, AscendingOrder);
                ELSE
                    SortTheTree(LeftPointer, AscendingOrder);
                END (*if*);
            END (*with*);
        END (*if*);
    END SortTheTree;



VAR
    NewNumber : INTEGER;

    Reply : CHAR;
    AscendingSort : BOOLEAN;

PROCEDURE GetNewNumber;
    BEGIN (*GetNewNumber*)
        WriteString('Enter a number: ');    ReadInt(NewNumber);
    END GetNewNumber;


BEGIN (*BinaryTree*)
    TreeRoot := NIL;
    GetNewNumber;
    WHILE (*ReadInt was*) Done (*properly, i.e. not eof*) DO
        TreeSearch( (*for*) NewNumber, (*starting at*) TreeRoot);
        GetNewNumber;
    END (*while*);

    WriteLn;  WriteString('Sort in ascending order (Y/N)? ');
    Read(Reply);
    AscendingSort := CAP(Reply) = 'Y';
    SortTheTree( (*starting at*) TreeRoot, (*in*) AscendingSort);
END BinaryTree.
```

The procedures of the sample program can be used for any data storage and retrieval that requires a binary tree formulation. Although we defined the data section of the node in the Tree record as Data : INTEGER; this was for simplicity of example. Typically, the tree node would be made up of a search key (Data, in our case), a data element of any structure and complexity, and the left/right pointers.

The procedure TreeSearch follows the 5-step word algorithm presented earlier almost exactly. If you can state in words what needs to be done, you should be able to convert those words to Modula-2 code very easily. Conversely, if you cannot describe the process, neither Modula-2 nor any other language is going to help. We feel that pseudo-code (a mixture of English and Modula-2 language elements, in this case) to describe an algorithm is far superior to flow-charting techniques for program development and documentation.

The procedure SortTheTree takes advantage of the special manner that data is stored in a binary tree to list the data in order. The trick of proceeding in ascending or descending order depends simply on whether the tree is traversed from left to right or from right to left. Books on the subject of data structures have much more to say on these topics.

SUMMARY

This completes the coverage of recursion using Modula-2. The key elements of recursion are

- procedures that call themselves (directly or indirectly),
- pointer types,
- dynamic data structures based on records and pointers, and
- recursive definition of the problem.

The subject of recursion is not essential to writing programs in Modula-2. However, the ability to formulate recursive solutions to problems is oftentimes very useful.

QUESTIONS AND PROBLEMS

1. Rewrite the binary tree example *without* using recursion.
2. Masochists only—program a recursive solution for the Towers of Hanoi.

SUPPLEMENTAL PROBLEMS

Problem 1

Investigate potential uses for recursion in your calculator program. Note the recursive call in the Subtract procedure in Appendix E.

Problem 2

Add a factorial function to your calculator. Do it with and without the use of recursion.

CHAPTER 11

LOW-LEVEL FACILITIES

NEW CONCEPTS: Concurrent Processes, Tasks, Monitors
ISSUES: Synchronization

11.1 OVERVIEW

Traditionally, high-level structured languages were used for application programs while detailed work, such as implementing an operating system, was done in assembly language. The assembly language programmer was required to code one assembly language instruction for each machine language instruction produced in the final program. Hence, assembly language programmers did not have the structured programming and data abstraction benefits that come with higher level languages. Perhaps the most compelling reason for the use of assembly language to code important system routines was the fact that humans could generally produce more efficient assembly language programs than could be generated by a compiler from a source program written in a high-level language. However, as compiler optimization techniques improved, this was no longer necessarily true. Yet, most operating systems continue to be coded in assembly language, primarily because many of the popular high-level languages lack the ability to express the types of data structures and procedural operations that are involved in coding an operating system. Modula-2 was intended to eliminate this gap found in other high-level languages. Modula-2's low-level facilities permit the expression of many programming concepts that previously required the use of assembly language.

Although the design issues for operating systems are beyond the scope of this book, an understanding of Modula-2's low-level facilities can be helpful in

265

a wide variety of computer applications. With increased emphasis on user interfaces, such as the trends toward windows and integrated software packages, the distinction between single purpose application programs and multitasking operating systems is vanishing. More application programs will interact with users through their operating systems on an increasingly sophisticated level. Hence, a programming language, such as Modula-2, which permits both high-level and low-level communication with its environment can offer the flexibility necessary to adapt to these trends. As an example of the power of Modula-2's low-level facilities, the entire operating system for Wirth's Lilith minicomputer was written in Modula-2.

One difficulty in defining a high-level language for system programming is that many programming details are machine specific. For example, some computers have an 8-bit word length while others have a 32-bit length. Although these differences cannot be ignored, the module concept makes a standardized approach toward machine-specific details possible. All machine-specific details have been isolated in a standard library module. When Modula-2 is implemented on a new machine, the vendor merely has to provide the machine-specific module with his software package. This chapter will review these standard modules. We will also review Modula-2's facilities for manipulating specific machine locations (which is frequently required for controlling input/output devices), and we will also examine library routines that support concurrent processing. Concurrent processing is a technique for performing more than one function at a time by switching between the functions so that the computer is kept fully utilized.

Although this chapter will introduce little by way of new syntax or data types, it provides a useful review of material already covered and a glimpse at a future trend in high-level programming. This chapter is not intended to be a comprehensive treatment of a low-level programming, nor of Modula-2's low-level facilities. These topics are beyond the scope of this book.

11.2 MACHINE-LEVEL DATA REPRESENTATION

System-dependent features in Modula-2 arise on two fronts. First, a program might have to deal with nonstandard data representation (which might come from an input device or another machine.) Or, second, a Modula-2 program might have to override the normal assignment of variables to memory locations in order to assure that a variable is stored in the exact memory address specified by the programmer.

Let's take a moment to review how data is stored in a computer. The computer's memory is divided into words. Typically each variable is assigned to one or more words, with different data types requiring different amounts of memory. Chapter 9 introduced three procedure functions from the System module that provide information about how variables are stored. SIZE(v) returns a CARDINAL value with the number of memory positions (but not necessarily WORDs) that the variable v occupies. TSIZE(t) returns the number of positions that variables of TYPE t will occupy. ADR(v) returns a pointer value to where variable v is located in storage.

But these functions merely help locate the words of data representing a variable. How is the data stored and how can it be manipulated? Each WORD contains a series of binary digits (bits). The number of bits depends upon the implementation. Each data type has a special convention for representing the type's values as bits. For example, BOOLEAN variables merely store a 0 or 1 in the least significant bit. REAL variables divide the storage into two parts to represent both the exponent and fractional part of a number.

Low-level programming requires a detailed understanding of how your implementation represents data types. Regardless of what data types your program will manipulate, Modula-2 provides a high-level tool for expressing operations on the individual bits in each word. If your data is transferred to a variable of type BITSET (see Chapter 6), then each binary digit will be represented by the presence or absence of a number in the BITSET variable. The bits are numbered from 0 to 15 for a 16-bit computer, where bit 0 is the least significant and 15 is the most significant bit. The representation of the BITSET value {15,3,1} is shown by:

15	14	13	12	11	10	9	8	7	6	5	4	3	2	1	0
1	0	0	0	0	0	0	0	0	0	0	0	1	0	1	0

11.2.1 Loosening Type Restrictions

In order to assure that Modula-2 programs can be transported between different types of computers, programmers generally avoid relying upon the specific details of how various types of data are encoded in the computer's memory. There are numerous exceptions to this guideline. For example, the ASCII coding scheme for characters is so common that most programmers assume ASCII character sets when using the ORD and CHR standard procedures. Another potential problem area is the REAL number. Not only does the internal representation of a REAL number vary from system to system, but the amount of memory allocated to each variable can also change. Similarly, with character strings the number of characters stored in each computer word is system dependent.

Some of these system-dependent features are described in the library module SystemTypes. This module defines constants for the smallest and largest INTEGER values, and the largest CARDINAL value. Two other constants that are useful if address arithmetic must be performed are the number of machine-addressable locations per WORD and the number of characters that can be stored in one WORD. The definitions from SystemTypes for the Volition Systems implementation on the Apple are in Listing 11.1.

LISTING 11.1

```
(* Listing 11.1 - System dependent data definitions *)


DEFINITION MODULE SystemTypes;

EXPORT QUALIFIED
  MinInt, MaxInt, MaxCard, AdrsPerWord, CharPerWord;

  CONST
    MinInt = -32768;
    MaxInt = 32767;
    MaxCard = 65535;
    AdrsPerWord = 2;
    CharPerWord = 2;

END SystemTypes.
```

Aside from these constants, a programmer is on his own in coping with system-dependent features. However, unlike certain strongly typed languages such as Pascal, Modula-2 will get out of the way of a programmer who is willing to accept complete responsibility for coping with internal representations. Modula-2 offers two alternative methods for suspending its type checking, which usually prevents values that are not assignment compatible from being mixed. The first device is type transfer functions, which were introduced in Section 4.1.2. A type transfer function can be used with any data types that occupy identical amounts of memory, including those defined by a programmer. For example, consider Listing 11.2, which we will discuss one part at a time.

In Listing 11.2, procedure HashKey illustrates the use of type transfer functions. The user-defined type called hash is used to convert data that is in the form of record type EmpRec into type hash. With a type transfer function, the name of the destination data type is used as if it were a previously defined

LISTING 11.2

```
(* Listing 11.2 - use of type transfer function *)

MODULE Convert;

  FROM InOut IMPORT  WriteString, WriteCard, WriteInt, WriteHex, WriteLn

  FROM SYSTEM IMPORT WORD, ADR, ADDRESS, SIZE, TSIZE;

  FROM SystemTypes IMPORT AdrsPerWord;

  TYPE
    EmpRec = RECORD
               name : ARRAY[0..7] OF CHAR;
               WorkLoc : CARDINAL;
               id : CARDINAL;
               END;

    hash = ARRAY[0..5] OF INTEGER;

  VAR
    employee : EmpRec;
    key      : INTEGER;

  (* dump memory to demonstrate the effect of type transfer *)
  PROCEDURE MemDump(ptr: ADDRESS; size: CARDINAL);
  BEGIN
    WriteString("Starting address:");
    WriteHex(CARDINAL(ptr),6);
    WriteString(", Size = ");
    WriteCard(size,4);
    WriteLn;
    size := (size+1) DIV AdrsPerWord;
    WHILE size>0 DO
      WriteHex(CARDINAL(ptr^),6);
      INC(ptr, TSIZE(WORD)); (* move on to next word *)
      DEC(size);
    END;
    WriteLn;
  END MeDump;

  (* a context where a type transfer function might be applied *)
  PROCEDURE HashKey(ee:EmpRec):INTEGER;
    VAR
      reckey  : hash;
      i,j     : INTEGER;
    BEGIN
      MemDump(ADR(ee),SIZE(ee));  (* Display the incoming data *)
      reckey := hash(ee);   (* type transfer function *)
      MemDump(ADR(reckey),SIZE(reckey));
      (* The following is an arbitrary arithmetic combination
         of the data to generate a key number to be used
         in some other storage scheme *)
      := reckey[0];
```

LISTING 11.2 (continued)

```
    FOR i := 1 TO 5  DO
        j := CARDINAL(BITSET(j + reckey[i]) * {0..12});
    END;  (* FOR *)
    RETURN(j);
END HashKey;


BEGIN
    WITH employee DO
        id := 4994;
        name := 'Smith';
        WorkLoc := 43;
    END;
    key := HashKey(employee);
    WriteString("key = ");
    WriteInt(key,6);
END Convert.
```

function procedure that has only one parameter—a source variable of any type. Note that a type transfer function does not actually perform any conversions. It merely avoids a compiler error for incompatible types. The differences in internal representation must be handled by the program.

Procedure HashKey contains several other examples of type transfer functions. The HashKey procedure is designed to add up all of the memory locations in an EmpRec and produce a INTEGER value that can be used in a storage scheme. Although devising appropriate hashing functions to perform this function is beyond the scope of this book, HashKey uses a simple calculation to illustrate the use of the standard data type BITSET.

After every addition, we want to drop the three most significant bits in the sum. As a result our key will be an integer in the range of 0..4095. The assignment statement in the FOR loop adds each successive word to j, and then considering that value as a set of bits, performs the equivalent of a BOOLEAN AND operation with a word with 1's in every bit except the bit positions of the three most significant bits. Using set notation, this is the BITSET value {0..12}, i.e., 1's in the first 13 positions. The * operator performs a set intersection with the sum of j and reckey[i]. This has the effect of dropping the 3 most significant bits of the internal representation of that sum. Because the result is of type BITSET, another type transfer function is needed to make the result assignment compatible with CARDINAL variable j.

A second device for writing code that avoids the usual data type restrictions consists of two data types that can be imported from Module SYSTEM. (SYSTEM is not a normal library module; it is really a part of the compiler that provides a means for expressing a number of low-level facilities.) SYS-

TEM offers a generic data type called WORD which is compatible with any data type that occupies a single machine word (typically 16-bits long). The characteristics of WORD are found in the constants AdrsPerWord and Chars-PerWord in Module SystemTypes. WORD typically appears as a formal procedure parameter type when the procedure is intended to function regardless of the actual parameter's type (see Chapter 8). If the variable to be passed to the procedure is longer than WORD's defined length, then an open-array parameter can be specified so as to accommodate just about any data object. For example,

```
PROCEDURE HandleAnything(VAR a: ARRAY OF WORD);
```

WORD also frequently appears in conjunction with a second type defined in the Module System that is called ADDRESS. ADDRESS is defined as

```
TYPE ADDRESS = POINTER TO WORD;
```

Think of an ADDRESS variable as a generic pointer that refers to objects of no particular data type.

Listing 11.2 includes PROCEDURE MemDump, which displays the contents of a specified number of contiguous memory locations beginning at a specified address. This procedure illustrates simple address arithmetic. Addresses can be used with certain operators just as if they were CARDINALS. Caution is required because, as with the case of dynamic variables and pointers, the system does not prevent you from altering unintended memory locations. This alteration could include destroying the copy of your program or the operating system itself that is in memory.

In MemDump, the constant AdrsPerWord is used to determine the number of words to be displayed. (Recall that SIZE returns the number of bytes.) The selected memory location is then displayed by WriteHex one word at a time. Because WriteHex expects a CARDINAL parameter, a type transfer function is used to convert from type WORD to type CARDINAL. The results displayed by the two calls to MemDump demonstrate that the hash type transfer function does *not* alter the internal representation of the converted data. (See Listing 11.2a.)

11.2.2 Dealing with Specific Addresses

The computer's memory is accessed by reference to internal numbers called addresses. Both pointer variables and ADDRESS variables store numbers that

LISTING 11.2a

```
(* Listing 11.2a, output from type transfer function program *)

Starting address:  77E0, Size =   12
  6D53  7469  0068  9A6A  002B  1382
Starting address:  77EC, Size =   12
  6D53  7469  0068  9A6A  002B  1382
key =   4155
```

correspond to the value required by the computer's hardware to retrieve data. Ordinarily, Modula-2 programs never refer to specific machine addresses because the compiler automatically allocates memory to each variable and these addresses are not ordinarily available to the application program. Even when using dynamic variables and pointers, a programmer does not need to know the actual contents of a pointer variable. Only the object that the pointer references is of interest. For this reason, Modula-2 provides only one pointer constant, NIL, to signify that a pointer variable is not referring to any object. However, some computers use a form of input/output where the input/output devices are assigned machine addresses as though the device was a part of the computer's memory. Operating systems and input/output routines have to be able to refer to specific memory locations in order to operate such devices. As a result, Modula-2 includes the ability to access specific computer addresses. In a sense, this feature is the equivalent of pointer constants.

For example, suppose a memory dump was needed of a special system area, called the stack, which always occupies an area beginning with machine address 100H. (Machine addresses are usually specified in hexadecimal notation.) How could the MemDump routine in Listing 11.2 be incorporated into a program to achieve this task? Modula-2's low-level facilities permit variables to be declared as occupying specific memory locations. If the variable stack were declared to occupy the proper address, then the ADR function will pass the address of the start of the stack to the pointer variable ptr in the MemDump routine. For example,

```
VAR stack[100H] : WORD;
:
:
MemDump(ADR(stack), 256);
```

Note that stack is declared just like any other variable except that a numeric constant expression, enclosed in square brackets, follows the name of the identifier.

Similarly, if a system defines a particular address as having a given input/output function, those functions can be accessed through variables allocated to memory locations. Using the Apple as an example, the following lines will produce a buzzing sound:

```
VAR speaker[OCO30H] : WORD; (* Toggles speaker when read *)
    keybdchar[OCO00H]: CHAR; (* Character typed at keyboard *)
    keywaiting[OCO10H]: BITSET; (* Read to reactivate keyboard *)
    :
FOR i := 1 TO BuzzLength DO
    j := speaker;
END; (* for *)
```

Similarly, accesses to keybdchar and keywaiting will read a character from the keyboard. Of course, because these addresses are specific to the Apple II, this program cannot be transported to other computers. In fact, there is no guarantee that other computers will have addresses that perform equivalent functions.

The data type of variables that are assigned to input/output locations should be selected with care. When the mere accessing of memory performs the input/output, as is the case with the Apple speaker, type WORD works. But if the location represents a control register whose binary digits will be examined or reset, consider using BITSET. In cases such as a keyboard device generating characters, type CHAR makes subsequent programming easier. Note that the amount of space occupied by type WORD is system dependent. In some implementations there is the possibility that you may be accessing more or less memory than was intended. This could particularly arise when a word occupies more than one memory location, as measured in terms of separately addressed units (i.e. AdrsPerWord>1).

11.3 CONCURRENT PROGRAMMING—PROCESSES

Up to this point, every sample program has executed statements in a given sequence. Although control structures modify the sequence of execution, the computer still performs only one step at a time. Increasingly, programs are expected to do more than one thing at a time, a feature called *multiprogramming* or *multitasking*. For example, a user may want to use a word processor to prepare a new document while another routine is busy printing an already completed document.

The technique of performing more than one task during a given length of time is called *concurrent processing*. Concurrent processing may involve the coordination of several processors or pieces of hardware, or it may involve sharing a single processor between a number of different tasks. Most micro-computer applications involve the latter situation. All that is necessary to make a user think that two routines are running simultaneously is the careful sche-duling of the activities of the routines so that the processor will work on one routine while another is waiting for input/output or for some other event. The program that schedules each of these concurrent tasks is called a *monitor* or *process scheduler*. The Modula-2 tasks that operate concurrently actually share the attention of a single processor, and are called *coroutines*. Each *coroutine* that acts independently of the remainder of the program is called a *process*.

11.3.1 Coroutines

Several items imported from the System module implement coroutines in Modula-2. Type PROCESS represents a sequence of activities that will be ex-ecuted independently of the sequential execution of the main portion of the program. A Modula-2 program can have a number of different coroutines ac-tive at the same time, but each coroutine must be represented by a PROCESS variable. In addition to having a PROCESS variable, each coroutine needs a work area in memory to store temporary variables and to keep track of its own status between activations by the scheduling mechanism. Work areas generally need to be at least 100 words long.

Finally, a coroutine must have a series of instructions to execute. These instructions are coded as a normal Modula-2 procedure except for the fact that the procedure may not have parameters and if the computer reaches the end of the procedure, execution of the program terminates. As a result, coroutine procedures generally take the form of an infinite loop that does not have a ter-mination condition. Special procedure calls within the loop shift control to other coroutines.

Given a PROCESS variable, a work area, and a procedure to be executed, everything is ready to create a new process. Procedure NEWPROCESS from the System module creates processes. NEWPROCESS is defined with the fol-lowing parameters:

```
PROCEDURE NEWPROCESS(PR : PROC; A : ADDRESS; S : CARDINAL;
                     VAR PV : PROCESS);
```

where PR is the coroutine procedure, A is the address of the work area, S is the size of the work area, and PV is the PROCESS variable for this coroutine. Note that calling NEWPROCESS does not commence execution of the coroutine, it merely initializes the PROCESS variable.

A coroutine is activated by calling procedure TRANSFER, which is another element of the System module. TRANSFER has the following parameters:

```
PROCEDURE TRANSFER(VAR Pfrom,Pto: PROCESS);
```

where Pfrom is a PROCESS variable for saving the status of the current process, and Pto is the process variable to be activated. When TRANSFER is called, the execution of the Pfrom coroutine is suspended, and execution of the Pto routine commences where it left off when it was last suspended. Note that the execution status of the current coroutine is assigned to Pfrom only after all the information is extracted from Pto. As a result, the statement

```
TRANSFER(PV,PV);
```

is legal. Procedure TRANSFER is used to call the coroutine procedure rather than calling the procedure directly. TRANSFER will execute the procedure last associated with the Pto process variable. (Recall that NEWPROCESS initializes the PROCESS variable by associating it with a procedure.) In this sense, a coroutine call is different from procedure calls. In a normal procedure call, control will return at the conclusion of the called procedure. But control never returns from TRANSFER. Instead, it passes to the routine marked by the second PROCESS variable.

Listing 11.3 illustrates the use of NEWPROCESS and TRANSFER. This program has two coroutines that display the letters A and B on the screen. The A will move vertically until it collides with B, in which case it shifts to another column. The letter B will move horizontally, changing directions once every 50 moves. Both letters will appear to be moving simultaneously.

The main body of the program module Concurrent defines the initial positions of A and B and then initializes the two PROCESS variables, ProcessA and ProcessB. Having set everything up, execution of the module ceases, and its status is preserved in PROCESS variable Main. Procedure WriteA implements coroutine ProcessA. After writing the letter A in a new position, it calls TRANSFER to activate ProcessB. The status of the old coroutine is saved in ProcessA. Similarly, B performs its function and activates ProcessA, using a

LISTING 11.3

```
(* Listing 11.3, concurrency demo *)
MODULE Concurrent;

  FROM SYSTEM IMPORT
    WORD, ADR, SIZE, PROCESS, NEWPROCESS, TRANSFER;

  FROM Terminal IMPORT Write, WriteLn;

  FROM Screen IMPORT GotoXY;

  CONST MaxRow = 39;
        MaxCol = 23;
        MaxLoop = 1000;

  VAR i: CARDINAL;
      ProcessA, ProcessB, Main: PROCESS;
      A, B: ARRAY [1..200] OF WORD;
      ax, ay, bx, by : CARDINAL;
      delta          : INTEGER;

  PROCEDURE WriteA;
  BEGIN
    LOOP GotoXY(ax,ay);
      Write(' '); (* erase old a *)
      IF ay<MaxCol THEN
        ay := ay + 1;
      ELSE
        ay := 0;
      END;
      (* Collision routine *)
      IF (ax=bx) AND (ay=by) THEN
        ax := ax + 1;
        IF ax>MaxRow THEN ax :=0 END;
      END;
      GotoXY(ax,ay);
      Write('A');
      TRANSFER(ProcessA,ProcessB);
    END;
  END WriteA;

  PROCEDURE WriteB;
  BEGIN
    LOOP GotoXY(bx,by);
      Write(' ');
      bx := INTEGER(bx) + delta;
      IF bx>MaxRow THEN bx := 3 END;
      IF bx<3 THEN bx := MaxRow END;
      GotoXY(bx,by);
      Write('B');
      INC(i);
      IF i > MaxLoop THEN
        WriteLn; EXIT;
      END;
```

```
    (* Reverse direction every 50 moves *)
    IF i MOD 50 = 0 THEN delta := -delta END;
    TRANSFER(ProcessB,ProcessA);
  END;
END WriteB;


BEGIN  i := 0;
  ax := 5; ay := 12; bx :=20; by := 3;
  delta := 1;
  NEWPROCESS(WriteA, ADR(A), SIZE(A), ProcessA);
  NEWPROCESS(WriteB, ADR(B), SIZE(B), ProcessB);
  TRANSFER(Main, ProcessA);
END Concurrent.
```

TRANSFER procedure call at the end of its loop. The two routines continue
to exchange control until the IF i>Maxloop statement in WriteB exits the
loop. When the END WriteB statement is executed, the program terminates.
Try revising this program to add a third moving object or more elaborate pat-
terns.

11.3.2 Communication Between Processes

Note that the two coroutines communicate only through the global variables
ax, ay, bx, and by. Procedure WriteA uses these variables to test for a collision.
A global variable is one of two methods for communicating between coroutines. SIGNALS are the other method. Data type SIGNAL is defined in
Wirth's recommended library module Processes. Signals are used to synchro-
nize the operation of coroutines and processes. Instead of representing data,
signals represent the fact that an event has occurred. A process may either send
a signal or wait for its arrival. Because every signal denotes a particular event or
condition, arrival of the signal forms the basis for the receiving process to assume that the condition is satisfied.

Signals are necessary because of the side effect problems, which we have
repeatedly mentioned, that stem from global variables. For example, suppose
that one process listens to the keyboard until a complete command is typed
and the return key pressed. Depending upon the command, the process would
activate another process to process the command, which is stored in a global
variable. If the process for implementing the commands trys to interpret the
global command string before a value is placed there, undesired effects arise.
However, if the input process sends a signal to the implementing process to
indicate that a valid command is present in the global variable, then the actions of both coroutines will be successfully synchronized.

Wirth recommends five procedures as part of the Processes module:

1. PROCEDURE StartProcess(P:PROC;N:CARDINAL); Starts a concurrent process with procedure P and work area of size N.
2. PROCEDURE SEND(VAR S: SIGNAL); Sends a signal; causes one of the processes waiting for signal S to resume execution.
3. PROCEDURE WAIT(VAR S: SIGNAL); Suspends execution of the process until an S signal is received.
4. PROCEDURE Awaited(S: SIGNAL): BOOLEAN; Returns a TRUE if at least one process is waiting for signal S.
5. PROCEDURE Init(VAR S: SIGNAL); Initializes the signal variable S. Every signal variable must be initialized with this procedure before it is used.

Given these routines, a more sophisticated form of concurrent processing can be programmed than is available through just the use of the TRANSFER procedure. However, two programming techniques must be observed:

1. In order to give other processes a chance to execute, whenever a process is waiting for an event (such as input), a call to WAIT should be used instead of a delay loop. In effect, a call to WAIT has the effect of TRANSFERing to other processes that have tasks to perform. Similarly, a call to SEND may have the effect of TRANSFERing control to a process that has been waiting for the signal variable.
2. One process should be designated as a monitor. A monitor is a separate MODULE with a priority number designated in square brackets after the module name. All shared variables between the different processes should be encapsulated in the monitor module. The variables should be hidden in the monitor module and accessible only by calling procedures contained in the monitor. In this manner, the programmer can be assured that only one process will be accessing the shared variables at any given moment. This is guaranteed by the fact that only one procedure in the monitor module can be active at any given time.

Note the following difference between the process approach just described and the coroutine approach illustrated in Listing 11.3:

1. In coroutines, the processor (computer) shifts from working on one routine to the other through explicit calls to TRANSFER. When the

processor returns to the suspended routine, it resumes where it left off after the transfer.

2. With true processes, the sending and receiving of signals determines that control will shift between routines, but a monitor is necessary to direct control to the highest priority routine that is waiting for a signal.

The most logical application for processes are in device driver routines to service interrupt-driven input/output devices. Because the details of such devices are very much installation dependent, you should consult the implementation documentation before attempting to write such Modula-2 routines.

SUMMARY

This has been a quick sketch of the issues involved with low-level programming and Modula-2's facilities for handling these issues. A detailed treatment of these topics is beyond the scope of this book. Operating system texts and the Modula-2 implementation documentation for your particular system should provide more details and specifics.

SUPPLEMENTAL PROBLEMS

Problem 1

Extend the calculator program to do real (fractional) arithmetic rather than just whole numbers.

Problem 2

Can you think of any applications of the features of Modula-2 discussed in this chapter to the calculator?

CHAPTER 12

PUTTING IT ALL TOGETHER

INTRODUCTION

In the previous chapters we introduced the components of Modula-2. Now it's time to put all of the bits and pieces together. This is necessary in order to understand how the elements of the language work together when combined to form a program. It is especially important in the case of Modula-2, whose chief features and advantages can be best appreciated in the context of a large programming project.

To learn a language such as English, we begin by studying the basics of grammar and vocabulary. In the previous chapters, we have studied the grammar and vocabulary of Modula-2. In English, these basics are not the end objective, but a means to an end. Similarly, we study programming languages in order to be able to write programs. Learning the grammar is an essential first step.

In order to learn how to write programs, it is helpful to study sample programs. We need to examine complete Modula-2 programs in order to understand the differences between Modula-2 and other languages. Many important differences can only be understood and appreciated when viewed in the context of a complete program.

Most Modula-2 language elements, when viewed individually, do not appear to be dramatically different from similar components of other languages.

Superficially, many languages seem to offer similar capabilities. For example, how much difference is there among

Modula-2	Pascal	BASIC
FOR I := 1 TO 10 DO	FOR I := 1 TO 10 DO	10 FOR I = 1 TO 10 DO
N := N + I	N := N + I;	20 N = N + I
END;		30 NEXT I

In these examples of loop structures, the apparent differences among the languages are trivial. The real differences are obvious only when the language is looked at as a whole. So that is our objective in this chapter—to examine the complete language based on our understanding of the elements and grammar that comprise it.

This chapter presents a word processor as an example program. In describing the design and implementation of this word processor, we will point out the system-level features of Modula-2 that make it well-suited for the development of large, reliable, maintainable systems.

12.1 BASIC WORD PROCESSING FEATURES AND FUNCTIONS

Before getting into the program, let's define some terms related to word processing so that we are all talking the same language. What is a word processor? What are its basic features and functions? A word processing program allows textual material to be created, edited, and formatted for transmission to a variety of output devices. We can view the creating of text as a special form of editing and thus consider two basic word processing functions—Editing and Output Formatting. The output process should include all output devices—consoles, disks, tapes, etc.—as well as printers. Commercial word processing programs provide one or both of these functions although they do not always call themselves either text editors or output formatters when only one function is provided. The program we will be considering provides both functions as well as the input/output file utility functions that are necessary to get your text to and from a variety of file sources and destinations.

12.1.1 Text Editors

There are two basic types of text editors—line and full screen. With a line editor, the lines of the text are numbered. For example,

1. This is a sample file from a line editor.
2. Notice how each line is preceeded by a number.
3. This number is not part of the text. It exists solely
4. to allow the user to specify what portion of
5. the text is to be affected by an editing command.

In order to perform an editing operation, you must specify which line (or lines) is to be affected. For example, in order to change the word "file" in line one to "text," a typical command would be to type

```
1 R /file//text/
```

where the 1 signifies the line to be edited, R indicates that the editing operation is a replacement, and /file//text/ describes the text to be replaced and the replacement text. The editor searches the text for the line and then performs the operation. The line to be edited does not have to be displayed on the screen before it can be edited. You can be working on line 500 and still perform the change to line 1 described above.

A full-screen editor does not use line numbers. An operation is performed by moving the cursor to the screen location of the text to be edited and performing the operation directly. In the example above, we would move the cursor over the letter f in the word file, enter the exchange mode, and then type text. Full screen editors are more flexible and easier to use than line editors (unless you happen to be using a hard copy terminal, in which case moving the cursor is a problem). The program in this chapter includes a full-screen editor for use on a CRT terminal.

In order to be useful, any text editor must support at least two basic functions—text insertion and text deletion. Practically speaking, a capability to perform text replacement or exchange in the manner described in the sample above is also desirable. The alternative to a separate exchange mode is to first delete the text to be replaced and then to insert the new text. Insert, delete, and exchange are the essential features of an editor. There are other features, but their chief purpose is to provide more convenient operation.

12.1.2 Output Formatters

Similar to editors, output formatters come in two basic flavors. On the one hand, there is the "what you see is what you get" type. As an example, if we were to print the edited text with one of these systems, the printed page would be identical to the text as it appeared in the text editor (but without the line editor's line numbers). For the example above, this type of formatter would produce

```
This is a sample file from a line editor.
Notice how each line is preceeded by a number.
This number is not part of the text. It exists solely
to allow the user to specify what portion of
the text is to be affected by an editing command.
```

But isn't that what we want? Maybe, and maybe not. Suppose we needed to change the format of a page, such as page length or left, right, top, and bottom margins? Suppose we wanted a left margin of 15 and a right margin of 65 with right justification (a smooth right edge) similar to the following

```
This  is  a  sample  file  from  a  line  editor.  Notice
how  each  line  is  preceeded  by  a  number.  This  number
is  not  part  of  the  text.  It  exists  solely  to  allow
the  user  to  specify  what  portion  of  the  text  is  to
be  affected  by  an  editing  command.
```

With the "what you see" system, you may have to do the reformatting by going back and re-editing the original text. Inconvenient! So what is the alternative? The second category of formatter uses embedded commands in the text. In this approach, the text does not have to be reformatted using the editor. We would specify the format depicted in the paragraph above by preceeding the text with

```
.lm15 .rm65 .rj
```

starting in the first column of the line preceeding the affected text.

In an embedded command formatter, the presence of a special character in the first column, such as the period in the above example, indicates that a format command follows. In the example, three format commands are shown: left margin of 15, right margin of 65, and right-justified text. If we decide later that the left margin should be at column 5, we simply change .lm15 to .lm5 and it's all ready to go. We never have to make any changes to the text proper.

The text is prepared once and never has to be changed again in order to output it in any format that may be required. This is more convenient than the "what you see" editor but not very natural for a secretary who is accustomed to just typing textual material. The typical user is not used to having to include special commands within the body of typed material. Also, there is the added problem of not seeing the material in its final form until after it has been printed

A hybrid of the two formatter extremes is a good solution. Our output formatter can be used in the equivalent of either of the two extremes and serves as a good basis for developing a more sophisticated hybrid system. In its current form, the formatter can give you "what you see". It can also handle embedded commands (which include the ability to turn "what you see" on/off within different portions of the text). Lastly, default commands can be specified when the program is run by means of a menu without the need to actually embed the commands within the text. This last option is useful if one set of margins, with no special tabbed columns, is acceptable for the entire document. Suggested changes to extend the features and capabilities of the word processor will be indicated as we proceed through the chapter.

12.2 BUILDING A WORD PROCESSING PROGRAM

As we describe the word processing program, we will also discuss the program design and development process used to develop large programs. This process is the top-down design approach with stepwise refinement normally associated with structured programming. In this approach we start with a brief, top level description of the program and then fill out the details (refine the description) one step at a time. This approach is necessary for the efficient development of large, reliable, maintainable programs. (The word processor has over 1000 lines of code, not including the general purpose utility modules that it uses.)

A key element in this approach is a programming language that supports modular development and separately compiled parts. To illustrate that structured programming using Modula-2 works, the word processing program (exclusive of the File I/O and CRT utility modules) was written over a weekend in about 20 hours. This would have been difficult, if not impossible, with a language such as BASIC.

In top-down design, we start with the forest and not the trees. In the case of the word processor, we specify the major functions to be performed, i.e. text editing and output formatting, and ignore until later the details of exactly how these functions are to be implemented. We also define the approach by which the user gains access to these functions, i.e. the user interface.

The user interface is a paramount consideration which should be addressed explicitly at every step of the development. If we wait until the program is developed before paying attention to the details of interaction with the user, it will be too late. This is especially true in a program such as a word processor, where interaction with the user is the very essence of the program. The CRT utility module, which is used extensively in the program, was developed to handle the user interface.

12.2.1 The Main Program

The main program for the word processor is shown in Listing 12.1. Every detail of the program is left to three separately compiled modules: CRT, TextEditor, and TextFormatter. TextEditor and TextFormatter definition and implementation modules will be presented in this chapter. The CRT module was described in Chapter 9.

The main program presents an error-proof menu to the user, interprets the menu selection, and directs the program execution to the appropriate module. This same basic menu selection/control process is repeated within the TextEditor and TextFormatter modules for error trapping and program control. Thus, a consistent interface is presented to the user throughout the program. The consistency is made possible through the use of the same CRT module both by the main program and by all of the modules that the main program imports (uses). The CRT module is a general purpose program that provides the majority of functions needed by most programs in order to handle user screen input/output in a friendly, error-free manner.

The modules TextEditor and TextFormatter provide the editing and formatting functions. Although these modules are fairly specific to this program, they can be imported into any other program that requires either or both of these functions. The decision as to whether to provide these functions by means of separate modules, or within the word processor proper, is fairly subjective. However, we prefer the separate module approach any time there are multiple functions whose code is large or complex. If nothing else, savings in compilation time during the development and debugging phases can be substantial.

The TextEditor and TextFormatter modules use a large number of the CRT procedures. The main program only uses the PROCEDURES ClearTheScreen and Prompt and the TYPE CharSet, as specified in the program's IMPORT statement. ClearTheScreen does exactly what the name suggests. Prompt causes the string presented as the first argument, in this case the string

'MAIN MENU > E(ditor, F(ormatter, Q(uit:'

to be centered and displayed on the top line of the CRT. It also causes the

LISTING 12.1

```
MODULE WordProcessor;

FROM CRT IMPORT
        CharSet,
        ClearTheScreen,
        Prompt;

FROM TextEditor IMPORT
        Editor;

FROM TextFormatter IMPORT
        Formatter;


VAR
  AllDone : BOOLEAN;


(*********************************************************************
Our "main program" is limited to acting on the response to the main word
processor menu which it displays.  Options are to EDIT text, OUTPUT text,
or QUIT.  The editor & formatter are imported.
*********************************************************************)

BEGIN
  AllDone := FALSE;
  REPEAT
    ClearTheScreen;
      CASE CAP(Prompt('MAIN MENU > E(ditor, F(ormatter, Q(uit : ',
                       CharSet('E', 'e','F', 'f', 'Q', 'q')))  OF
        'E' : Editor;
        'F' : Formatter;
        'Q' : AllDone := TRUE;
      END (*case*);
  UNTIL AllDone;
  ClearTheScreen;
END WordProcesser.
```

system to wait until one of the characters (of TYPE CharSet) in the second
argument

{ 'E', 'e', 'F', 'f', 'Q', 'q' }

is entered from the keyboard. This procedure traps all erroneous input, i.e.
anything not specified in the second argument. The user has a choice of using
the E(ditor, the F(ormatter, or Q(uitting. The program will ignore any keys
that are pressed except upper-and lower-case E, F, and Q. Similar menu
prompts will be used throughout the program when the user must make a

choice. The prompts all begin with an identification of the current program module, MAIN MENU in the above case, to assist the user in navigating through the program.

When E(ditor or F(ormatter is selected, control shifts to the appropriate imported procedure. This process is continued indefinitely in the REPEAT ... UNTIL loop until the Q(uit option is selected. Typing a Q, for Q(uit, causes the BOOLEAN variable AllDone to be set to TRUE in the CASE statement, and thus the REPEAT ... UNTIL loop terminates and the program ends.

A major advantage of Modula-2 is that a procedure needs to be written and compiled only one time. It can then be placed in a library module for subsequent use by any client program. (See Chapter 8 for details on modules and procedures.) The importing program (and programmer) does not have to know or care how the function is implemented. Only the definition of the interface to the procedure (its name and formal parameters) is needed by the programmer in order to use the procedure.

The word processor extensively uses two general purpose utility library programs, CRT and FileStuff. FileStuff handles file procedures such as creating new files, opening existing files, closing files, and assigning files to external devices such as printers, terminals, and disks. The FileStuff library module is described in Chapter 9.

We can change the implementation code for an exported procedure for reasons of efficiency, or whatever, at any time with no effect on importing client programs so long as the interface (specified in the definition module) is not changed. If the interface is changed, recompilation of the definition module is required, followed by recompilation of the implementation module. After this recompilation, no program that imports anything from the newest version of this unit will work until it has also been recompiled. In this way, Modula-2 enforces compatibility among the parts of a large program.

12.2.2 Overview of the Editor and Formatter Modules

The definition modules for the editor and the formatter are shown in Listing 12.2 and 12.3 respectively. These two modules represent the simplest form of a definition module. They each export a single procedure without parameters. The sole function of these modules is to allow client programs access to the editor and formatter. If it were not for the desire to make the editor and formatter accessible to other programs, we could just as easily have written them as stand-alone programs. In fact, they were developed as stand alones.

LISTING 12.2

```
DEFINITION MODULE TextEditor;

EXPORT QUALIFIED
        Editor;

PROCEDURE Editor;

END TextEditor.
```

The development strategy for these two functions, which represent the heart of the word processor, was to first create each of them as separate programs. Subsequent to their development, the definition modules were written and the program modules were recompiled into library modules. This approach reduces development time by cutting down on the size of the program that must be handled (comprehended, edited, compiled, tested, and debugged) at any one time. This approach might also be dictated for reasons of computer memory space at compilation time if a program gets very large. Separate compilation is also needed for large programs that are developed by several programmers, each working independently. A language such as Modula-2, with its separately compiled programs, is ideally suited for such tasks. We will have more to say about these modules when we introduce their implementation sections.

12.2.3 Word Processor Overview Summary

This concludes the overview of the word processor. In terms of our top-down design approach, we have defined

1. a main program for user interaction and program control,

LISTING 12.3

```
DEFINITION MODULE TextFormatter;

EXPORT QUALIFIED
        Formatter;

PROCEDURE Formatter;

END TextFormatter.
```

2. two primary modules, TextEditor and TextFormatter, to perform the main word processing functions, and

3. two utility modules, CRT and FileStuff, to handle user input/output interactions and file operations.

The process of specifying the implementation details comes next.

12.3 WORD PROCESSOR IMPLEMENTATION DETAILS

We will discuss the word processor implementation in two major sections. First we will consider the TextEditor and TextFormatter modules and assume that the utility modules CRT and FileStuff are available and that they work as specified in their definition modules. We will identify the editor and formatter functions that we want our system to have, and then describe the program that provides these functions.

12.3.1 Editor Functions

The basic editor capabilities are text insertion, deletion, and exchange. As a matter of choice, we will use a full-screen editor rather than a line editor. The full-screen system is more difficult to implement but is easier and more flexible to use. Having made these choices, what functions must be implemented in the program, and how should these functions be organized?

Let's first consider overall program organization. Almost every program can be divided into the following three basic areas, which follow in sequence:

- program initialization,
- performing the major function(s) of the program, and
- program wrap up.

In terms of the editor, this organization equates to

- determining what the user wants to edit (old or new files) and getting the system ready by opening necessary files, loading them into memory, and initializing variables;
- performing text insertion, deletion, and exchange; and
- saving the edited text for future use or output.

In Listing 12.4, we present PROCEDURE Editor. This is a further stage in our top-down, stepwise refinement process. We have progressed from defining a function called Editor in the main program to further refining Editor into three smaller procedures (StartUp, ProcessText, and FinishUp), which accomplish the three steps defined above. Editor goes through these three steps in sequence and then returns to the main program. The majority of the time and effort will be spent in PROCEDURE ProcessText since that is what the editor is all about.

The three procedures in Editor use a number of imported elements. Also, the TextEditor module requires a number of global variables. Listing 12.4 shows the Editor procedure in the context of the entire TextEditor implementation module, so the imported parameters and global variables can be reviewed.

LISTING 12.4

```
IMPLEMENTATION MODULE TextEditor;

FROM ASCII IMPORT (*Some ASCII control characters that the editor will use*)
        bs,
        cr,
        esc,
        etx;

IMPORT CRT;       (*Import the entire CRT module*)

FROM Files IMPORT (*This is the same system module that was used by the*)
        Create, (*FileStuff definition module;  the operating system*)
        FILE,   (*is intelligent and only imports common elements ONCE*)
        Open;

FROM FileStuff IMPORT    (*See the earlier discussion of this module*)
        StringType,
        TextFileOpen,
        TextFileClose,
        FProc;

FROM Strings IMPORT      (*Another system module*)
        Length;

IMPORT Terminal;         (*Terminal handles terminal read & writes*)

FROM Texts IMPORT        (*System module for text stream input/output*)
        EOT,
        TEXT,
        ReadLn,
        WriteLn,
        WriteString;
```

LISTING 12.4 (continued)

```
CONST
  TermHeight = 25;              (*# of rows on the terminal*)
  TermWidth = 80;               (*# of columns on the terminal*)
  MaxRow = TermHeight - 1;      (*number the rows from 0..24*)
  MaxColumn = TermWidth -1;     (*number the columns from 0..79*)
  MaxLines = 100;               (*demo program, keep text file size small*)
  MaxString = TermWidth;        (*text line length <= screen width*)
  MaxCopy = 20;                 (*max # of lines in copy buffer*)
  Up = 310C;                    (*next 6 are IBM PC unique for cursor control*)
  Down = 320C;
  Left = 313C;                  (*a better way to do this is to use an*)
  Right = 315C;                 (*operating system that allows access to*)
  PageFwd = 321C;               (*to system "global" parameters*)
  PageBack = 311C;

TYPE
  mode = (insert, delete, exchange, output, command);
  textline = ARRAY [0..MaxString] OF CHAR;  (*basic text unit = line of char*)

VAR
  Buffer : ARRAY [1..MaxLines] OF textline;  (*text memory area = 100 lines*)
  CopyBuffer : ARRAY [1..MaxCopy] OF textline;  (*copy buffer = 20 lines*)
  EditMode : mode;        (*flag to identify what we're doing at any instant*)



PROCEDURE IOError(strg : ARRAY OF CHAR);

(************************************************************************
This is the final resting ground for all text file i/o errors.
************************************************************************)

  BEGIN (* IOError *)
    CRT.ClearTheScreen;
    CRT.CenterLine(10, 'FATAL ERROR');
    CRT.CenterLine(11, strg);
    HALT;                                    (*ABNORMAL EXIT*)
  END IOError;



PROCEDURE DisplayText(firstline, lastline, column, row : CARDINAL);

(************************************************************************
Start at row "firstline" of textbuffer; start at position "row, col"
of screen; do until end of screen or end of file, whichever comes first.
************************************************************************)

  VAR
    NmbrOfLines,
    i, j : CARDINAL;

  BEGIN (*DisplayText*)
    IF firstline > lastline THEN RETURN END;
    CRT.ClearEos(column, row);
```

```
  NmbrOfLines := lastline - firstline;
  IF NmbrOfLines >= (MaxRow - row) THEN
    NmbrOfLines := MaxRow - row;
  END;
  lastline := firstline + NmbrOfLines;
  j := column;
  FOR i := firstline TO lastline DO
    WHILE Buffer[i, j] # 0C DO
      Terminal.Write(Buffer[i, j]);     (*do this faster later*)
      INC(j);                           (*by leaving out j index*)
    END (*while*);
    j := 0;
    IF i # lastline THEN
      Terminal.WriteLn;
    END (*if i*);
  END (*for*);
END DisplayText;
```

```
+----------------------------------------------------+
:                                                    :
:        The rest of TextEditor, i.e. StartUp,       :
:                                                    :
:        ProcessText and FinishUp, belong here.      :
:                                                    :
+----------------------------------------------------+
```

```
PROCEDURE Editor;

(***********************************************************************
This is what gets exported; cycles thru 3 main steps (start, edit, save)
and then back to the calling program.

***********************************************************************)

  VAR
    NmbrOfLines : CARDINAL;
    TextToSave : BOOLEAN;

  BEGIN (*Editor*)
    StartUp(NmbrOfLines);
    ProcessText(NmbrOfLines, TextToSave);
    IF TextToSave THEN
      FinishUp(NmbrOfLines);
    END;
  END Editor;


BEGIN       (*Main body, executed at startup of client program, does nothing*)
END TextEditor.
```

The following observations regarding the overall implementation module
should be made here:

1. Listing 12.4 describes the shell of the TextEditor. It identifies the imported elements, and it declares the global parameters, i.e. constants,

types, and variables. Two procedures used by several main parts of the module are defined. Lastly, the TextEditor's exported procedure, Editor, is given. None of the details of TextEditor are visible to any program that imports the Editor procedure. There can be no side effects caused by interactions between elements of the client programs and TextEditor.

2. Listing 12.4 uses both forms of IMPORT, i.e. qualified and unqualified. In the case of Terminal, this was necessary in order to avoid conflicts with elements of Texts (e.g. a procedure named WriteLn is imported from both Terminal and Texts). This is an example of why exports from a definition module must be qualified. Otherwise, conflicts between identically named items could not be resolved.

3. Key design parameter values and system-specific values are defined as constants for ease of update and change.

4. Several limiting editor design decisions are seen in the variable declaration. The edited text is being kept entirely in memory, which limits the size of the largest text file that can be handled. Also, the text file data structure is an array of text lines, which is not the most efficient way to utilize the available memory. Improvements to these two potential problem areas are left to the reader.

5. The main body of TextEditor, which is executed when the word processor is first run, does nothing. Compare this to the main body of the TextFormatter module in the next section.

Editor StartUp

Since initialization is the first thing to be done by Editor, let's look at PROCEDURE StartUp first. This procedure determines if the user wants to edit an existing file or create new text. If the choice is an existing file, then procedure StartUp gets the name of the file, opens the file, and reads it into memory. Once the old file has been obtained, or if the user's choice is to create a new text file, editor variables are initialized.

This part of the program, like many others, places a premium on reliable and error-free user interaction and file operations. That is why the CRT and FileStuff modules are so important. This demonstrates, once again, the value of a language that supports libraries of separately compiled programs. The complete listing of procedure StartUp is shown in Listing 12.5. We will review the procedure to see what it does (and does not) do and to see how Modula-2 enhances our ability to perform these functions.

LISTING 12.5

```
PROCEDURE StartUp(VAR nmbrlines : CARDINAL);

(*********************************************************************
Menu to control "old/new" file; if old, open the file & read into memory.
*********************************************************************)


  PROCEDURE GetFile(VAR nmbrlines : CARDINAL);

  (*********************************************************************
  Open old file; depend on filestuff module imports for most of work.
  *********************************************************************)

    VAR
      InText : TEXT;
      InFile : FILE;


    PROCEDURE DiskToRam(VAR nmbrlines : CARDINAL);

    (*********************************************************************
    Read the disk file into memory.
    *********************************************************************)

      BEGIN (* DiskToRam *)
        nmbrlines := 1;
        Terminal.WriteLn;  Terminal.WriteString('Reading input file');
        LOOP
          IF nmbrlines MOD 10 = 0 THEN
            Terminal.Write('.');                  (*let user know we're alive*)
          END (*if*);                             (*takes too long*)
          ReadLn(InText, Buffer[nmbrlines]);
          IF (EOT(InText)) OR (nmbrlines = MaxLines) THEN
            DEC(nmbrlines);
            EXIT;
          END (*if*);
          INC(nmbrlines);
        END (*loop*);
      END DiskToRam;


    BEGIN (* GetFile *)
      IF NOT TextFileOpen(Open, InText, InFile, PromptIs,
                          'Enter name of file : ') THEN
        IOError('opening text file');
      ELSE
        DiskToRam(nmbrlines);
      END (*if*);
      IF NOT TextFileClose(InText, InFile) THEN
        IOError('closing text file');
      END;
      CRT.ClearTheScreen;
    END GetFile;
```

LISTING 12.5 (continued)

```
VAR
  i : CARDINAL;




BEGIN (* StartUp *)
  CRT.ClearTheScreen;
  FOR i := 1 TO MaxLines DO       (*Set length of each text line to zero*)
    Buffer[i, 0] := 0C;
  END;
  CASE CAP(CRT.Prompt('EDIT >   O(ld file,  N(ew file,  or Q(uit : ',
          CRT.CharSet('O', 'o', 'N', 'n', 'Q', 'q'))) OF
    'O' :  GetFile(nmbrlines)!
    'N' :  nmbrlines := 1!
    'Q' :  HALT                  (*ABNORMAL EXIT POINT*)
  END (*case*);
END StartUp;
```

As we look at Startup, we see that it is made up of three parts with the following program structure:

```
PROCEDURE StartUp
   PROCEDURE GetFile
      PROCEDURE DiskToRam,
```

StartUp initializes the main text storage area, Buffer, and then provides the user with the EDIT menu choices that are to edit an O(ld file, create a N(ew file, or Q(uit. This menu technique is a repeat of the process used in the main program.

In order to edit an O(ld file, the file must be identified, opened, and read into memory (into Buffer which was initialized earlier in StartUp). In StartUp, a user input of O calls the procedure GetFile. GetFile is straightforward. Module FileStuff's procedure OpenTextFile is used to obtain the name of the file to be edited from the user and to open the file. Once this is done, DiskToRam is called to transfer the file to the memory's text storage area—variable Buffer.

On returning to GetFile from DiskToRam, the file is closed since it is no longer required. GetFile, and the FileStuff procedures that it uses, interact as necessary with the user to trap errors involved in opening and closing files. For example, OpenTextFile will inform the user when a file cannot be opened (usually because it does not exist) and prompts the user to try again or to give up and return to the main menu.

DiskToRam is a file copy procedure that has broader applications than procedure StartUp. The procedure reads a file one line at a time using the system Texts module's standard input/output facilities. DiskToRam also counts the number of lines in the file since this variable is returned to the main program by StartUp.

The ReadLn procedure used by DiskToRam is convenient, but it is also very slow, as is noted in the listing comments. You will notice that the program sends a message to the user during the process of transferring the file from disk to the computer's memory. The message includes printing a dot on the screen following every ten lines that are read into memory. This is another aspect of user interaction. We do not want the user to think that the program or the computer has died.

A long-range solution is to make this section faster. It is not necessary now though. The first objective is to get something that works. Later we can come back and make improvements. This once again illustrates the benefit of separately compiled modules. The user is insulated from the details of how DiskToRam is implemented. Therefore, later on we can make the necessary go-fast changes with no impact on the client programs such as the word processor.

Editor Text Processing

The primary function of a word processor is to create text. The TextEditor procedure ProcessText provides the essential text creation functions for our word processor. Procedure ProcessText is shown in Listing 12.6.

The procedure begins by displaying the first page of the text buffer. This would be a blank screen for a new file. Next, a menu-driven control loop is entered. The user has a choice of

Edit Menu > I(nsert, D(elete, X(chng, Q(uit, Cursor move.

At this point, text can be entered, deleted, or replaced, or the user may quit. Quitting returns the user to the main program menu. An additional option is available. This option is identified as Cursor move.

In a screen-oriented editor, the process for adding, deleting, or replacing text requires moving the cursor to the location of the text to be edited before performing the edit function. This means that procedures for controlling movement of the cursor are very important in this type of editor. Furthermore, it is important that the screen display be updated as the cursor is moved, particularly as the cursor is moved past the top or bottom of the screen. This display update, known as scrolling, and cursor movement control are major implementation differences from a line editor. It is these differences that make a screen editor more difficult to implement.

LISTING 12.6

```
PROCEDURE ProcessText(VAR nmbrlines : CARDINAL; VAR texttosave : BOOLEAN);

(************************************************************************
This is the main editor control section; insert, delete, exchange & quit are
all selected/controlled from here.
*************************************************************************)

  CONST
    MainPrompt = 'Edit Menu > I(nsert, D(elete, X(chng, Q(uit, Cursor move : ';

  VAR
    Response : CHAR;
    Column,
    Row,
    TopLine : CARDINAL;

  BEGIN (* ProcessText *)
    Column := 0;          (*Row & Column are the cursor screen coordinates*)
    Row := 1;
    TopLine := 1;         (*line of text buffer which is at top of screen*)
    DisplayText(TopLine, nmbrlines, Column, Row);
    CRT.CenterLine(0, MainPrompt);

    REPEAT
      CRT.GoToxy(Column, ((Row - 1) MOD MaxRow) + 1);
      Terminal.Read(Response);
      CRT.GoToxy(Column, ((Row - 1) MOD MaxRow) + 1);
      IF Buffer[Row, Column] IN CRT.Printables THEN
        Terminal.Write(Buffer[Row, Column]);
      ELSE
        Terminal.Write(' ');
      END (*if*);
      Response := CAP(Response);
      CASE Response OF
        'I'   : EditMode := insert;
                Insert(Column, Row, TopLine, nmbrlines);
                CRT.CenterLine(0, MainPrompt)|
        'D'   : EditMode := delete;
                Delete(Column, Row, TopLine, nmbrlines);
                CRT.CenterLine(0, MainPrompt)|
        'X'   : EditMode := exchange;
                Exchange(Column, Row, TopLine, nmbrlines);
                CRT.CenterLine(0, MainPrompt)|
        'Q'   : texttosave := (Column > 0) OR (Row > 1) OR (nmbrlines > 1);
      ELSE
        EditMode := command;
        MoveTheCursor(Response, Column, Row, TopLine, nmbrlines, Column, Row);
      END (*case*);
    UNTIL Response = 'Q';
  END ProcessText;
```

Before examining each of the editing procedures in more detail, let's take a look at the control loop for ProcessText. Here we REPEAT UNTIL a Q is entered from the keyboard. As each keystroke is entered, the top of the loop restores whatever text happened to be under the cursor when a key was pressed. Next, a CASE statement interprets the keystroke. If the entry is I, D, or X, we set the variable EditMode, call the appropriate procedure, and then redisplay the menu prompt upon returning from the procedure. User interaction in this loop is fully error-trapped using the CRT module techniques.

Moving the Cursor

Let's turn to the specifics of the edit procedures. First, MoveTheCursor handles any keystroke other than I, D, or X. This procedure is shown in Listing 12.7. Basically, MoveTheCursor

- accepts a character, the formal parameter called direction, which indicates what key was pressed;
- modifies the values of the current cursor coordinates by means of a case statement (e.g. if the direction is Up, then decrement the value of y, provided $y > 1$) and returns the new x and y;
- changes the screen display if a page border is crossed (see the procedures ScreenUp and ScreenDown); and
- filters out all entries that are not valid cursor directions.

The cursor can be moved up, down, left, and right. In addition to moving one row or column at a time, PageFwd and PageBack allow the cursor to be moved ahead or back one full screen (24 or 25 lines, depending on the type of computer). A carriage return causes a move down and to the left margin, as you would expect. A right move from the end of the current line moves to column zero of the next line. Similarly, a left move from the beginning of the current line takes the cursor to the end of the previous line. Any time that the next cursor line is off the current screen, the screen is "paged."

Examination of Listing 12.7 shows that we must provide for a number of special cases. These are dependent on the EditMode and boundary conditions (top and bottom) of the screen.

Thinking back to the CASE statement in ProcessText, we recall that MoveTheCursor is responsible for all key entries except I, D, and X. Notice that the ELSE clause of the MoveTheCursor CASE statement covers all cases

LISTING 12.7

```
PROCEDURE MoveTheCursor(direction : CHAR; VAR x, y, topline : CARDINAL;
                        nmbrlines, x0, y0 : CARDINAL);


(**************************************************************************
Interpret & perform cursor moves for editor.
**************************************************************************)



PROCEDURE PageUp(VAR topline : CARDINAL; nmbrlines : CARDINAL);

(**************************************************************************
Display the previous screen page.
**************************************************************************)

    BEGIN (* PageUp *)
      topline := topline - MaxRow;
      IF topline < 0 THEN
        topline := 0;
      END;
      IF EditMode # insert THEN
        DisplayText(topline, nmbrlines, 0, 1);
      END;
    END PageUp;



  PROCEDURE PageDown(VAR topline : CARDINAL; nmbrlines : CARDINAL);

(**************************************************************************
Display the next screen page.
**************************************************************************)

    BEGIN (* PageDown *)
      topline := topline + MaxRow;          (*WHAT IF > NMBRLINES??*)
      IF EditMode # insert THEN
        DisplayText(topline, nmbrlines, 0, 1);
      END;
    END PageDown;



  PROCEDURE WrapUpMove;

(**************************************************************************
Clean up after performing the cursor moves.
**************************************************************************)

    BEGIN (*WrapUpMove*)
      IF EditMode # insert THEN
        IF x > Length(Buffer[y]) THEN
          x := Length(Buffer[y]);
        END (*if x*);
```

```
        END (*if ed...*);
        IF y < topline THEN
          PageUp(topline, nmbrlines);
        ELSIF y > (topline + MaxRow - 1) THEN
          PageDown(topline, nmbrlines);

        END;
        CRT.GoToxy(x, ((y - 1) MOD MaxRow) + 1);
      END WrapUpMove;



BEGIN (* MoveTheCursor *)
    CASE direction OF                    (*put tabs & repeat moves in later*)
      Up          : IF y > 1 THEN DEC(y) END;
      Down,
      cr          : IF direction = cr THEN
                        IF (y = nmbrlines) & (EditMode # insert) THEN
                          x := Length(Buffer[nmbrlines]);
                        ELSE
                          x := 0;
                        END(* if y...*);
                      END (*if dir...*);
                      IF (y < nmbrlines) OR (EditMode = insert) THEN INC(y) END;
      bs,
      Left        : IF x > 0 THEN
                        DEC(x);
                      ELSIF y > 1 THEN
                        DEC(y);
                        IF EditMode # insert THEN
                          x := Length(Buffer[y]);
                        ELSE
                          x := Length(CopyBuffer[1+ y - y0]);
                        END;
                      END (*if x*);
      Right       : IF x < Length(Buffer[y]) THEN
                        INC(x);
                      ELSIF y < nmbrlines THEN
                        INC(y);
                        x := 0;
                      END (*if x*);
      PageFwd     : x := 0;
                      IF y < (nmbrlines- MaxRow) THEN
                        INC(y, MaxRow);
                      ELSE
                        y := nmbrlines;
                      END (*if y*);
      PageBack    : x := 0;
                      IF y > MaxRow THEN
                        DEC(y, MaxRow);
                      ELSE
                        y := 1;
                      END (*if y*);
      ELSE          (*do nothing; avoid run time error*)
    END (*case*);

    WrapUpMove;
END MoveTheCursor;
```

except the valid cursor directions. The ELSE clause in this case is a null statement that does nothing—exactly what we want done in this case.

It is important to include the ELSE statement in this situation, or a run-time error would occur anytime that a non-valid cursor direction key was entered. Once again, we see that all possible user responses have been accounted for, and all errors are trapped.

In summary, we pass the current cursor coordinates and the move direction to MoveTheCursor. It updates the coordinates and returns them to the calling program. The responsibility for actually moving the cursor on the screen rests with the calling program (by a call to CRT.GoToxy) if an actual move is appropriate. MoveTheCursor is called by Insert, Delete, and Xchange, in addition to ProcessText.

A number of enhancements can be considered for MoveTheCursor. These could include commands to move the cursor to the beginning of the file, to the end of the file, to the beginning or end of the current line, to the next word, to the next sentence, and so on. The current modularized implementation makes these enhancements easy to do. For example, a jump to the start of the file [you must define a command for this, e.g. B(eginning to indicate that pressing B is required] is accomplished by setting x to zero and y to one within MoveTheCursor's CASE statement (CASE direction OF beginning).

Text Insertion

Probably the most fundamental text editing function is the ability to add (insert) text to a file. A new file is created by inserting text on what is initially a blank screen (an empty file). Text deletion, replacement, and formatting have no meaning if you cannot add the text to begin with.

The ProcessText Procedure that handles text addition is Insert. This procedure is shown in Listing 12.8. Insert is the most complicated of the procedures that will be presented. Basically, what it must do is

- keep track of where, within the existing text, the insertion began (beginning, middle, end?).
- make room on the screen when new text is inserted prior to the end of the current file.
- read and interpret every keystroke.
- place inserted text into a special buffer (CopyBuffer).
- perform cursor moves as required.
- merge the new text with the old when the insert is completed.

LISTING 12.8

```
PROCEDURE Insert(VAR x, y, topline, nmbrlines : CARDINAL);

(*************************************************************************
One of the 3 main edit functions; adds new text.
*************************************************************************)

  TYPE
    splittype = (none, active, inactive);

  CONST
    SubPrompt = 'INSERT - <CTRL-C> accepts,  <Esc> escapes : ';

  VAR
    Ch : CHAR;
    Y0, X0 : CARDINAL;
    TempBuffer : textline;
    SplitLine : splittype;


  PROCEDURE RightJustify(strg : ARRAY OF CHAR; row : CARDINAL);

  (*************************************************************************
  If 1st insert is before end of line, drop remainder of line down 1 row and
  move to far right so user can see where new insertions fits.
  *************************************************************************)

    VAR
      Column : CARDINAL;

    BEGIN (*RightJustify*)
      IF row <= MaxRow THEN
        Column := TermWidth - Length(strg);
        CRT.GoToxy(Column, row);
        Terminal.WriteString(strg);
      END (*if*);
    END RightJustify;


  PROCEDURE MergeBuffers(n, nmbrlines, X0, Y0 : CARDINAL;
                         splitline : splittype; tempbuffer : textline);

  (*************************************************************************
  Combine the original text in "buffer" with the newly inserted text in "copy
  buffer" to finish up the insert.
  *************************************************************************)

    VAR
      i, m : CARDINAL;

    BEGIN (* MergeBuffers *)
      IF nmbrlines > Y0 THEN        (*FOR BOOK; CARD +/- # NEG RESULT*)
```

LISTING 12.8 (continued)

```
          FOR i := 0 TO (nmbrlines - Y0 - 1) DO
            Buffer[nmbrlines + n - i] := Buffer[nmbrlines - i];
          END (*for*);
        END (*if*);
        FOR i := 1 TO n DO

          Buffer[Y0 + i] := CopyBuffer[1 + i];
        END (*for*);
        i := X0;
        REPEAT
          Buffer[Y0, i] := CopyBuffer[1, i];
          INC(i);
        UNTIL CopyBuffer[1, i] = 0C;
        Buffer[Y0, i] := 0C;
        IF splitline # none THEN
          m := Length(CopyBuffer[1 + n]);       i := 0;
          REPEAT
            Buffer[Y0 + n, m + i] := tempbuffer[i];
            INC(i);
          UNTIL (tempbuffer[i] = 0C) OR ((m + i) = TermWidth);
          Buffer[Y0 + n, m + i] := 0C;
        END (* if split*);
      END MergeBuffers;



PROCEDURE InitInsert;

(************************************************************************
Initialize the insert procedure paramenters.
************************************************************************)

  VAR
    i : CARDINAL;

  BEGIN (*InitInsert*)
    FOR i := 0 TO x DO
      CopyBuffer[1, i] := 40C;   (*1st line is blank out to point of insert*)
    END;
    CopyBuffer[1, i] := 0C;
    FOR i := 2 TO MaxCopy DO
      CopyBuffer[i, 0] := 0C;    (*length of each copy buffer line is 0*)
    END;
    CRT.CenterLine(0, SubPrompt);
    CRT.ClearEos(x, ((y - 1) MOD MaxRow) + 1);
    Y0 := y;    X0 := x;
    IF X0 < Length(Buffer[Y0]) THEN
      SplitLine := active;
      FOR i := X0 TO Length(Buffer[Y0]) DO
        TempBuffer[i - X0] := Buffer[Y0, i];
      END (*for*);
      RightJustify(TempBuffer, Y0 MOD MaxRow + 1);
    ELSE
      SplitLine := none;
    END (*if*);
    CRT.GoToxy(x, ((y - 1) MOD MaxRow) + 1);
  END InitInsert;
```

```
PROCEDURE WrapUpInsert;

(**************************************************************************
Clean up the debris after insert is complete.
***************************************************************************)
    BEGIN (*WrapUpInsert*)
      IF Ch = esc THEN
        y := Y0;  x:=X0;
        DisplayText(y, nmbrlines, x, ((y - 1) MOD MaxRow) + 1);
      ELSE
        MergeBuffers(y - Y0, nmbrlines, X0, Y0, SplitLine, TempBuffer);
        nmbrlines := nmbrlines + y - Y0;
        DisplayText(topline, nmbrlines, 0, 1);
      END;
    END WrapUpInsert;



  BEGIN (* Insert *)
    InitInsert;

    REPEAT
      Terminal.Read(Ch);
      CASE Ch OF
        40C..176C : CopyBuffer[1 + y - Y0, x] := Ch;
                    IF x < MaxString THEN INC(x) END;
                    CopyBuffer[1 + y - Y0, x] := 0C!
        Left, bs  : IF NOT((y = Y0) & (x = X0)) THEN
                      MoveTheCursor(Ch, x, y, topline, nmbrlines + y - Y0,
                                      X0, Y0);
                      CopyBuffer[1 + y - Y0, x] := 0C;
                      Terminal.Write(' ');
                      CRT.GoToxy(x, ((y - 1) MOD MaxRow) + 1);
                    END (*if*)!
        cr        : CopyBuffer[1 + y - Y0, x] := 0C;
                    IF SplitLine = active THEN
                      CRT.ClearLine(Y0 MOD MaxRow + 1);
                      SplitLine := inactive;
                    END (*if*);
                    MoveTheCursor(Ch, x, y, topline, nmbrlines + y - Y0,
                                    X0, Y0);
                    CopyBuffer[1 + y - Y0, x] := 0C!
        esc, etx  : (*do nothing until end of repeat..until loop*);
      ELSE
        Terminal.Write('?');
        CopyBuffer[1 + y - Y0, x] := '?';
        IF x < MaxString THEN INC(x) END;
        CopyBuffer[1 + y - Y0, x] := 0C;
      END (*case*);
    UNTIL (Ch = esc) OR (Ch = etx);

    WrapUpInsert;
  END Insert;
```

As implemented, Insert calls InitInsert which

- initializes CopyBuffer and other Insert variables.
- displays the Insert menu prompt, which allows the following three options:
  Enter a character (including cursor moves).
  Press the escape key to "bail out."
  Press (CTRL-C) to add the insert to the permanent buffer.
- blanks the screen from the point of the insertion.
- redisplays the right half of the original line down one line and shifted all the way to the right of the screen if the insertion started in the middle of an existing line. This provides the user information regarding how much room there is for insertion in the current line.

Next, the Insert procedure *repeats* reading and interpreting the keyboard *until* either escape or control C is entered. Four possible cases are considered:

- A printable character is entered, and put in the copy buffer.
- A cursor move is entered and the cursor moved.
- An invalid entry is made. The symbol ? is displayed on the screen and the symbol ? is put in the copy buffer.
- The user quits by entering Escape, which restores everything to as it was before Insert was entered; i.e. the insertion is undone.
- Entering <CTRL-C>, which merges CopyBuffer with Buffer, i.e. merge the new text with the old and put it all in Buffer.

The current implementation of Insert has the following shortcomings:

- There is no word wrap. The user must provide a carriage return at the end of each line. This is easy to improve.
- CopyBuffer, like Buffer, is an array of text lines and thus suffers from the same problems that were given earlier for Buffer.
- After using insert in the middle of existing text, the right margins tend to get very uneven. Except for esthetics, this is not a serious problem. It is readily cured by the "fill" option of the formatter. A neater solution calls for text to be remargined within the editor. (Calling the formatter from the editor is the simplest solution.)

- Backing up over inserted text that crossed over the bottom of the screen needs improvement. Currently it is not allowed.
- An enhancement, which would be very valuable, is to allow the contents of the CopyBuffer (inserted text) to be copied to other places in the text. This is easy to do. Move the cursor to the new location and enter the appropriate command such as C(opy. At this point, only a little more than a call to MergeBuffers is needed.

Text Deletion

Now that we have covered moving the cursor and adding text, let's consider the problem of deleting text. Listing 12.9 shows the procedure to perform the delete function.

Delete allows us to delete individual characters and/or entire lines. The process is straightforward. There are essentially three steps to perform:

- Mark the spot in the text where the deletion begins.
- Mark the spot in the text where the deletion ends.
- Merge the remaining sections of text back into a single entity.

As a user moves the cursor from the start to the end of the area of text to be deleted, the text should disappear from the screen. Further, a user should be able to back up, and in the process, retrieve the original text that had disappeared. Lastly, if a user changes his mind entirely and decides that he did not really want to delete text, he should be able to get out gracefully to the way things were before the deletion started.

Examining the Delete procedure listing, we first of all notice the same REPEAT. . .UNTIL menu control structure that we have encountered in every other procedure. The choices are

1. to move the cursor right and delete a character,
2. to move the cursor left and restore a previously deleted character,
3. to enter a carriage return to delete an entire line,
4. to enter control-C to make the deletion permanent, and
5. to enter escape in order to bail out of the delete operation.

LISTING 12.9

```
PROCEDURE Delete(VAR x, y, topline, nmbrlines : CARDINAL);

(************************************************************************
2nd of the 3 main edit functions; delete characters and/or entire lines.
************************************************************************)

  CONST
    SubPrompt = 'DELETE - <CTRL-C> accepts, <Esc> escapes : ';

  VAR
    Ch : CHAR;
    YO, XO : CARDINAL;


  PROCEDURE DeleteBuffer(x, y, nmbrlines, XO, YO : CARDINAL);

  (************************************************************************
  Restore the text into a single piece after delete operation is done.
  ************************************************************************)

    VAR
      i : CARDINAL;
      (*n : INTEGER;*)

    BEGIN (*DeleteBuffer*)
      i := 0;
      WHILE (Buffer[y, x + i] # 0C) & ((XO + i) < TermWidth) DO
        Buffer[YO, XO + i] := Buffer[y, x + i];
        INC(i);
      END (*while*);
      Buffer[YO, XO +.i] := 0C;

      (*n := y - YO - 1;  IF (n > 0) THEN        this doesn't work*)
      IF y > YO THEN
        FOR i := 1 TO nmbrlines - y DO
          Buffer[YO + i] := Buffer[y + i];
        END (*for*);
      END (*if*);
    END DeleteBuffer;



  PROCEDURE WrapUpDelete;

  (************************************************************************
  Clean up after delete is done.
  ************************************************************************)

    BEGIN (*WrapUpDelete*)
      IF Ch = esc THEN
        y := YO;   x:=XO;
        DisplayText(y, nmbrlines, x, ((y - 1) MOD MaxRow) + 1);
      ELSE
        DeleteBuffer(x, y, nmbrlines, XO, YO);
```

```
    nmbrlines := nmbrlines - (y - Y0);
    IF Length(Buffer[nmbrlines]) = 0 THEN
      DEC(nmbrlines);
    END (*if*);
    x := X0;            y := Y0;

      DisplayText(topline, nmbrlines, 0, 1);
    END;
  END  WrapUpDelete;



BEGIN (* Delete *)
  CRT.CenterLine(0, SubPrompt);
  CRT.GoToxy(x, ((y - 1) MOD MaxRow) + 1);
  Y0 := y;    X0 := x;

  REPEAT
    Terminal.Read(Ch);
    CASE Ch OF
      Right     : CRT.GoToxy(x, ((y - 1) MOD MaxRow) + 1);
                  Terminal.Write(' ');
                  MoveTheCursor(Ch, x, y, topline, nmbrlines, X0, Y0);
      cr        : CRT.GoToxy(x, ((y - 1) MOD MaxRow) + 1);
                  CRT.ClearEoln(x, ((y - 1) MOD MaxRow) + 1);
                  MoveTheCursor(Ch, x, y, topline, nmbrlines, X0, Y0);
      Left, bs  : IF NOT((y = Y0) & (x = X0)) THEN
                    MoveTheCursor(Ch, x, y, topline, nmbrlines, X0, Y0);
                    CRT.GoToxy(x, ((y - 1) MOD MaxRow) + 1);
                    Terminal.Write(Buffer[y, x]);
                    CRT.GoToxy(x, ((y - 1) MOD MaxRow) + 1);
                  END (*if*);
      esc, etx  : (*do nothing until end of repeat..until loop*);
    ELSE
      CRT.GoToxy(x, ((y - 1) MOD MaxRow) + 1);
      Terminal.Write(Buffer[y, x]);
      CRT.GoToxy(x, ((y - 1) MOD MaxRow) + 1);
    END (*case*);
  UNTIL (Ch = esc) OR (Ch = etx);

  WrapUpDelete;
END Delete;
```

Text Exchange

The final function of the editor to be considered is text change. This allows a user to change existing text without having to first delete the part to be changed, and to then add the new (changed) text. Listing 12.10 shows this procedure.

LISTING 12.10

```
PROCEDURE Exchange(VAR x, y : CARDINAL; topline, nmbrlines : CARDINAL);

(****************************************************************************
3rd of the 3 main edit functions; exchange of characters limited to one
line at a time.
****************************************************************************)

  CONST
    SubPrompt = 'XCHG -  <CTRL-C> accepts,  <Esc> escapes : ';

  VAR
    Ch : CHAR;
    i, X0 : CARDINAL;

  PROCEDURE WrapUpXchg;

  (****************************************************************************
  Finish up the exchange operation.
  ****************************************************************************)

    BEGIN (*WrapUpXchg*)
      IF Ch = esc THEN
        x:=X0;
        DisplayText(y, nmbrlines, x, ((y - 1) MOD MaxRow) + 1);
      ELSE
        IF x > X0 THEN
          FOR i := X0 TO x - 1 DO
            Buffer[y, i] := CopyBuffer[1, i];
          END (*for*);
        END (*if*);
        DisplayText(topline, nmbrlines, 0, 1);
      END;
    END  WrapUpXchg;


  BEGIN (* Exchange *)
    CRT.CenterLine(0, SubPrompt);
    CRT.GoToxy(x, ((y - 1) MOD MaxRow) + 1);
    X0 := x;

    REPEAT
      Terminal.Read(Ch);
      CASE Ch OF
        40C..176C : IF x < Length(Buffer[y]) THEN
                      CopyBuffer[1, x] := Ch;
                      INC(x);
                    ELSE          (*BETTER CHECK FOR COL 79 HERE!!!*)
                      CRT.GoToxy(x, ((y - 1) MOD MaxRow) + 1);
                      Terminal.Write(' ');
                      CRT.GoToxy(x, ((y - 1) MOD MaxRow) + 1);
                    END;
        Left, bs  : IF NOT(x = X0) THEN
                      DEC(x);
```

```
                    CRT.GoToxy(x, ((y - 1) MOD MaxRow) + 1);
                    Terminal.Write(Buffer[y, x]);
                    CRT.GoToxy(x, ((y - 1) MOD MaxRow) + 1);
                    END (*if*);
          cr        : CRT.GoToxy(x, ((y - 1) MOD MaxRow) + 1);

            esc, etx  : (*do nothing until end of repeat..until loop*);
          ELSE
            CRT.GoToxy(x, ((y - 1) MOD MaxRow) + 1);
          END (*case*);
       UNTIL (Ch = esc) OR (Ch = etx);

       WrapUpXchg;
    END Exchange;
```

Exchange is the simplest of the three editor functions. It reads the new text into the copy buffer, and when control-C is entered, it overwrites the appropriate portion of the text buffer with the contents of the copy buffer. As was the case in Delete, if the user backs the cursor over changed text, the original text is restored.

12.3.2 Formatter Functions

The format of a text file includes the following:

- Size of the text page. For example, a fairly standard page size is 66 lines long and 80 columns wide.
- Size of the page margins (e.g., left, right, top, and bottom).
- Margin justification, i.e. smooth or ragged edges.
- Paragraph indentation.
- Line spacing (single or double).
- Page numbering, titles, headers, and footers.

Ideally, users should be able to change the above parameters for a text file without actually having to rearrange the pages, lines, and words that are affected by the change. Imagine the amount of work required just to change the left and right margins of a letter from columns 10 and 70 to columns 15 and 65. If users had to manually re-edit every line, the work required would be significant for anything longer than a short memo.

Users want to be able to compose the text, and once the text has been composed, to print the material in any reasonable output format without having to make any changes to the basic textual material. Accomplishment of this function is the job of a text formatter.

The text formatter described in this section uses embedded commands to specify the output format for the text. An embedded command is a special command symbol followed by one or more command characters. This command sequence is placed (embedded) within the textual material that is to be formatted. Consider the following example:

```
.L14 .R66 .F+
This is an embedded command formatter example. The
three items in the first line are embedded
commands. They are
distinguished by the period in the
first column which says to
the formatter, "I'm an embedded command. Don't
print me."
```

When the above text is presented to the formatter for printing, the following output results:

```
This is an embedded command formatter example.
The three items in the first line are embedded commands.
They are distinguished by the period in the first
column which says to the formatter, "I'm an embedded
command. Don't print me."
```

The commands .L14 and .R66 set the left and right margins to columns 14 and 66. The command .F+ turns on a feature known as filling. The filling process converts the uneven length lines of the input file to uniform output format lengths and margins. The output lines are filled with the words from the input text. The filling process starts at the left margin and continues until the right margin is reached.

The above example illustrates the portion of the formatter functions that deal with the format of lines and paragraphs. The format of a page is equally important, and must also be handled by the formatter. At a minimum, the formatter must be able to accommodate different page lengths. This is necessary in order to allow top and bottom page margins. The ability to number pages and place titles or headers at the top of each page is also a desirable option.

In addition to providing some or all of the features that have been mentioned, the ability to provide different formats within the same document is also required. For example, the same margin may not be appropriate for an entire document.

The outer shell of the formatter module is given in Listing 12.11. This listing shows us that the TextFormatter module consists of

- a module main body,
- imported elements similar to those in TextEditor,
- global parameters,
- the procedure Formatter, which is exported from the module, and
- two local procedures, FormatterMenu and FileOutput.

As in the TextEditor, the implementation details of TextFormatter are invisible to client programs. A procedure, Formatter, is exported. There can be no adverse interaction between the module and the calling program. Formatter is another black box that provides a service to its clients. The client program neither knows nor cares how the formatting function is implemented.

As we examine the TextFormatter module, there is an important observation to be made. When the editor was presented, we commented that the main body of the TextEditor module did nothing. It was an empty BEGIN END statement sequence. The TextFormatter module body, in contrast, initializes a number of formatter variables. The initialization takes place when the formatter's client program, the word processor, is executed. Once initialized, these variables retain their values (i.e. they continue to exist) even when the TextFormatter module is not being executed. See Chapter 8 for details.

In our application, we want to provide default values for a number of format parameters. We do this in the main body of TextFormatter. For example, we set the page length to 66. The Formatter procedure allows the user to modify the setting of these same parameters during execution of the program.

The user may change the page length value to 50. We would prefer not to make the user reset the value to 50 every time that the Formatter is called by the word processor. Why shouldn't the program remember the most recent setting? It can, using modules as we have done here. However when using a procedure, either the user would reset the values every time that Formatter was called, or all of the format parameters would have to be global variables of the calling program.

As was described in Chapter 8, the separation of the program and variable existence is a major difference between modules and procedures. Variables declared in a procedure are created when the procedure is called and destroyed when the procedure is exited. Thus the existence of such a variable is tied to the existence (execution) of the procedure. If the value of any of these variables must be retained from one call of the procedure to another, those variables must be made global variables of the program that calls the proce-

LISTING 12.11

```
IMPLEMENTATION MODULE TextFormatter;

FROM CRT IMPORT
        CharSet,
        ClearEoln,
        ClearEos,
        ClearTheScreen,
        GoToxy,
        Prompt,
        UpperLower,
        UserInput;

FROM Files IMPORT
        Open,
        Create,
        FILE;

FROM FileStuff IMPORT
        StringType,
        TextFileOpen,
        TextFileClose;

FROM InOut IMPORT
        ReadCard,
        WriteCard;

FROM Strings IMPORT
        Length;

IMPORT Terminal;

FROM Texts IMPORT
        EOT,
        ReadLn,
        TEXT,
        Write,
        WriteInt,
        WriteLn,
        WriteString;

CONST
  CommandChar = '.';

TYPE
        textline = ARRAY[0..80] OF CHAR;
        direction = (LeftToRight, RightToLeft);

VAR
        InText,
        OutText : TEXT;
        Outbuf : textline;
        Direction : direction;
        Number,
        Justify,
```

```
          Space,
          Fill,
          FormFeed,
          Scroll : BOOLEAN;
          TempIndent,
          Words,
          NextColumn,
          LineNmbr,
          PageLength,
          LeftMargin,
          RightMargin,
          TopMargin,
          BottomMargin : CARDINAL;
          Header : ARRAY [0..80] OF CHAR;


     +-----------------------------------------------------------+
     :                                                           :
     :            PROCEDURE FileOutput    (listing 12.12)        :
     :                                                           :
     :                         and                               :
     :                                                           :
     :            PROCEDURE FormatterMenu (listing 12.12)        :
     :                                                           :
     :                       go here.                            :
     :                                                           :
     +-----------------------------------------------------------+


PROCEDURE Formatter;

(*************************************************************************
This is what we export; put up a menu & control the options from here.
*************************************************************************)

  CONST
    M = 'OUTPUT MENU >   S(et parameters, O(utput file, Q(uit : ';

  VAR
    Done : BOOLEAN;

  BEGIN (*Formatter*)
    REPEAT
      ClearTheScreen;
      CASE CAP(Prompt(M, CharSet('S','O','Q','s','o','q'))) OF
        'S' :   FormatterMenu!
        'O' :   FileOutput!
        'Q' :   Done := TRUE;
      END (*case*);
    UNTIL Done;
    ClearTheScreen;
  END Formatter;



BEGIN (*TextFormatter*)

(*************************************************************************
In a module this gets done ONE time - at execution time.
*************************************************************************)
```

LISTING 12.11 (continued)

```
    Number := FALSE;
    Justify := FALSE;
    Space := FALSE;
    Fill := FALSE;
    FormFeed := FALSE;
    Scroll := TRUE;
    PageLength := 66;
    LeftMargin := 1;
    RightMargin := 79;
    TopMargin := 2;
    BottomMargin := 2;
    Header[0] := 0C;
END TextFormatter.
```

dure. This can lead to problems with side effects, in which instructions outside of the procedure cause changes to the procedure's variables.

The next parts of the module, the imports and globals, are similar to what we have already seen in the TextEditor module. The imports are primarily for the purpose of input, output, and file handling operations. The global types and variables are used in the procedures FileOutput and FormatterMenu. Many of these variables, for example PageLength, control the format. The main body sets their default value. Procedure FormatterMenu allows the user to modify their value. Procedure FileOutput uses the variables to determine the format of the text file that is being output.

The procedure Formatter is all that is exported to the client program. Formatter is almost identical to the control portion of the word processor program. There is a menu

'OUTPUT MENU > S(et Parameters, O(utput file, Q(uit'

and a REPEAT. . .UNTIL loop to interpret and respond to user inputs. The user can select S(et parameters, O(utput file, or Q(uit. No other input is accepted by Formatter.

The S(et parameters selection calls the procedure, FormatterMenu, and allows the user to modify format settings. O(utput file results in the execution of the procedure, FileOutput, which prompts the user for the name of the file to be formatted. Once the file has been opened, FileOutput sends the formatted document to the destination (printer, screen, disk) specified by the user. This process continues until the user Q(uits and the system returns to the main word processor menu.

Setting Format Procedures

The procedure FormatterMenu allows the user to modify format parameter values. The values set here are used by the program unless overridden by embedded commands in the text file to be processed. In this way, if the document requires a uniform set of margins and page lengths throughout, we can specify those values here and not have to bother with embedded commands in the text file proper.

The formatter was used to print the drafts of this book. A single set of format values were used throughout. These values were specified through the use of FormatterMenu. The only embedded commands in the text were used to turn the filling and right justification options on and off. In the off mode of these two parameters, the formatter became "what you see is what you get," and allowed special format requirements to be accommodated.

Listing 12.12 shows the FormatterMenu procedure. Once again, we have a REPEAT. . .UNTIL menu control loop. In this instance, the menu options are more extensive than in the previous cases that we have encountered. However, the control procedure is identical.

The format menu displays all of the format parameters along with their current values. There are three basic parameter types:

- On/Off, such as filling and right justification.
- Integer values, e.g. page length.
- Text string, the optional page title.

The on/off parameters are toggled when the user selects them. If F(illing is entered, the value of filling is toggled to its opposite state. Procedures Rite and ReRite take care of flipping the value of BOOLEAN variables that are passed as arguments. The allowable values of the integer variables are displayed together with the current settings. The system will accept values in the specified range and reject all others. Procedure ReadData handles this task. The valid input range for each variable is easily modified within the FormatterMenu control loop that calls ReadData.

The implementation of this section is straightforward. The code is highly modularized, and can be changed easily to add additional format parameters or to modify existing ones. The process to ensure a user-friendly, error-free interface is worth close examination. All information regarding format parameter values is clearly displayed and easily changed. Mental errors are easily corrected. All other input errors are fully trapped.

LISTING 12.12

```
PROCEDURE FormatterMenu;

(*****************************************************************************
2nd of the 2 formatter choices; allows error proof, user friendly modification
of the formatter parameters to comtrol format of output text.
*****************************************************************************)

  CONST
    HTab = 36;

  VAR
    Finished : BOOLEAN;

  PROCEDURE Rite(IO : BOOLEAN; N : CARDINAL);

    BEGIN
      GoToxy(HTab, N);
      IF IO THEN
        Terminal.WriteString('    ON');
      ELSE
        Terminal.WriteString('    OFF');
      END;
    END Rite;



  PROCEDURE Rerite(VAR IO : BOOLEAN; N : CARDINAL);

    BEGIN
      ClearEoln(HTab, N);
      IO := NOT(IO);
      Rite(IO, N)
    END Rerite;



  PROCEDURE Init;

  (*****************************************************************************
  Write the menu once & leave it up until user is done with it.
  *****************************************************************************)

    BEGIN
      ClearEos(0, 0);
      Terminal.WriteString('Parameter menu - ');
      Terminal.WriteString('Enter option listed below or Q(uit : ');

      GoToxy(0,1);
      Terminal.WriteString('Page N(umbering                    : ');
      Rite(Number, 1);

      GoToxy(0,2);
      Terminal.WriteString('J(ustification                    : ');
      Rite(Justify, 2);
```

```
   GoToxy(0,3);
   Terminal.WriteString('S(pacing (double) (not impl)     : ');
   Rite(Space, 3);

   GoToxy(0, 4);
   Terminal.WriteString('F(illing                         : ');
   Rite(Fill, 4);

   GoToxy(0, 5);
   Terminal.WriteString('Z(ip to top of page at end       : ');
   Rite(FormFeed, 5);

   GoToxy(0, 6);
   Terminal.WriteString('C(ontinuous scroll (not impl)    : ');
   Rite(Scroll, 6);

   GoToxy(0, 7);
   Terminal.WriteString('P(age Length      1-65000        : ');
   GoToxy(HTab, 7);
   WriteCard(PageLength, 6);

   GoToxy(0, 8);
   Terminal.WriteString('T(op Margin       0-10           : ');
   GoToxy(HTab, 8);
   WriteCard(TopMargin, 6);

   GoToxy(0, 9);
   Terminal.WriteString('B(ottom Margin    0-10           : ');
   GoToxy(HTab, 9);
   WriteCard(BottomMargin, 6);

   GoToxy(0, 10);
   Terminal.WriteString('L(eft Margin      0-99           : ');
   GoToxy(HTab, 10);
   WriteCard(LeftMargin, 6);

   GoToxy(0, 11);
   Terminal.WriteString('R(ight Margin     1-100          : ');
   GoToxy(HTab, 11);
   WriteCard(RightMargin, 6);

   GoToxy(0, 12);
   Terminal.WriteString('H(eader   (max length = 80 char) : ');
   GoToxy(0, 13);
   Terminal.WriteString(Header);

   Finished := FALSE
 END Init;



PROCEDURE ReadData(VAR D : CARDINAL; Y, N, M : CARDINAL);

(**************************************************************************
Read numeric data, trap errors, force data (D) to be  N <= D <= M.
**************************************************************************)
```

LISTING 12.12 (continued)

```
BEGIN (*readdata*)
  REPEAT
    ClearEoln(HTab, Y);
    ReadCard(D);
  UNTIL (D >= N) & (D <= M);
  ClearEoln(HTab, Y);
  WriteCard(D, 6)


  END ReadData;



BEGIN  (*FormatterMenu*)
  Init;

  REPEAT
    GoToxy(54, 0);
    CASE UserInput(CharSet('Q','C','Z','P','L','R','T','B','N','H','J',
                          'S','F'), Upper) OF
      'N' :  Rerite(Number, 1)¦
      'J' :  Rerite(Justify, 2)¦
      'S' :  Rerite(Space, 3)¦
      'F' :  Rerite(Fill, 4)¦
      'Z' :  Rerite(FormFeed, 5)¦
      'C' :  Rerite(Scroll, 6)¦
      'P' :  ReadData(PageLength, 7, 1, 65000)¦
      'T' :  ReadData(TopMargin, 8, 0, 10)¦
      'B' :  ReadData(BottomMargin, 9, 0, 10)¦
      'L' :  ReadData(LeftMargin, 10, 0, 99)¦
      'R' :  ReadData(RightMargin, 11, 1, 100)¦
      'H' :  ClearEoln(0, 13);
             Terminal.ReadLn(Header)¦
      'Q' :  Finished := TRUE
    END  (*case*)
  UNTIL Finished
END FormatterMenu;
```

Document Formatting

The final section of the output formatter is procedure FileOutput. Listing 12.14 shows this procedure. Procedure FileOutput queries the user for the name of the file to be output and the name of the destination file, calls procedure FileCopy, and closes all open files once the process has been completed.

The real work horse of this procedure is FileCopy. FileCopy employs a LOOP. . .END construct. It reads text from the file being formatted until the end of file is reached, at which time the LOOP is EXITed. As each line is read, three possible output conditions are tested within an IF. . .ELSIF. . .ELSE statement sequence.

LISTING 12.13

```
PROCEDURE FileOutput;

(******************************************************************************
One of 2 formatter options - does the actual file output to any legal device
including printer, screen or disk.
******************************************************************************)


  PROCEDURE SkipLines(nmbr : CARDINAL);

  (****************************************************************************
  Skips nmbr lines on output device.
  ****************************************************************************)

    VAR
      i : CARDINAL;

    BEGIN (* skiplines *)
      FOR i := 1 TO nmbr DO
        WriteLn(OutText);
      END (*for*);
    END SkipLines;



  PROCEDURE WriteHeader(header : ARRAY OF CHAR; nmbr : CARDINAL);

  (****************************************************************************
  Place optional header at top of each output page.
  ****************************************************************************)

    BEGIN (* header *)
      WriteString(OutText, header);
      IF Number THEN
        WriteString(OutText, '  -  Page ');
        WriteInt(OutText, nmbr, 1);
      END;
      WriteLn(OutText);
    END WriteHeader;



  MODULE PageStuff;

  (****************************************************************************
  Controls actions for top of page incl. top margin, header, linecount
  initialization; NOTE embedded local module within a procedure which is in
  turn within a library module - not necessary, more for example purposes.
  ****************************************************************************)

    IMPORT  WriteHeader,
            SkipLines,
            Header,
            Number,
            TopMargin;
```

LISTING 12.13 (continued)

```
   EXPORT  PageTop;

   VAR

   PageNmbr : CARDINAL;


PROCEDURE PageTop(VAR linenmbr : CARDINAL);

(************************************************************************
This is where the nested local module's work gets done.
************************************************************************)

   BEGIN (* pageinit *)
     INC(PageNmbr);
     SkipLines(TopMargin);
     IF (Header[0] # 0C) OR Number THEN
       WriteHeader(Header, PageNmbr);
       SkipLines(TopMargin);
       linenmbr := TopMargin + TopMargin + 1;
     ELSE
       linenmbr := TopMargin;
     END;
   END PageTop;


 BEGIN (*pagestuff*)
   PageNmbr := 0;
 END PageStuff;



PROCEDURE PutLine(strg : ARRAY OF CHAR);

(************************************************************************
Single place within FileCopy to do all of the writing of text data; also
updates linecount, does double space if rqd, & watches for bottom of page.
************************************************************************)

   VAR
     i : CARDINAL;

   BEGIN (*PutLine*)
     IF Fill OR Justify THEN
       FOR i := 1 TO LeftMargin + TempIndent DO
         Write(OutText, ' ');
       END (*for*);
     END (*if*);
     WriteString(OutText, strg);     WriteLn(OutText);
     INC(LineNmbr);
     IF LineNmbr >= (PageLength - BottomMargin) THEN
       SkipLines(PageLength - LineNmbr);
       LineNmbr := 0;
```

```
      ELSIF Space THEN
        WriteLn(OutText);
        INC(LineNmbr);
        IF LineNmbr >= (PageLength - BottomMargin) THEN
          SkipLines(PageLength - LineNmbr);
          LineNmbr := 0;
        END (*if line...*);
      END (*if line...*);
  END PutLine;

PROCEDURE Break;

(*###############################################################################
Line break; flushes current line buffer.
###############################################################################*)

  BEGIN (*Break*)
    IF Outbuf[0] # 0C THEN
      PutLine(Outbuf);
      Outbuf[0] := 0C;
    END (*if out*);
    IF LineNmbr = 0 THEN
      PageTop(LineNmbr);
    END;
    Words := 0;
    NextColumn := 0;
    TempIndent := 0;
  END Break;




PROCEDURE FillAndJustify(tempbuf : textline);

(*****************************************************************************
Large procedure within FileCopy to handle Text filling & right justification.
*****************************************************************************)

  TYPE
    CharSet = SET OF CHAR;

  VAR
    Word : textline;
    index,
    Position : CARDINAL;




  PROCEDURE NextWord(strg : textline; i : CARDINAL; VAR word: textline) :
                     CARDINAL;

  (*****************************************************************************
  Gets one word at a time for output line from current input line; strips
  interior blanks.
  *****************************************************************************)

    VAR
      j : CARDINAL;
```

LISTING 12.13 (continued)

```
BEGIN (* NextWord *)
  WHILE NOT(strg[i] IN CharSet{0C, 41C..176C}) DO
    INC(i);
  END (*while*);

  j := 0;
  WHILE strg[i] IN CharSet{41C..176C} DO
    word[j] := strg[i];
    INC(i);   INC(j);
  END (*while*);
  word[j] := 0C;

    IF strg[i] = 0C THEN
      RETURN 0;
    ELSE
      RETURN i;
    END (*if*);
  END NextWord;



PROCEDURE AddSpaces(VAR strg : textline; words : CARDINAL);

(****************************************************************************
Adds extra spaces within current output line if right justifying.
****************************************************************************)

  VAR
    i, j, k,
    Gap,
    Blanks,
    Holes : CARDINAL;

  BEGIN (*AddSpaces*)
    IF Direction = LeftToRight THEN
      Direction := RightToLeft;
    ELSE
      Direction := LeftToRight;
    END (*if*);
    Gap := RightMargin + 2 - LeftMargin - NextColumn - TempIndent;
    Holes := words - 1;

    i := Length(strg) - 2;        j := NextColumn + Gap - 2;
    strg[j + 1] := 0C;
    WHILE (j > i) (*& (Gap > 0) & (Holes > 0)*) DO
      strg[j] := strg[i];

      IF strg[i] = ' ' THEN
        IF Direction = LeftToRight THEN
          Blanks := Gap DIV Holes;
        ELSIF Holes > 1 THEN
          Blanks := Gap DIV Holes + 1;
        ELSE
          Blanks := Gap DIV Holes;
        END (*if*);
```

```
        DEC(Gap, Blanks);
        DEC(Holes);
        WHILE Blanks > 0 DO
          DEC(j);
          strg[j] := ' ';
          DEC(Blanks);
        END (*while*);
      END (*if*);
      DEC(i);    DEC(j);
    END (*while*);

  END AddSpaces;

  PROCEDURE FillLine(strg : ARRAY OF CHAR);

  (**************************************************************************
  Builds current output line a word at a time; outputs the line when the
  next word recieved would cause the line length to be too long.
  **************************************************************************)

    VAR
      i,
      Width : CARDINAL;

    BEGIN (* FillLine *)
      Width := Length(strg);
      IF LeftMargin + NextColumn + Width + TempIndent > RightMargin THEN
        IF Justify THEN AddSpaces(Outbuf, Words) END;
        PutLine(Outbuf);
        Outbuf[0] := 0C;          (*??not needed??*)
        Words := 0;
        NextColumn := 0;
        TempIndent := 0;
        IF LineNmbr = 0 THEN
          PageTop(LineNmbr);
        END (*if*);
      END (*if*);
      FOR i := 0 TO Width - 1 DO
        Outbuf[NextColumn + i] := strg[i];
      END (*for*);
      Outbuf[NextColumn + Width] := ' ';
      Outbuf[NextColumn + Width + 1] := 0C;
      NextColumn := NextColumn + Width + 1;
      INC(Words);
    END FillLine;


PROCEDURE LeadingBlank(VAR strg : textline);

(**************************************************************************
Strips leading blanks from line & remembers size of indent for output.
**************************************************************************)

  VAR
    i, j : CARDINAL;
```

LISTING 12.13 (continued)

```
BEGIN (*LeadingBlank*)
  TempIndent := 0;
  WHILE strg[TempIndent] = ' ' DO      (*count blanks*)
    INC(TempIndent);
  END (*while*);

  j := Length(strg) - TempIndent;      (*strip off leading blanks*)
  FOR i := 0 TO j DO
    strg[i] := strg[TempIndent + i];
  END;
END LeadingBlank;



BEGIN (*FillAndJustify*)
  IF (tempbuf[0] = ' ') OR (tempbuf[0] = 0C) THEN

    Break;
    LeadingBlank(tempbuf);
  END (*if temp*);

  IF tempbuf[0] = 0C THEN
    PutLine(tempbuf);
  ELSE
    Position := 0;
    REPEAT
      Position := NextWord(tempbuf, Position, Word);
      IF Length(Word) > 0 THEN FillLine(Word) END;
    UNTIL Position = 0;
  END (*if temp*);
END FillAndJustify;



PROCEDURE ParseCommand(strg : textline);

(*##############################################################################
Parse embedded format commands.
##############################################################################*)

  BEGIN (*ParseCommand*)
    CASE CAP(strg[1]) OF
      'B'  :  Break;
      'F'  :  IF strg[2] = '+' THEN
                Fill := TRUE;
              ELSE
                Break;
                Fill := FALSE;
              END;
      'J'  :  IF strg[2] = '+' THEN
                Justify := TRUE;
              ELSE
                Break;
                Justify := FALSE;
              END;
```

```
    END (*case*);
  END ParseCommand;



PROCEDURE FileCopy;

(***********************************************************************
Read input lines & output directly or via "Fill&Justify".
***********************************************************************)

  VAR
    Strg : textline;

  BEGIN (*filecopy*)
    Words := 0;
    NextColumn := 0;
    TempIndent := 0;
    Outbuf[0] := 0C;
    Direction := LeftToRight;
    PageTop(LineNmbr);

      LOOP
        ReadLn(InText, Strg);
        IF EOT(InText) THEN
          EXIT
        END (*if*);

        IF LineNmbr = 0 THEN
          PageTop(LineNmbr);
        END (*if*);

        IF Strg[0] = CommandChar THEN
          ParseCommand(Strg);
        ELSIF NOT(Fill) & NOT(Justify) THEN
          PutLine(Strg);
        ELSE
          FillAndJustify(Strg);
        END (*if*);
      END (*loop*);

      IF Length(Outbuf) > 0 THEN
        IF LineNmbr = 0 THEN
          PageTop(LineNmbr);
        END (*if*);
        PutLine(Outbuf);
      END (*if*);
      IF FormFeed AND (LineNmbr > 0) THEN
        SkipLines(PageLength - LineNmbr);
      END (*if*);
    END FileCopy;



  VAR
          InFile,
          OutFile : FILE;
```

LISTING 12.13 (continued)

```
BEGIN (*FileOutput*)
  IF NOT TextFileOpen(Open, InText, InFile, PromptIs, 'Input file? ') THEN
    HALT END;
  IF NOT TextFileOpen(Create, OutText, OutFile, PromptIs, 'Output file? ')
    THEN HALT END;

  FileCopy;

  IF NOT TextFileClose(InText, InFile) THEN HALT END;
  IF NOT TextFileClose(OutText, OutFile) THEN HALT END;
END FileOutput;
```

Each line must first be tested to see if it is a command line. Is the first character a period? If this is a command, then we must interpret it by calling the ParseCommand procedure. The current implementation of ParseCommand handles a subset of the format parameters. The implementation makes extending this set a trivial job.

If the line is not a command, then one of two other cases exist. The simplest case is when filling and justify are off. In this case, the line is printed as is. If filling *or* justify are on, then we must build output lines. Procedure FillAndJustify does this for us.

FillAndJustify takes each line read by FileCopy and decomposes it into its component words with the help of procedure NextWord. It passes the words, one at a time, to FillLine. FillLine builds the next output line within the bounds of the line width specified by the left and right margins. FillLine continues to accept words from FillAndJustify until it reaches the point where the next word would exceed the right margin.

Once FillLine's current output line has been filled, it checks to see if right justification is required. If so, the current output line is passed to procedure AddSpaces. AddSpaces adds blanks between words of the output line so that the line exactly equals the specified line width. The spaces are added first from right to left between the words of a line, and then from left to right on alternating lines of text. This is done to achieve an even distribution of whiteness over a page. Once the line is justified, it is sent to procedure PutLine for output.

All output from FileOutput, regardless of the setting of filling and justify, is done by procedure PutLine. This is important for a number of reasons. First of all, there is the matter of page format control. It is important to know which is the current page line number. Are we at the top of the page? If we are, is there a header or page number to print? Is there a top or bottom of page margin? Every time a line is output, the page line number increases and all of these questions must be answered. It is much easier to deal with these questions if we consolidate all of the output in one location. It is much easier to debug problems if we only have one place to check when the problems crop up.

There are a number of other procedures in FileOutput. SkipLines and WriteHeader do just about what you would expect from their names. In addition, there is Procedure PageTop. PageTop is interesting from the viewpoint that it is exported from a LOCAL module.

Although the module PageStuff, which exports PageTop, was not essential in this implementation, it illustrates several points. First, local modules do exist. In a local module, the exports do not have to be qualified. The module's variable, PageNmbr, which is set to zero in PageStuff's main body when FileOutput is called, is incremented each time PageTop is executed. The current value of PageNmbr is remembered even after PageTop is exited. Again, this is the idea of module variable existence being separate from module existence.

Note that although TextFormatter's variable values are retained even when control passes back to the word processor, this is not true for PageNmbr. Recall that the variable exists as long as its surrounding program exists. In the case of TextFormatter, the surrounding program is the word processor. In the case of PageNmbr, the surrounding program is FileOutput. Therefore, each time O(utput file is selected from the Formatter procedure control loop, PageNmbr is reinitialized to zero. This is exactly the action that is desired. Otherwise, the first page in every document would be numbered where the previous document left off.

SUMMARY

This completes our study of Modula-2. The emphasis on the language basics in the early chapters, coupled with the example provided by the word processor of this chapter, should provide a solid basis for exploring all aspects of Modula-2. If you have not yet written any programs, you have not learned much about Modula-2. Get to a computer!

PROBLEMS

An excellent mechanism for expanding and testing your understanding of the language is to modify and refine the word processing program. The program modularity lends itself to easy expansion. You should attempt at least two of the following problems that were discussed during this chapter.

1. Combine the formatter with the editor so that page properties such as margins, indentations, and spacing are displayed while the editing function is in progress. The object is to "see what you will get" while the document is being created and not just when it is printed.

2. We mentioned that the text file array data structure used in the editor was not the most efficient technique that could be used for this application. Modify the editor to solve the problems caused by the use of the array structure.

3. The ReadLn procedure used by DiskToRam in the editor is slow. Use an alternative technique in DiskToRam to dramatically improve the speed of this process.

4. Implement some of the enhancements to MoveTheCursor that were suggested in the text such as moving to the beginning or end of the file, moving to the beginning or end of the paragraph, moving to the beginning or end of the line, and moving to the beginning or end of the next word.

5. Implement the CopyBuffer enhancement suggested at the end of the text insertion section.

6. Extend the list of embedded commands that the formatter can recognize.

7. Add a feature to FormatterMenu that allows the current format values to be saved to a file that is loaded by the word processor program at execution time. This would allow users to customize the defaults to their needs.

8. Use the low-level features of Chapter 11 to allow the editor to be interrupted in order to use the calculator that we have been developing. For a more advanced application, implement a "windowing" option so that the editor and the calculator are both visible and accessible at the same time.

Appendices

APPENDIX A

MODULA-2 SYNTAX DIAGRAMS

This appendix contains the complete set of syntax diagrams for the Modula-2 language. An index to the diagrams is also included. The purpose and use of syntax diagrams is explained in Chapter 2.

The syntax diagrams are presented in the same order as they appear in Wirth's syntax for Modula-2. This was done to allow easy cross-reference with the standard definition for the language. Wirth presents the syntax in Extended Backus Naur Form (EBNF).

334   APPENDICES

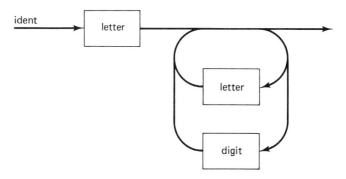

FIGURE A.1

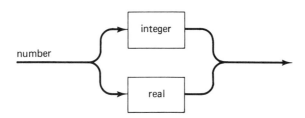

FIGURE A.2

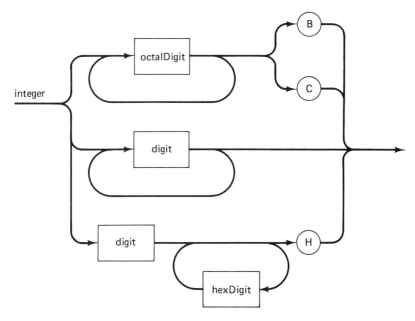

FIGURE A.3

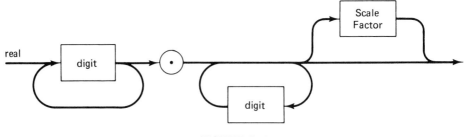

FIGURE A.4

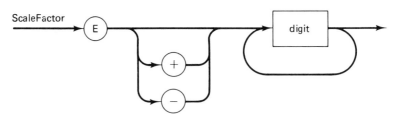

FIGURE A.5

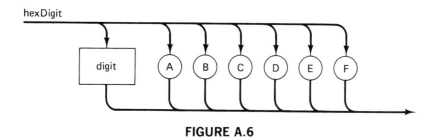

FIGURE A.6

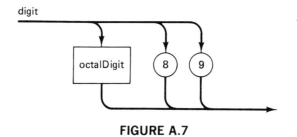

FIGURE A.7

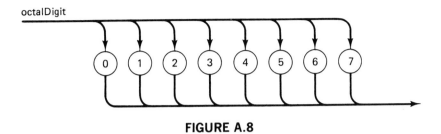

FIGURE A.8

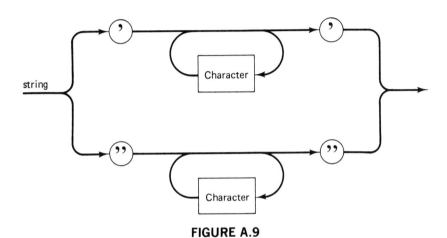

FIGURE A.9

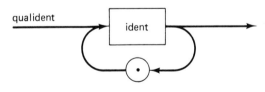

FIGURE A.10

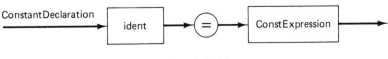

FIGURE A.11

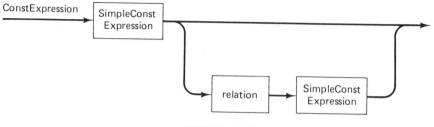

FIGURE A.12

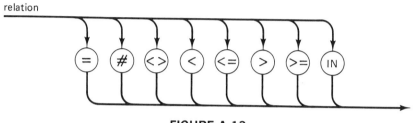

FIGURE A.13

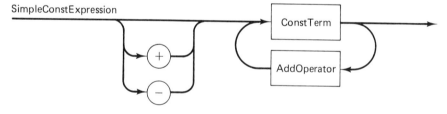

FIGURE A.14

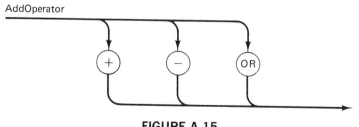

FIGURE A.15

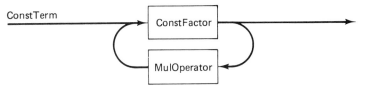

FIGURE A.16

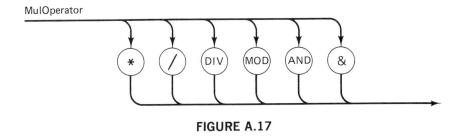

FIGURE A.17

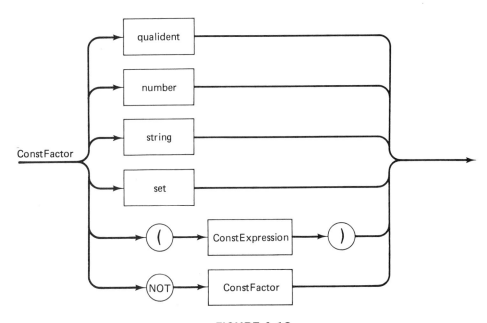

FIGURE A.18

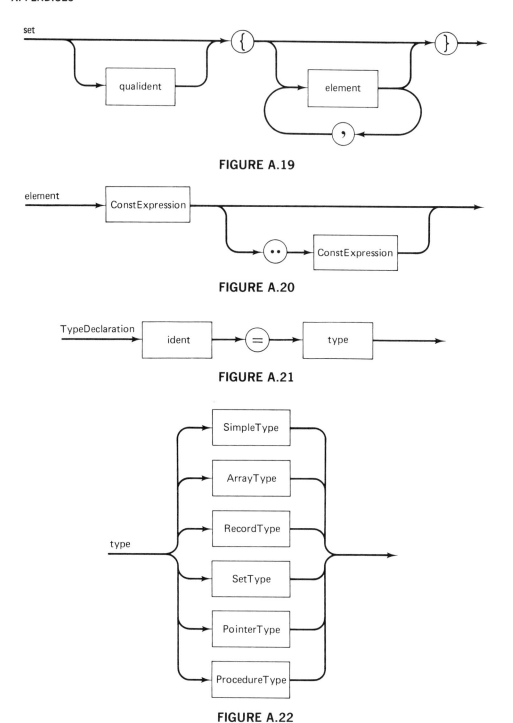

FIGURE A.19

FIGURE A.20

FIGURE A.21

FIGURE A.22

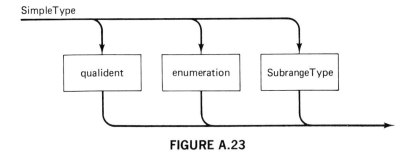

FIGURE A.23

FIGURE A.24

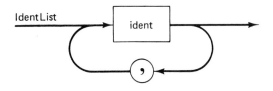

FIGURE A.25

FIGURE A.26

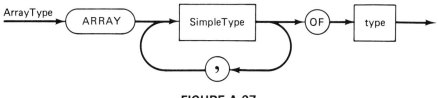

FIGURE A.27

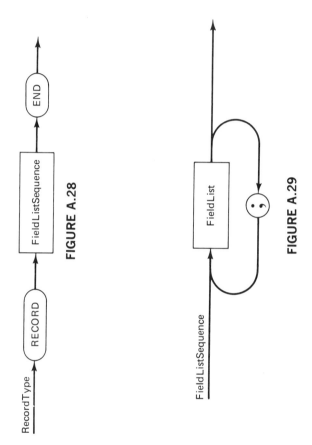

FIGURE A.28

FIGURE A.29

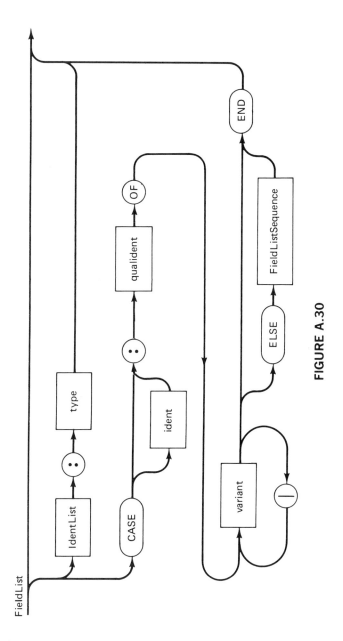

FIGURE A.30

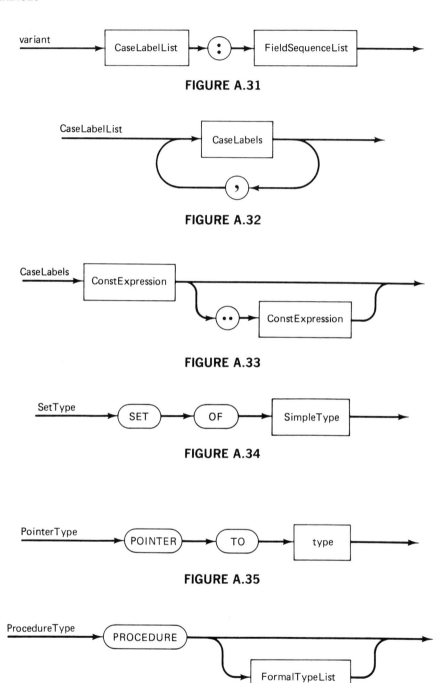

FIGURE A.31

FIGURE A.32

FIGURE A.33

FIGURE A.34

FIGURE A.35

FIGURE A.36

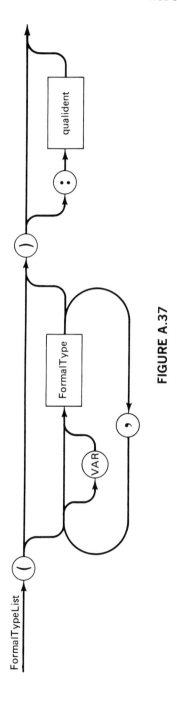

FIGURE A.37

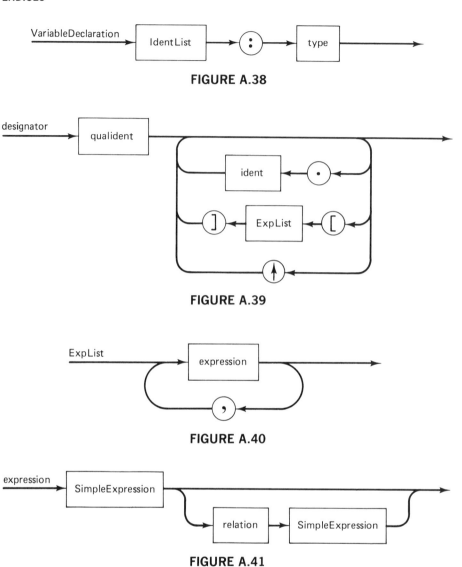

FIGURE A.38

FIGURE A.39

FIGURE A.40

FIGURE A.41

FIGURE A.42

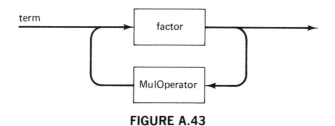

term
factor
MulOperator

FIGURE A.43

factor
number
string
set
designator
ActualParameters
(
expression
)
NOT
factor

FIGURE A.44

ActualParameters
(
ExpList
)

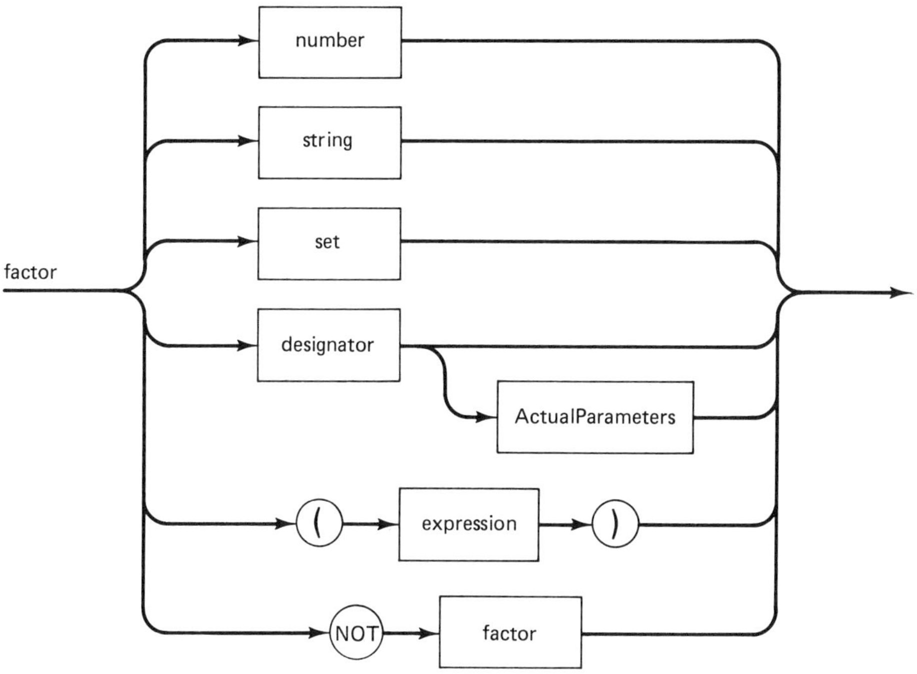

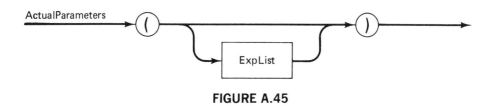

FIGURE A.45

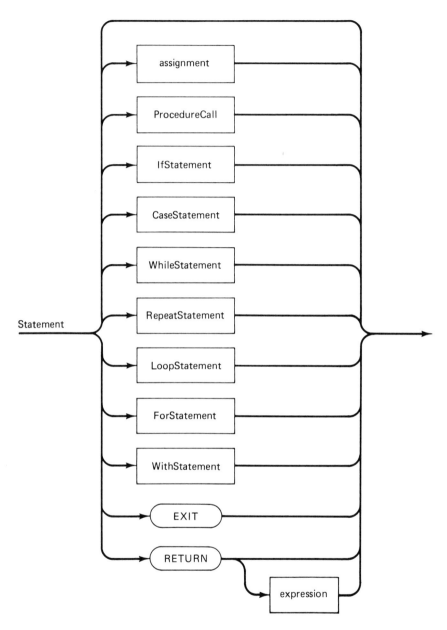

FIGURE A.46

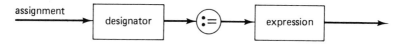

FIGURE A.47

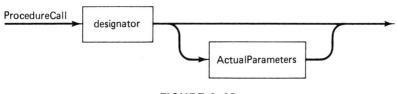

FIGURE A.48

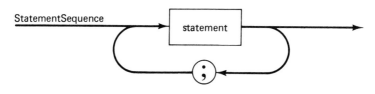

FIGURE A.49

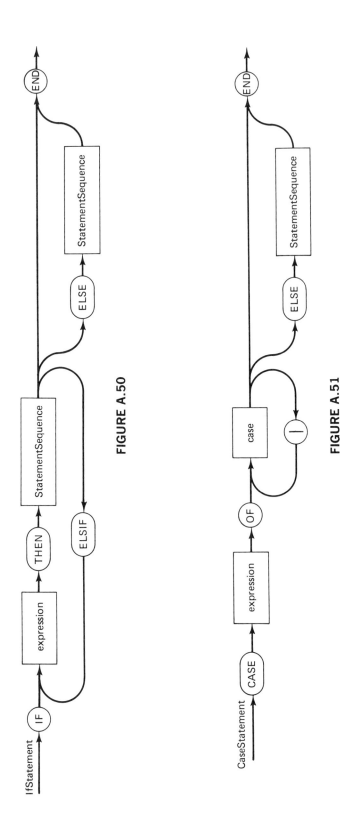

FIGURE A.50

FIGURE A.51

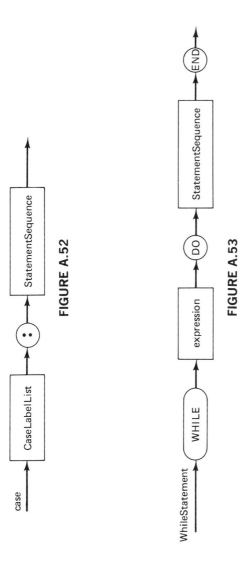

FIGURE A.52

FIGURE A.53

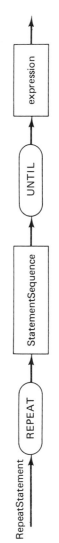

FIGURE A.54

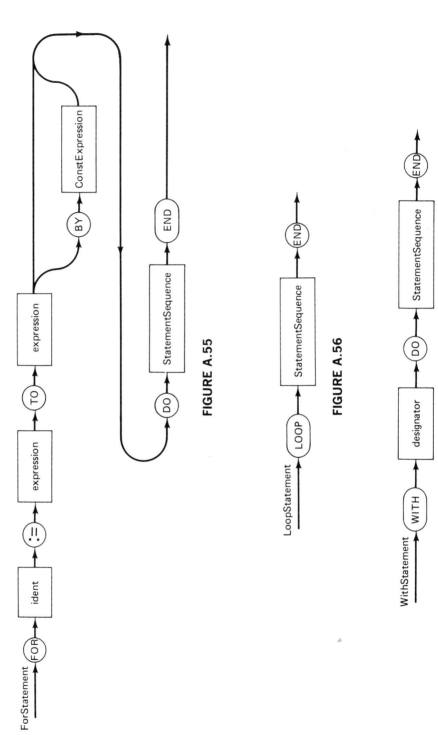

FIGURE A.55

FIGURE A.56

FIGURE A.57

352

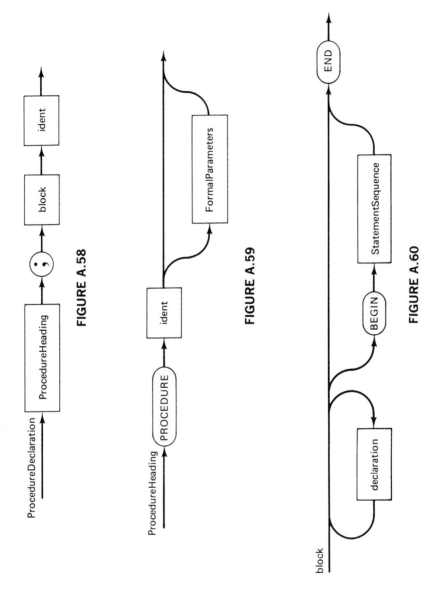

ProcedureDeclaration

FIGURE A.58

FIGURE A.59

FIGURE A.60

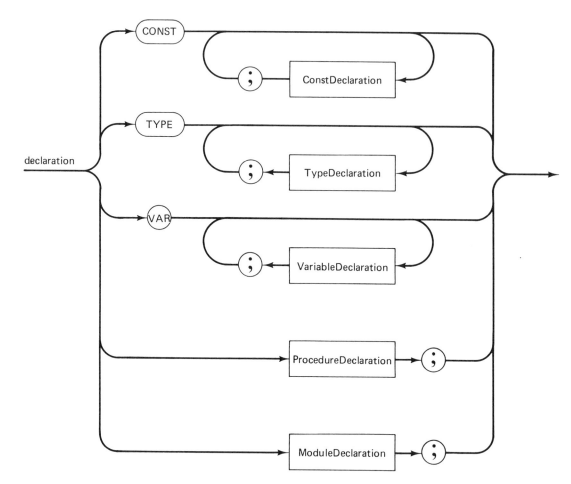

FIGURE A.61

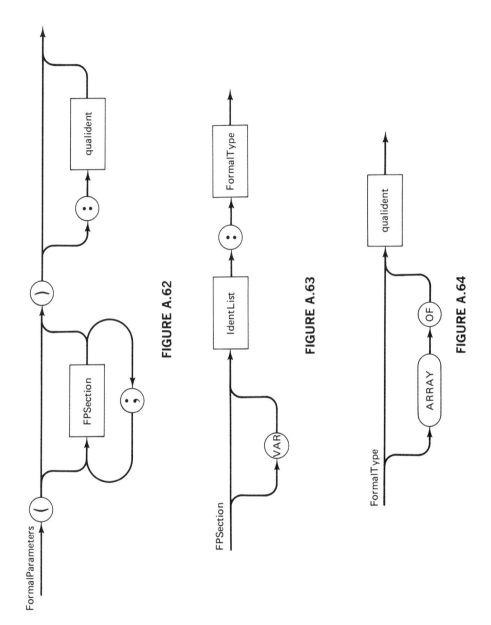

FIGURE A.62

FIGURE A.63

FIGURE A.64

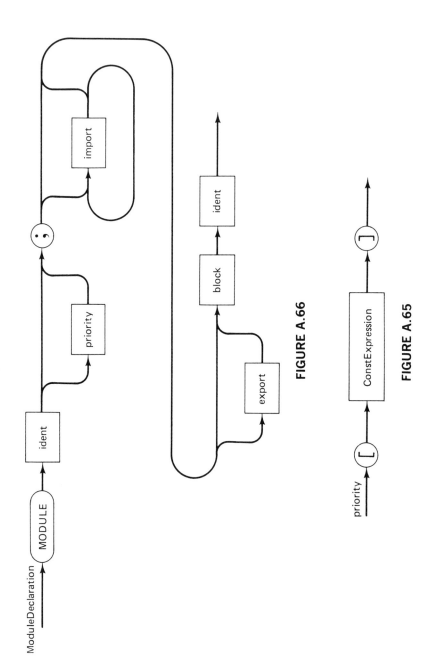

FIGURE A.66

FIGURE A.65

356

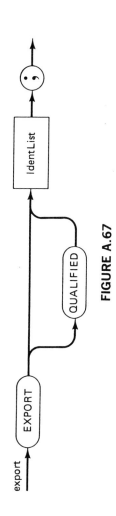

FIGURE A.67

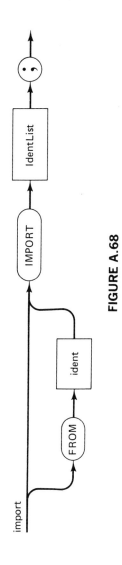

FIGURE A.68

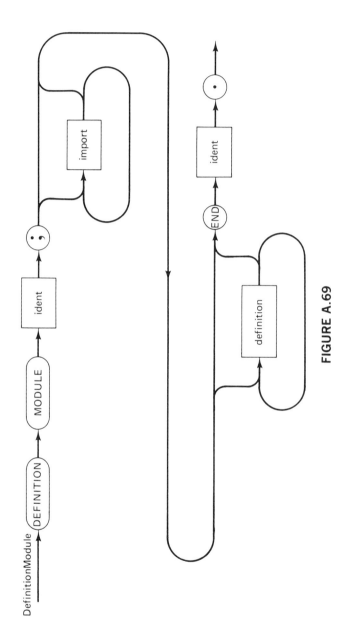

FIGURE A.69

358

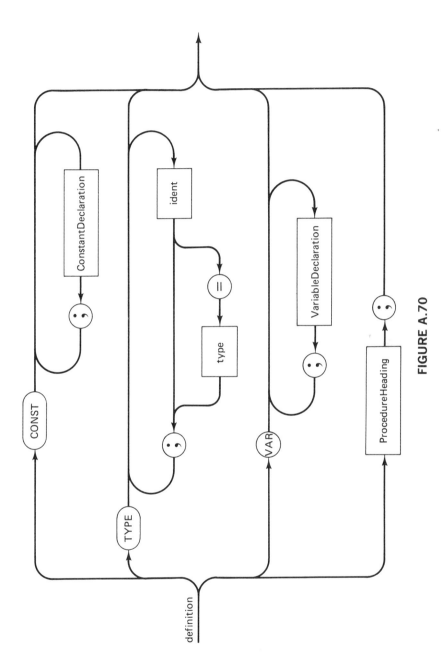

FIGURE A.70

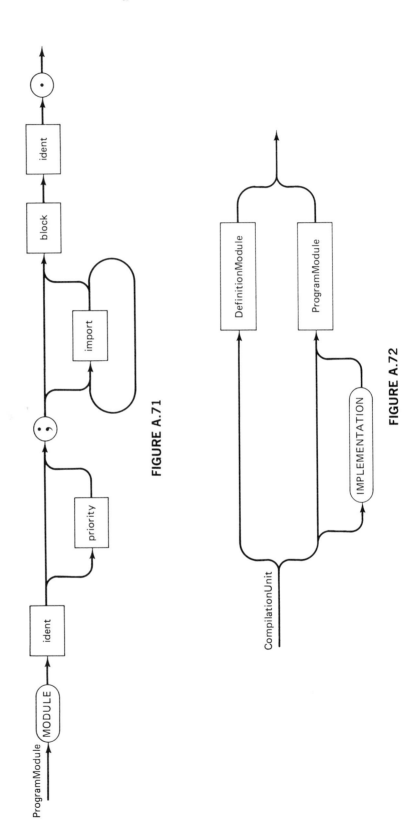

FIGURE A.71

FIGURE A.72

APPENDIX B

THE ASCII CHARACTER SET

		000000	000020	000040	000060	000100	000120	000140	000160
000000		nul	dle		0	@	P	`	p
000001		soh	dc1	!	1	A	Q	a	q
000002		stx	dc2	"	2	B	R	b	r
000003		etx	dc3	#	3	C	S	c	s
000004		eot	dc4	$	4	D	T	d	t
000005		enq	nak	%	5	E	U	e	u
000006		ack	syn	&	6	F	V	f	v
000007		bel	etb	'	7	G	W	g	w
000010		bs	can	(	8	H	X	h	x
000011		ht	em	)	9	I	Y	i	y
000012		lf	sub	*	:	J	Z	j	z
000013		vt	esc	+	;	K	[	k	{
000014		ff	fs	,	<	L	\	l	|
000015		cr	gs	−	=	M	]	m	}
000016		so	rs	.	>	N	^	n	~
000017		si	us	/	?	O	—	o	del

The above table is the complete ASCII character set. The row and column headings are given in octal to correspond to Modula-2 syntax for character representation.

```
    Name[017B] := 'si ';      Name[020B] := 'dle';      Name[021B] := 'dc1';
    Name[022B] := 'dc2';      Name[023B] := 'dc3';      Name[024B] := 'dc4';
    Name[025B] := 'nak';      Name[026B] := 'syn';      Name[027B] := 'etb';
    Name[030B] := 'can';      Name[031B] := 'em ';      Name[032B] := 'sub';
    Name[033B] := 'esc';      Name[034B] := 'fs ';      Name[035B] := 'gs ';
    Name[036B] := 'rs ';      Name[037B] := 'us ';      Name[177B] := 'del';
  END Printer;


  PROCEDURE Heading;

    VAR
      i : CARDINAL;

    BEGIN (*Heading*)
      InOut.WriteString('  Appendix B'); InOut.WriteLn;
      InOut.WriteString('  The ASCII Character Set');
      InOut.WriteLn;
      InOut.WriteLn;
      FOR i := 0 TO 7 DO
        InOut.Write(' ');
      END (*for i*);
      FOR i := 0B TO 160B BY 16 DO
        InOut.WriteOct(i, 8);
      END (*for i*);
      InOut.WriteLn;
    END Heading;



VAR
  AsciiChar,
  Char : CHAR;

BEGIN (*ASCII*)
  Heading;
  FOR AsciiChar := 0C TO 17C DO
    InOut.WriteLn;
    InOut.WriteOct(ORD(AsciiChar), 8);
    FOR Char := AsciiChar TO CHR(ORD(AsciiChar) + 160B) BY 16 DO
      PrintCharacter(Char);
    END (*for char*);
  END (*for asciichar*);
END ASCII.
```

APPENDIX C

VOLITION SYSTEMS LIBRARY MODULES

This appendix contains the definition modules for the Volition Systems Standard Library and Utility Library modules. These modules comprise the library routines that coincide with Wirth's recommendations for standard library units.

The Volition Systems implementation of Modula-2 contains a number of modules in addition to those shown in this appendix. Most of the other modules tend to be machine specific. For example, the Screen module that implements full-screen operations such as Gotoxy, ClearScreen, etc. is machine specific.

```
DEFINITION MODULE InOut;

EXPORT QUALIFIED
  EOL, Done, termCH,
  OpenInput, OpenOutput, CloseInput, CloseOutput,
  Read, ReadString, ReadInt, ReadCard,
  Write, WriteLn, WriteString, WriteInt, WriteCard, WriteOct, WriteHex;

CONST EOL = 15C;   (* system dependent *)

VAR Done: BOOLEAN;
VAR termCH: CHAR;

PROCEDURE OpenInput  (defext: ARRAY OF CHAR);
PROCEDURE OpenOutput (defext: ARRAY OF CHAR);
PROCEDURE CloseInput;
PROCEDURE CloseOutput;
```

```
PROCEDURE Read        (VAR ch: CHAR);
PROCEDURE ReadString  (VAR s: ARRAY OF CHAR);
PROCEDURE ReadInt     (VAR x: INTEGER);
PROCEDURE ReadCard    (VAR x: CARDINAL);

PROCEDURE Write       (ch: CHAR);
PROCEDURE WriteLn;
PROCEDURE WriteString (s: ARRAY OF CHAR);
PROCEDURE WriteInt    (x: INTEGER; n: CARDINAL);
PROCEDURE WriteCard   (x,n: CARDINAL);
PROCEDURE WriteOct    (x,n: CARDINAL);
PROCEDURE WriteHex    (x,n: CARDINAL);

END InOut.




DEFINITION MODULE RealInOut;

EXPORT QUALIFIED
  ReadReal, WriteReal, WriteRealOct, Done;

VAR Done: BOOLEAN;

PROCEDURE ReadReal(VAR x: REAL);
PROCEDURE WriteReal(x: REAL; n: CARDINAL);
PROCEDURE WriteRealOct (x: REAL);

END RealInOut.




DEFINITION MODULE Texts;

FROM Files IMPORT FILE;

EXPORT QUALIFIED
  TEXT, input, output, console, Connect, Disconnect,
  EOT, EOL, TextStatus, TextState, SetTextHandler,
  Read, ReadInt, ReadCard, ReadLn, ReadAgain,
  Write, WriteString, WriteInt, WriteCard, WriteLn;

TYPE TEXT;

VAR input, output, console: TEXT;      (* Predeclared text files *)

PROCEDURE EOT (t: TEXT): BOOLEAN;       (* End of text read *)
PROCEDURE EOL (t: TEXT): BOOLEAN;       (* End of line read *)

TYPE TextState = (TextOK, FormatError, FileError, ConnectError);

PROCEDURE TextStatus (t: TEXT): TextState;

TYPE TextHandler = PROCEDURE (TextState);
```

```
PROCEDURE SetTextHandler (t: TEXT; handler: TextHandler);

PROCEDURE Connect     (VAR t: TEXT; f: FILE): TextState;
PROCEDURE Disconnect  (VAR t: TEXT): TextState;

PROCEDURE Read        (t: TEXT; VAR ch: CHAR);
PROCEDURE ReadInt     (t: TEXT; VAR i: INTEGER);
PROCEDURE ReadCard    (t: TEXT; VAR c: CARDINAL);
PROCEDURE ReadLn      (t: TEXT; VAR s: ARRAY OF CHAR);
PROCEDURE ReadAgain   (t: TEXT);

PROCEDURE Write       (t: TEXT; ch: CHAR);
PROCEDURE WriteString (t: TEXT; s: ARRAY OF CHAR);
PROCEDURE WriteInt    (t: TEXT; i: INTEGER; n: CARDINAL);
PROCEDURE WriteCard   (t: TEXT; c, n: CARDINAL);
PROCEDURE WriteLn     (t: TEXT);

END Texts.



DEFINITION MODULE Reals;

FROM Texts IMPORT TEXT;

EXPORT QUALIFIED RealToStr, StrToReal, ReadReal, WriteReal;

PROCEDURE ReadReal    (t: TEXT; VAR r: REAL);

PROCEDURE WriteReal   (t: TEXT; r: REAL;
                        n: CARDINAL; digits: INTEGER);

PROCEDURE RealToStr   (r: REAL; digits: INTEGER;
                        VAR s: ARRAY OF CHAR): BOOLEAN;

PROCEDURE StrToReal   (s: ARRAY OF CHAR;
                        VAR r: REAL): BOOLEAN;

END Reals.



DEFINITION MODULE Files;

FROM SYSTEM IMPORT WORD, ADDRESS;

EXPORT QUALIFIED
    FILE, EOF, FileStatus, FileState, SetFileHandler,
    Open, Create, Close, Release, Rename, Delete,
    FilePos, SetPos, GetPos, SetEOF, GetEOF, CalcPos,
    Read, Write, ReadRec, WriteRec, ReadBytes, WriteBytes;

TYPE FILE;

PROCEDURE EOF (f: FILE): BOOLEAN;    (* End of file encountered *)
```

```
TYPE FileState = (FileOK, NameError, UseError, StatusError, DeviceError, EndError);

PROCEDURE FileStatus (f: FILE): FileState;   (* file I/O status *)

TYPE FileHandler = PROCEDURE (FileState);

PROCEDURE SetFileHandler (f: FILE; handler: FileHandler);

PROCEDURE Open    (VAR f: FILE; name: ARRAY OF CHAR): FileState;
PROCEDURE Create  (VAR f: FILE; name: ARRAY OF CHAR): FileState;

PROCEDURE Close   (VAR f: FILE): FileState;
PROCEDURE Release (VAR f: FILE): FileState;

PROCEDURE Delete  (name: ARRAY OF CHAR): FileState;
PROCEDURE Rename  (old, new: ARRAY OF CHAR): FileState;

TYPE FilePos;

PROCEDURE GetPos (f: FILE; VAR pos: FilePos);
PROCEDURE GetEOF (f: FILE; VAR pos: FilePos);

PROCEDURE SetPos (f: FILE; pos: FilePos);
PROCEDURE SetEOF (f: FILE; pos: FilePos);

PROCEDURE CalcPos (recnum, recsize: CARDINAL; VAR pos: FilePos);

PROCEDURE Read      (f: FILE; VAR ch: CHAR);
PROCEDURE ReadRec   (f: FILE; VAR rec: ARRAY OF WORD);
PROCEDURE ReadBytes (f: FILE; buf: ADDRESS; nbytes: CARDINAL): CARDINAL;

PROCEDURE Write     (f: FILE; ch: CHAR);
PROCEDURE WriteRec  (f: FILE; VAR rec: ARRAY OF WORD);
PROCEDURE WriteBytes (f: FILE; buf: ADDRESS; nbytes: CARDINAL): CARDINAL;

END Files.




                DEFINITION MODULE Terminal;

                EXPORT QUALIFIED  Read, BusyRead, ReadAgain, ReadLn,
                                  Write, WriteString, WriteLn;

                PROCEDURE Read     (VAR ch: CHAR);
                PROCEDURE ReadLn   (VAR s: ARRAY OF CHAR);
                PROCEDURE BusyRead (VAR ch: CHAR);
                PROCEDURE ReadAgain;

                PROCEDURE Write       (ch: CHAR);
                PROCEDURE WriteString (s: ARRAY OF CHAR);
                PROCEDURE WriteLn;

                END Terminal.
```

```
DEFINITION MODULE Storage;

FROM SYSTEM IMPORT ADDRESS;

EXPORT QUALIFIED ALLOCATE, DEALLOCATE, Available;

PROCEDURE ALLOCATE    (VAR p: ADDRESS; size: CARDINAL);

PROCEDURE DEALLOCATE (VAR p: ADDRESS; size: CARDINAL);

PROCEDURE Available       (size: CARDINAL): BOOLEAN;

END Storage.
```

```
DEFINITION MODULE Program;

EXPORT QUALIFIED
   Call, CallMode, ErrorMode, CallResult,
   Terminate, SetEnvelope, EnvMode;

TYPE CallResult = (NormalReturn, ProgramHalt, RangeError, SystemError,
                   FunctionError, StackOverflow, IntegerError,
                   DivideByZero, AddressError, UserHalt, CodeIOError,
                   UserIOError, InstructionError, FloatingError,
                   StringError, StorageError, VersionError,
                   MissingProgram, MissingModule, LibraryError,
                   NotMainProcess, DuplicateName);

TYPE CallMode  = (Shared, Unshared);
TYPE ErrorMode = (SystemTrap, CallerTrap);

PROCEDURE Terminate (exception: CallResult);

PROCEDURE Call (programName: ARRAY OF CHAR;
                calltype    : CallMode;
                errors      : ErrorMode): CallResult;

TYPE EnvMode = (AllCalls, UnsharedCalls, FirstCall);

PROCEDURE SetEnvelope (init, term: PROC; mode: EnvMode);

END Program.
```

```
DEFINITION MODULE Processes;

EXPORT QUALIFIED SIGNAL, StartProcess, SEND, WAIT, Awaited, Init;

TYPE SIGNAL;
```

```
PROCEDURE StartProcess (P: PROC; n: CARDINAL);
(*start a sequential process with program P
        and workspace of size n*)

PROCEDURE SEND (VAR s: SIGNAL);
(*one process waiting for s is resumed*)

PROCEDURE WAIT (VAR s: SIGNAL);
(*wait for some other process to send s*)

PROCEDURE Awaited (s: SIGNAL): BOOLEAN;
(*Awaited(s) = 'at least one process waiting for s'*)

PROCEDURE Init (VAR s: SIGNAL);
(*compulsory initialization*)

END Processes.
```

```
        DEFINITION MODULE MathLib0;

        EXPORT QUALIFIED
          sqrt, exp, ln, sin, cos, arctan, real, entier;

        PROCEDURE sqrt      (x: REAL): REAL;
        PROCEDURE exp       (x: REAL): REAL;
        PROCEDURE ln        (x: REAL): REAL;
        PROCEDURE sin       (x: REAL): REAL;
        PROCEDURE cos       (x: REAL): REAL;
        PROCEDURE arctan    (x: REAL): REAL;
        PROCEDURE real      (x: INTEGER): REAL;
        PROCEDURE entier    (x: REAL): INTEGER;

        END MathLib0.
```

```
DEFINITION MODULE Decimals;

EXPORT QUALIFIED
  DECIMAL, DecDigits, DecPoint, DecSep, DecCur, DecStatus,
  DecState, DecValid, StrToDec, DecToStr, NegDec, CompareDec,
  AddDec, SubDec, MulDec, DivDec, Remainder, SetDecHandler;

CONST   DecDigits = 19;
        DecCur    = '$';
        DecPoint  = '.';
        DecSep    = ',';

TYPE    DECIMAL;
        DecState = (NegOvfl, Minus, Zero, Plus, PosOvfl, Invalid);

VAR DecValid: BOOLEAN;  (* set after every operation *)
    Remainder: CHAR;    (* remainder digit - set after DivDec *)
```

```
PROCEDURE StrToDec   (String : ARRAY OF CHAR;
                      Picture: ARRAY OF CHAR): DECIMAL;

PROCEDURE DecToStr   (Dec     : DECIMAL;
                      Picture : ARRAY OF CHAR;
                      VAR RsltStr: ARRAY OF CHAR);

TYPE DecHandler = PROCEDURE (DecState);

PROCEDURE SetDecHandler (handler; DecHandler);

PROCEDURE DecStatus (Dec: DECIMAL): DecState;

PROCEDURE CompareDec (Dec0, Dec1: DECIMAL): INTEGER;

PROCEDURE AddDec   (Dec0, Dec1: DECIMAL): DECIMAL;

PROCEDURE SubDec   (Dec0, Dec1: DECIMAL): DECIMAL;

PROCEDURE MulDec   (Dec0, Dec1: DECIMAL): DECIMAL;

PROCEDURE DivDec   (Dec0, Dec1: DECIMAL): DECIMAL;

PROCEDURE NegDec   (Dec0, Dec1: DECIMAL): DECIMAL;

END Decimals.



DEFINITION MODULE Strings;

EXPORT QUALIFIED  STRING, Assign, Insert, Delete,
                  Pos, Copy, Concat, Length, CompareStr;

TYPE STRING = ARRAY [0..80] OF CHAR;

PROCEDURE Assign (VAR source, dest: ARRAY OF CHAR);

PROCEDURE Insert   (substr: ARRAY OF CHAR;
                    VAR str: ARRAY OF CHAR;
                    inx : CARDINAL);

PROCEDURE Delete   (VAR str: ARRAY OF CHAR;
                    inx: CARDINAL;
                    len: CARDINAL);

PROCEDURE Pos (substr, str: ARRAY OF CHAR): CARDINAL;

PROCEDURE Copy   (str: ARRAY OF CHAR;
                  inx: CARDINAL;
                  len: CARDINAL;
                  VAR result: ARRAY OF CHAR);

PROCEDURE Concat (s1, s2: ARRAY OF CHAR;
                  VAR result: ARRAY OF CHAR);
```

PROCEDURE Length (VAR str: ARRAY OF CHAR): CARDINAL;

PROCEDURE CompareStr (s1, s2: ARRAY OF CHAR): INTEGER;

END Strings.

DEFINITION MODULE Conversions;

FROM SYSTEM IMPORT WORD;

EXPORT QUALIFIED
    IntToStr, StrToInt, CardToStr, StrToCard, HexToStr, StrToHex;

PROCEDURE IntToStr   (i: INTEGER;
                       VAR s: ARRAY OF CHAR): BOOLEAN;

PROCEDURE StrToInt   (s: ARRAY OF CHAR;
                       VAR i: INTEGER): BOOLEAN;

PROCEDURE CardToStr   (c: CARDINAL;
                       VAR s: ARRAY OF CHAR): BOOLEAN;

PROCEDURE StrToCard   (s: ARRAY OF CHAR;
                       VAR c: CARDINAL): BOOLEAN;

PROCEDURE HexToStr   (w: WORD;
                       VAR s: ARRAY OF CHAR): BOOLEAN;

PROCEDURE StrToHex   (s: ARRAY OF CHAR;
                       VAR w: WORD): BOOLEAN;

END Conversions.

DEFINITION MODULE ASCII;

EXPORT QUALIFIED
        nul, soh, stx, etx, eot, enq, ack, bel,
        bs, ht, lf, vt, ff, cr, so, si,
        dle, dc1, dc2, dc3, dc4, nak, syn, etb,
        can, em, sub, esc, fs, gs, rs, us, del;

CONST
        nul = 00C; soh = 01C; stx = 02C; etx = 03C;
        eot = 04C; enq = 05C; ack = 06C; bel = 07C;
        bs = 10C; ht = 11C; lf = 12C; vt = 13C;
        ff = 14C; cr = 15C; so = 16C; si = 17C;
        dle = 20C; dc1 = 21C; dc2 = 22C; dc3 = 23C;
        dc4 = 24C; nak = 25C; syn = 26C; etb = 27C;
        can = 30C; em = 31C; sub = 32C; esc = 33C;
        fs = 34C; gs = 35C; rs = 36C; us = 37C;
        del = 177C;

END ASCII.

APPENDIX D

CHARACTER SET LIBRARY MODULE

Modula-2 does not specify the maximum number of elements that a set should be able to accommodate. Each implementation may differ in this regard. Some implementations restrict the maximum number of elements in a set to the word size (typically 16).

The examples in this book assume a larger set size than 16. The SET OF CHAR (set of all characters) is used extensively. If you have a requirement for a larger set size than your particular Modula-2 implementation can handle, the approach shown in Listings D.1 to D.3 can be used. Listings D.1 and D.2 provide a library module that handles sets of characters. Listing D.3 is a program that uses the character set library module to provide an alternate formulation of the program of Listing 6.5. Examination of the library module will show the general approach that can be taken, i.e. create an array of BITSETs together with the appropriate procedures to manipulate these data structures.

LISTING D.1

```
DEFINITION MODULE CharSet;

EXPORT QUALIFIED
        CHARSET,
        MakeEmpty, Union, Incl,
        IsMember, IsEqual, IsSubset;
```

```
CONST
      MaxIndex = 16;

TYPE
      CHARSET = ARRAY [0..MaxIndex] OF BITSET;   (* 256 elements *)

PROCEDURE MakeEmpty(VAR CSet : CHARSET);
(* Returns CSet as an empty set *)

PROCEDURE Union(ASet, BSet : CHARSET; VAR RSet : CHARSET);
(* Assigns RSet := ASet + BSet *)

PROCEDURE Incl(VAR CSet : CHARSET; E : CHAR);
(* Include the character E in set CSet *)

PROCEDURE IsMember(E : CHAR; CSet : CHARSET) : BOOLEAN;
(* Returns TRUE if E IN CSet *)

PROCEDURE IsEqual(ASet, BSet : CHARSET) : BOOLEAN;
(* Returns TRUE if ASet = BSet *)

PROCEDURE IsSubset(ASet, BSet : CHARSET) : BOOLEAN;
(* Returns TRUE if ASet <= BSet *)


END CharSet.
```

LISTING D.2

```
IMPLEMENTATION MODULE CharSet;


PROCEDURE MakeEmpty(VAR CSet : CHARSET);

  VAR
       i : CARDINAL;

  BEGIN (*MakeEmpty*)
    FOR i := 0 TO MaxIndex DO
      CSet[i] := {};
    END;
  END MakeEmpty;



PROCEDURE Union(ASet, BSet : CHARSET; VAR RSet : CHARSET);

  VAR
       i : CARDINAL;

  BEGIN (*Union*)
    FOR i := 0 TO MaxIndex DO
      RSet[i] := ASet[i] + BSet[i];
    END;
  END Union;
```

```
PROCEDURE DivideBy16(k : CARDINAL; VAR q, r : CARDINAL);
(*divide k by 16 giving quotient q and remainder r*)

  BEGIN (*DivideBy16*)
    q := k DIV 16;
    r := k MOD 16;
  END DivideBy16;



PROCEDURE Incl(VAR CSet : CHARSET; E : CHAR);

  VAR
        q, r : CARDINAL;

  BEGIN (*Incl*)
    DivideBy16(ORD(E), q, r);
    INCL(CSet[q], r);
  END Incl;



PROCEDURE IsMember(E : CHAR; CSet : CHARSET) : BOOLEAN;

  VAR
        q, r : CARDINAL;

  BEGIN (*IsMember*)
    DivideBy16(ORD(E), q, r);




    RETURN(r IN CSet[q]);
  END IsMember;



PROCEDURE IsEqual(ASet, BSet : CHARSET) : BOOLEAN;

  VAR
        i : CARDINAL;
        equal : BOOLEAN;

  BEGIN (*IsEqual*)
    equal := TRUE;
    i := 0;
    WHILE (equal) AND (i <= MaxIndex) DO
      equal := (ASet[i] = BSet[i]);
      INC(i);
    END (*while*);
    RETURN equal;
  END IsEqual;



PROCEDURE IsSubset(ASet, BSet : CHARSET) : BOOLEAN;
```

```
    VAR
        i : CARDINAL;
        subset : BOOLEAN;

    BEGIN (*IsSubset*)
      subset := TRUE;
      i := 0;
      WHILE (subset) AND (i <= MaxIndex) DO
        subset := (ASet[i] <= BSet[i]);
        INC(i);
      END (*while*);
      RETURN subset;
    END IsSubset;


END CharSet.
```

LISTING D.3

```
(*Alternate version of listing 6.5; uses library module CharSet*)
MODULE VowelTester;

FROM ASCII IMPORT
        bs;

FROM CharSet IMPORT
        CHARSET, Incl, IsMember, MakeEmpty;

FROM InOut IMPORT
        Read, Write, WriteString;

VAR
        i, Ch : CHAR;
        OKSet, Printables : CHARSET;


BEGIN
  MakeEmpty(Printables);
  FOR i := ' ' TO '}' DO
    Incl(Printables, i);
  END (*for*);
  MakeEmpty(OKSet);
  Incl(OKSet, 'A');
  Incl(OKSet, 'E');
  Incl(OKSet, 'I');
  Incl(OKSet, 'O');
  Incl(OKSet, 'U');

  WriteString('Please type a vowel to continue: ');
  REPEAT
    Read(Ch);
    IF IsMember(Ch, Printables) THEN
      Write(bs); Write(' '); Write(bs);
```

```
        END (*if*);
        Ch := CAP(Ch);
    UNTIL IsMember(Ch, OKSet);
    WriteString('Thank you.');
END VowelTester.
```

APPENDIX E

CALCULATOR EMULATION PROGRAM

This chapter provides the listing of a calculator emulation program that answers most of the questions posed in the supplemental problems of Chapters 1 through 11.

The reader is encouraged to answer the problems in the body of the book before referring to this listing. You will learn more about the construction of correct Modula-2 programs by first doing it on your own and then comparing your work against the program in this appendix.

There is no unique solution to a programming problem. The first criteria is—does it work? The next question is—is the style conducive to a reliable and maintainable program? The program in this appendix works and represents good programming practices. The comments are extensive (even to the point of possibly "cluttering" and reducing white space) and the program is essentially self-documented.

```
(***********************************************************************
*   Emulation of a Polish notation calcuator.  This implementation works only *
*   with integer (whole) numbers.  The maximum integer value is set by the    *
*   global constant MaxLength, and is system implementation independent.       *
*   "Numbers" are actually records composed of a string (i.e. ARRAY OF CHAR)   *
*   and an enumeration type.                                                    *
***********************************************************************)

MODULE Calculator;

FROM ASCII IMPORT       (* This is a system library module *)
    bel;                (* ASCII bel character to "beep" the speaker *)
```

```
FROM CRT IMPORT          (* User library module; see chapters 9 and 12 *)
   ClearTheScreen,       (* Clears the CRT and "homes" the cursor *)
   GoToxy,               (* Moves the cursor to coordinates x,y *)
   Input,                (* Sets up input "mask" and reads user input *)
   Justification,        (* Used in "Input" to position input data *)
   Message,              (* Puts msg at bottom of screen for 5 seconds *)
   PutLine;              (* Writes string starting at coordinates x,y *)
                         (* All the CRT functions do basic error checks to
                            ensure that screen boundaries are observed.  *)

FROM InOut IMPORT        (* System library module; covered in chapter 5 *)
   ReadString,
   Write,
   WriteLn,
   WriteString;

CONST
   MaxLength = 10;  (* Maximum length integer that calculator can handle *)
   OutColumn = 40 - MaxLength DIV 2; (* Center output on 80 column screen *)

TYPE
   String = ARRAY [0..MaxLength] OF CHAR;   (* Use this string IN PLACE of
                                             * actual integers!
                                             *)
   SignType = (Plus, Minus);            (* "Sign" of the "number" *)
   Number = RECORD          (* This is what the "integer" looks like *)
             Integer : String;   (* Change MaxLength to change size *)
             Sign : SignType;
          END;
(*-------------------------------------------------------------------------*)
(*-------------------------------------------------------------------------*)
MODULE Polish; (*  Local module for reverse Polish notation stack functions.
               *  Saves variable values between calls, and hides the stack
               *  implementation and access from other parts of the program
               *  except via procedure calls.  When we want to change the
               *  data structure of the stack from a fixed array to a
               *  dynamic pointer structure, this is where it's done. This
               *  could just as easily be a separately compiled module.  If
               *  it was, changing to pointers could be done with no impact
               *  (i.e. recompilation) on the rest of the program.
               *)
   IMPORT
      ClearTheScreen,           (* We need to import these elements   *)
      GoToxy,                   (* since modules can "see" only that   *)
      MaxLength,                (* which is imported.                  *)
      Message,                  (* Note difference of between          *)
      Number,                   (* "imports" here and in main program  *)
      OutColumn,                (* module; no "from" used here.        *)
      PutLine,
      SignType,
      Write,
      WriteLn,
      WriteString;

   EXPORT                  (* This is all the "outside" world sees *)
      Clear,
      DisplayStack,
      Pop,
      Push;
```

```
    CONST
        FirstStackAddress = 0;        (* Address of 1st stack location  *)
        FinalStackAddress = 15;       (* Address of last stack location *)
                                      (* Stack "grows" from 0-->15      *)
    VAR
        StackPointer : INTEGER;    (*  Points to current top of stack;
                                    *  this is the next EMPTY space to put
                                    *  things & NOT where the last element
                                    *  is located (it's 1 below here)
                                    *)
        Stack : ARRAY [FirstStackAddress..FinalStackAddress] OF Number;
        (* "The" stack implemented as an array *)
(*-------------------------------------------------------------------------*)
    PROCEDURE Clear();       (* Clear (i.e. empty) the stack *)

        BEGIN (* Clear *)
            StackPointer := FirstStackAddress;
        END Clear;
(*-------------------------------------------------------------------------*)
    PROCEDURE DisplayStack();    (*  Show stack contents beginning with the
                                  *  current top of stack.  If stack isn't
                                  *  full display the empty space.
                                  *)
        VAR
            i : INTEGER;

        BEGIN (* DisplayStack *)
            ClearTheScreen;

            (* Show contents of stack - from the last in to the 1st in *)
            i := StackPointer;       (* The current top (next EMPTY spot) *)
            WHILE i > FirstStackAddress  DO (* from top to FirstStackAddress *)
                GoToxy(OutColumn, StackPointer - i + 3); (* Where to write *)
                WriteString(Stack[i - 1].Integer); (* Write "integer" part *)
                IF Stack[i - 1].Sign = Minus THEN
                    GoToxy(OutColumn - 1, StackPointer - i + 3);
                    Write('-'); (* If number is negative, write a minus sign *)
                END (* if *);
                DEC(i);
            END (* while *);

            (* Give indication of empty stack space *)
            FOR i := 0 TO (FinalStackAddress - StackPointer) DO
                PutLine(OutColumn, StackPointer + i + 3, '**********');
            END (* for *);

        END DisplayStack;
(*-------------------------------------------------------------------------*)
    PROCEDURE Pop(VAR number : Number) : BOOLEAN; (* Pop next item off stack *)

        BEGIN (* Pop *)
            IF StackPointer > FirstStackAddress THEN (* stack isn't empty *)
                DEC(StackPointer);  (* Make stack one element smaller *)
                number := Stack[StackPointer]; (* Send caller current item *)
                RETURN TRUE;        (* Tell caller that all went well *)
            ELSE
                Message('Error --> stack empty'); (* "Beep" & display 5 sec. *)
                Clear();  (* May not want to do this; decisions, decisions *)
```

```
                    RETURN FALSE          (* Tell caller there was a problem *)
            END (* if*);
        END Pop;
    (*---------------------------------------------------------------------------*)
    PROCEDURE Push(number : Number);    (* Push new item on stack *)

        BEGIN (* Push *)
            IF StackPointer <= FinalStackAddress THEN (* there's room *)
                Stack[StackPointer] := number; (* Put it on the stack *)
                INC(StackPointer);  (* Make the stack one larger *)
            ELSE
                Message('Error --> stack full');
            END (* if *)
        END Push;
    (*---------------------------------------------------------------------------*)
BEGIN (* Polish *)
    Clear()    (* Initialize the stack at execution time *)
END Polish;
    (*---------------------------------------------------------------------------*)
    (*---------------------------------------------------------------------------*)
(* "Normalize" and its nested procedures take the character string input
 * from the user and right justify it.  Spaces to the left are filled in
 * in (padded) with the character '0'.  This is to line up the characters
 * in our pseudo "number" so the unit "digits", the tens (the hundreds...)
 * digits, etc. all line up.  We will take advantage of this alignment when
 * it comes time to do "arithmetic" on these numbers.
 *)
    TYPE
        SetOfChar = SET OF CHAR;
    VAR
        Digits : SetOfChar;    (* "Numeric" data *)

    PROCEDURE Normalize(VAR string : String);
    (*---------------------------------------------------------------------------*)
        PROCEDURE Length(string : String) : CARDINAL;
        (* Counts characters in the number string; a more general routine would
         * pass the string terminator(s) to Length rather than "Digits" below.
         *)

            VAR
                i : CARDINAL;

            BEGIN (* Length *)
                i := 0;      (* Initialize the length to zero *)

                (* Stop if not a "digit" (use the character set Digits),
                 * or if it is the Modula string terminator ASCII 0
                 *)
                WHILE (string[i] IN Digits) & (string[i] # 0C) DO
                    INC(i);      (* Increment the length *)
                END (* while *);
                RETURN i;    (* Works properly at boundaries, e.g. 0 length *)
            END Length;
    (*---------------------------------------------------------------------------*)
        PROCEDURE PadLeft(VAR string : String; length : CARDINAL);
        (* Right justify the "number" and fill spaces on left with '0's; we
         * could be more general by passing the "fill" character to the
```

```
            * procedure in parameter list instead of fixing it as a "0".
            *)
              VAR
                  i : CARDINAL;

              BEGIN (* PadLeft *)
                  FOR i := 1 TO length DO  (* right justify *)
                      string[MaxLength - i] := string[length - i];
                  END (* for *);
                  FOR i := 0 TO MaxLength - length - 1 DO (* pad with '0's *)
                      string[i] := '0';
                  END (* for *);
                  string[MaxLength] := 0C;  (* Set the string terminator *)
              END PadLeft;
(*-------------------------------------------------------------------------*)
    VAR
        StringLength : CARDINAL;

    BEGIN (* Normalize *)
        StringLength := Length(string);  (* Find out how long it is *)
        IF StringLength < MaxLength THEN (* Pad the short strings *)
            PadLeft(string, StringLength);
        END (* if *);
    END Normalize;
(*-------------------------------------------------------------------------*)
(*-------------------------------------------------------------------------*)
(* Compute sum := s1 + s2; notice the type for s1, s2 and sum -- they are NOT
 * actually numbers.  We do this to make the size of the largest number the
 * calculator can add implementation independent (and to demonstrate the
 * language).  We're going to add just like you do it with pencil and paper;
 * start at the rightmost digits & go right to left adding a pair of digits
 * at a time and remembering to carry "1" if the result is >= "10".  This is
 * probably "setting computers back" lots of years, but it's interesting. It
 * is trivial to convert this routine to a general purpose procedure which
 * can add two numbers from any base system (is it necessary to do any more
 * than just substitute a variable called for the constant "Base" below?).
 *)
PROCEDURE Add(s1, s2 : Number; VAR sum : Number);

    CONST
        Base = 10;  (* We're adding base 10 numbers *)
    VAR
        i : INTEGER;
        Temp, Carry : CARDINAL;  (* The ORD function (see below) likes CARD *)

    BEGIN (* Add *)
        i := MaxLength - 1; (* Start at the right *)
        Carry := 0;          (* Initialize the value of Carry *)
        WHILE i >= 0 DO      (* Right to left; a pair of digits at a time *)
        Temp := Carry + ORD(s1.Integer[i]) + ORD(s2.Integer[i])
                - (2 * ORD('0')) ;  (* Convert the character to a number *)
        Carry := Temp DIV Base;     (* If it's >= 10 we need to carry *)
        sum.Integer[i] := CHR(Temp MOD Base + ORD('0')); (* Convert the part
                        of the sum that's less than 10 back to CHAR *)
        DEC(i);        (* Next pair *)
    END (* while *);
    sum.Sign := s1.Sign;     (* Are we adding two "+" or "-" numbers? *)
```

```
                 IF Carry > 0 THEN        (* The sum is too large for our calculator *)
                     Message('Overflow error during addition');
                 END (* if *);
                 sum.Integer[MaxLength] := 0C;   (* Always set the string terminator *)
        END Add;
    (*----------------------------------------------------------------------------*)
    PROCEDURE Subtract(s1, s2 : Number; VAR diff : Number);
    (* Same idea as "Add"; compute diff := s1 - s2 the old fashioned way *)

        CONST
            Base = 10;
        VAR
            i : INTEGER;
            Temp, Borrow : CARDINAL;
            N1, N2 : Number;

        BEGIN (* Subtract *)
            N1 := s1;
            N2 := s2;    (* Save s1 & s2 in case we have to do diff := s2 - s1;
                            see the recursive call on Subtract below. *)
            i := MaxLength - 1;     (* Start at right as in Add *)
            Borrow := 0;            (* Initialize Borrow *)
            WHILE i >= 0 DO
                IF Borrow > 0 THEN (* we need to subtract 1 first *)
                    s1.Integer[i] := CHR(ORD(s1.Integer[i]) - 1);
                    (* Remember - CHAR is the basic unit of our "number" *)
                END (* if *);
                IF ORD(s2.Integer[i]) > ORD(s1.Integer[i]) THEN
                    Borrow := Base; (* just like the old fashioned way *)
                ELSE
                    Borrow := 0;
                END (* if *);
                Temp := Borrow + ORD(s1.Integer[i]) - ORD(s2.Integer[i]);
                diff.Integer[i] := CHR(Temp MOD Base + ORD('0')); (* back to CHAR *)
                DEC(i);     (* Next pair of digits *)
            END (* while *);
            diff.Sign := s1.Sign; (* Sign assumes s1 > s2 *)
            IF Borrow > 0 THEN  (* Above assumption was wrong; subtract again *)
                Subtract(N2, N1, diff);  (* Recursive call *)
            END (* if *);
            diff.Integer[MaxLength] := 0C;  (* Set string terminator *)
        END Subtract;
    (*----------------------------------------------------------------------------*)
    PROCEDURE Multiply(s1, s2 : Number; VAR product : Number);

        BEGIN (* Multiply *)
            product.Integer := '0000000000';   (* Left as an exercise *)
        END Multiply;
    (*----------------------------------------------------------------------------*)
    PROCEDURE Divide(s1, s2 : Number; VAR quotient : Number);
        BEGIN (* Divide *)
            quotient.Integer := '0000000000';   (* Left as an exercise *)
        END Divide;
    (*----------------------------------------------------------------------------*)
    (* Decide whether Add or Subtract should be called.  If the signs of the
     * two operands are the same it's an add regardless of whether the user
     * pressed the "+" or "-" key (and vice versa for Subtract)
     *)
```

```
PROCEDURE PreAdd(s1, s2 : Number; VAR tempstrg : Number);

   BEGIN (*PreAdd*)
      IF s1.Sign = s2.Sign THEN   (* This is always an add *)
         Add(s1, s2, tempstrg);
      ELSIF s1.Sign = Plus THEN   (* Subtract -- several options *)
         Subtract(s1, s2, tempstrg);
      ELSE
         Subtract(s2, s1, tempstrg);
      END (* if *);
   END PreAdd;
(*------------------------------------------------------------------------*)
PROCEDURE ChangeSign(VAR s1 : Number); (* Change the sign of s1 *)

   BEGIN (* ChangeSign *)
      IF s1.Sign = Plus THEN
         s1.Sign := Minus
      ELSE
         s1.Sign := Plus;
      END (* if *);
   END ChangeSign;
(*------------------------------------------------------------------------*)
PROCEDURE Exchange;   (* Exchange the order of top two items on stack *)

   VAR
     s1, s2 : Number;

   BEGIN (*Exchange*)
      IF Pop(s1) & Pop(s2) THEN   (* There were 2 numbers avail. to pop *)
         Push(s1);
         Push(s2);
      END (* if *);
   END Exchange;
(*------------------------------------------------------------------------*)
(* This is the user interface; gets the user's input and translates it.  The
 * library procedure "Input" gets the input; the remainder of the code
 * translates/processes the input and traps errors. All calculator options are
 * exercised and controlled here.  If new options are added -- e.g. change the
 * sign of the element at the top of the stack, or interchange the top two
 * elements in the stack -- , they are handled in this procedure.
 *)
PROCEDURE ProcessInput(VAR done : BOOLEAN);

   VAR
      Data : String;
      s1,
      s2,
      Result : Number;

   BEGIN (* ProcessInput *)

 Input(Data, OutColumn, 1, MaxLength, NoJustify);
 (* Place a mask MaxLength units long, starting at row 1 (centered) to
  * get user input. The mask is a series of dots; input is forced to
  * remain in this field (i.e. the user cannot enter more than MaxLength
  * characters.  Input is returned in Data, and no particular
  * justification (right/left) is assumed.
  *)
```

```
             CASE CAP(Data[0]) OF     (* Translate and process all legal inputs *)
                '0'..'9'  : Normalize(Data);     (* Input is a number; normalize *)
                            s1.Integer := Data; (* it & push it on the stack.   *)
                            s1.Sign := Plus;
                            Push(s1);
                '+', '-',
                '*', '/'  : IF (Pop(s1) & Pop(s2)) THEN (* It's a math operation,
                                                  & data is available on stack *)
                                CASE CAP(Data[0]) OF
                                      '+'       : PreAdd(s1, s2, Result);
                                      '-'       : ChangeSign(s1);
                                                  PreAdd(s1, s2, Result);
                                      '*'       : Multiply(s1, s2, Result);
                                      '/'       : Divide(s2, s1, Result);
                                END (* case *);
                                Push(Result);  (* Result of math op onto stack *)
                            END (* if *);
                'C'       : Clear();       (* Throw everything away *)
                'P'       : IF Pop(s1) THEN END;    (* Discard top stack element *)
                'S'       : IF Pop(s1) THEN  (* Change sign of item at stack top *)
                                ChangeSign(s1);
                                Push(s1);    (* Don't forget to put it back *)
                            END (* if *);
                'X'       : Exchange;    (* Exchange order of top 2 stack items *)
                'Q'       : (* null statement - get ready to quit *);
             ELSE
                Write(bel);  (* Beep at erroneous input *)
             END (* case *);

             done := CAP(Data[0]) = 'Q';      (* Tell main program if we're done *)
       END ProcessInput;
  (*------------------------------------------------------------------------*)
  (*------------------------------------------------------------------------*)
VAR
   Done : BOOLEAN;

BEGIN (* Calculator *)
   Digits := SetOfChar('0'..'9');  (* Used in Length *)
   REPEAT
       DisplayStack;                (* Show what we've got on the stack *)
       ProcessInput(Done);          (* Get user input, and process it *)
   UNTIL Done;                      (* Stop when a Q is entered *)
END Calculator.
```

INDEX